I0796013

IMAGES
of America

WASHINGTON COUNTY
ARKANSAS

Cover Photograph: Pictured are members of the West Fork Baseball team. The exact date is unknown. (Courtesy Collection of Opal Walker.)

IMAGES
of America

WASHINGTON COUNTY ARKANSAS

Velda Brotherton

ARCADIA
PUBLISHING

Copyright © 1999 by Velda Brotherton
ISBN 978-0-7385-008-9

Published by Arcadia Publishing
Charleston, South Carolina

Printed in the United States of America

Library of Congress Catalog Card Number: Applied For

For all general information contact Arcadia Publishing at:
Telephone 843-853-2070
Fax 843-853-0044
E-mail sales@arcadiapublishing.com
For customer service and orders:
Toll-Free 1-888-313-2665

Visit us on the Internet at www.arcadiapublishing.com

Contents

ACKNOWLEDGMENTS

This book is dedicated to the late Robert Winn, who shared so much of his knowledge of local history, and Harold Hutcheson, who founded *The Washington County Observer* and saw the importance of running "The Scrapbook" feature each week.

A special thank you to Boyce Davis, former owner and publisher of *The Cherokee Group* and *The Washington County Observer*, where most of these photos were first published in the 1970s. Thanks are extended to new owner Jerry Tanner and publisher Chris Rush. I would also like to thank Bob Beesom, Manon Wilson, and Brenda Smart of Shiloh Museum of Ozark History in Springdale, Winona Waggoner of the Elkins Historical Society, and Bob's Photography in Fayetteville for their cooperation in obtaining additional photos.

INTRODUCTION

On July 9, 1816, William and Peter Lovely purchased from the Osage Indians the lands lying between the western boundary of the Osage Cession of 1808 and the Verdigris River. In the meantime, the United States, by the treaty of July 8, 1817, granted to the Cherokee Nation a large tract of land north of the Arkansas River. When the lines of the grant were run, it was discovered that the grant included a large part of the Lovely Purchase; all white settlers were ordered to leave, with the exception of Peter Lovely, who acted as agent to the Native Americans.

On October 13, 1827, Governor Izard approved an act creating Lovely County, which included lands that extended from west of the Kings River to the western boundary of Arkansas into Indian Territory (now Oklahoma). Most of Lovely County was deeded to the Cherokee by the Treaty of 1828, and what was left became Washington County. Once certain financial disputes were settled between officials in the two counties, the county was established. In 1828, the first officials were appointed, including Larkin Newton, clerk; Lewis Evans, sheriff; and John Skelton, coroner.

A few white people had settled within the county limits before the organization, among them John Alexander, a man named Shannon, Mark Bean, two McGarrahs, and two Simpsons. They were evicted by soldiers from Fort Gibson in August 1826. After the Cherokee treaty was granted and the right to settle was undisputed, the settlers returned, and a number of families came from the Crystal Hill settlement (near present-day Little Rock) to live in Washington County, an area named in honor of George Washington. In March 1829, a post office was established in the county seat of Fayetteville, and Brazil Newton served as the first postmaster. By 1830, the county had a population of 2,182. Arkansas Territory became a state in 1836.

The history of Washington County would not be complete without the tragic story of the Cherokees, so many of whom once called this area home. Prior to the Trail of Tears, 900 Cherokees were driven from their homes in Georgia and into Arkansas, where they joined the 2,000 others who preceded them. The warring factions of the tribe—Chief John Ross leading one, Major Ridge the other—wanted to remain in Georgia but knew they had little choice. Chief Ross signed a treaty that agreed to the movement of his people, and in 1838, the Cherokee were removed to Indian Territory along the Trail of Tears. Its branches passed through Washington County.

On the night of June 20, 1839, the Ross Faction formed the Knights of Death, and 100 riders went to the home of John Ridge (son of Major Ridge), dragged him from his bed, and killed him. They then murdered Major Ridge and his close friend, Elias Bouginot (Boudinot), in Washington County, five miles from Cane Hill. For years, many members of the Cherokee tribe lived, worked with, and married into white families in the county. In 1849, Cherokee and white businessmen formed a wagon train and traveled to the gold mines in California, in search of gold to finance businesses in the area. The northern route they blazed became known as the Cherokee Trail and was used to drive thousands of herds of cattle west in the years that followed.

Though life continued to be harsh for most county residents, Northwest Arkansas was considered a very prosperous place to live. Settlers poured in from Tennessee, Kentucky, Georgia, and Eastern states, all looking for a better way of life in a place where they could own their own land. Looming on the distant horizon, though, was a tragedy that would rip apart the close-knit communities forming in this rural county. The Civil War divided them as nothing else ever could; families were torn apart as fathers declared for the South and sons traveled North to join Union troops. Brothers fought brothers, and mothers faced soldiers from both sides that moved across the county fighting one skirmish after another in the rugged wilderness. Bushwhackers, with no allegiance to either side, made life miserable for the women and children who were left to fend for themselves. Two terrible battles were fought in Northwest Arkansas—one at Pea Ridge and another at Prairie Grove in Washington County. The land on which wars are fought suffers dreadfully, and Washington County was no exception.

The Great Depression may have caused as much damage to the county as the Civil War; families moved out in droves, some simply walking out of their homes with what they could haul. Recovery eventually came in the 1950s, when the rural electric company wired the area with electricity. Telephone service was spotty, and it wasn't until the 1970s that party lines were abolished and remote areas were finally provided with telephones.

Since the turn of this century, the four counties in Northwest Arkansas have experienced enormous growth in both employment and population. Washington County is now comprised of over 150,000 residents, and it continues to grow. The county's boundaries encompass lush, green valleys cut by forks of the White River and mountainous regions that include, on the Southern boundary, a portion of the Boston Mountains of the Ozarks, the crest of which divides the flow of streams north and south. Farmers continue to raise cattle, poultry, and hogs. Local industry includes such companies as Campbell Soup, Levi Jeans, Tyson's, Jones Truck Lines, and Mexican Original; Wal-Mart headquarters are located in northern Benton County. The University of Arkansas, once referred to as the state university, resides on one of the seven hills of Fayetteville. A regional airport and new interstate are scheduled to open in winter 1998.

In compiling this history of the county, I have chosen photographs that best depict the lives of the majority of its residents from the 1800s through the 20th century. Unless otherwise indicated, photos featured in this collection are from "The Scrapbook," a weekly feature in the *Observer* for many years. Many of the images were originally supplied and captioned for the newspaper by the late Robert Winn, whose historical writings about the county are well known.

One

LEARNIN' THE THREE RS

When the Frisco Railroad laid tracks on a north/south route through the county in 1882, many small towns were born, flourishing until the stock market crash and the Great Depression. Schools located along the route prospered as a result of the taxes paid by the railroad company, while those scattered throughout the rugged wilderness barely managed to remain open three or four months out of the year. Washington County quickly took the lead in education, though there was little interest in the state of Arkansas. By the time the legislature enacted a new public school law in 1867, the county had already established a few districts and free public schools. Prior to that time, most schools functioned as subscription schools; only the children of families that could afford to pay tuition could receive even a rudimentary education. Some of those schools date back to the earliest part of the century; unfortunately, no official records were kept. After the state enacted a two-mill tax and a poll tax of $1 on every male citizen in 1868, the legislature established three-month schools. Even so, it would be a few more years before some of the remote areas could afford to build and maintain a one-room school and hire a teacher.

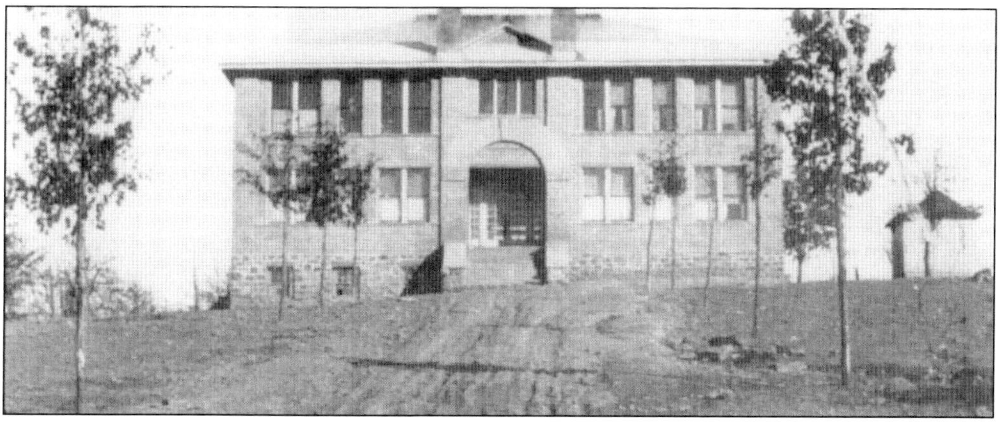

This brick school replaced the first white-frame school built in Winslow proper after it was destroyed by fire. Students attended school here from 1919 through 1929. The second building also burned; its remains were replaced by a rock school house that is still used today. There were earlier, one-room log schools scattered around the town prior to the first city school, which was built in 1894.

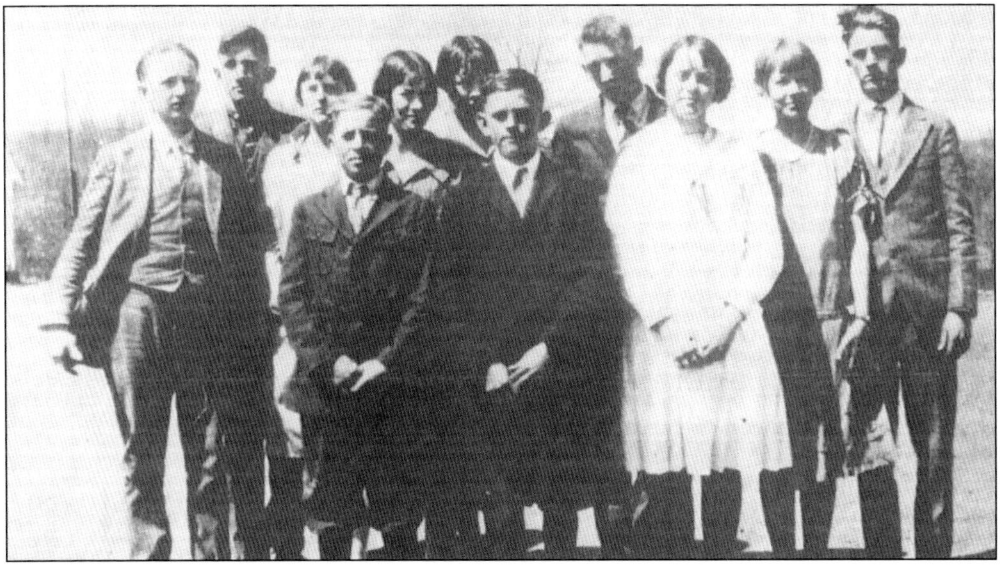

Winslow's eighth-grade class of 1926 is gathered on the grounds near the school for this photograph. From left to right are as follows: (front row) Frank Stoffer, Hal Innis, and Evelyn Crissman; (back row) Paul Stonesifer, Robert Adkins, Anna Smith, Pauline Westfall, Betsy Miller, Alex Smith, Margaret L. Crider, and Sanford Nott. The teacher, Carrie Alexander, is not pictured.

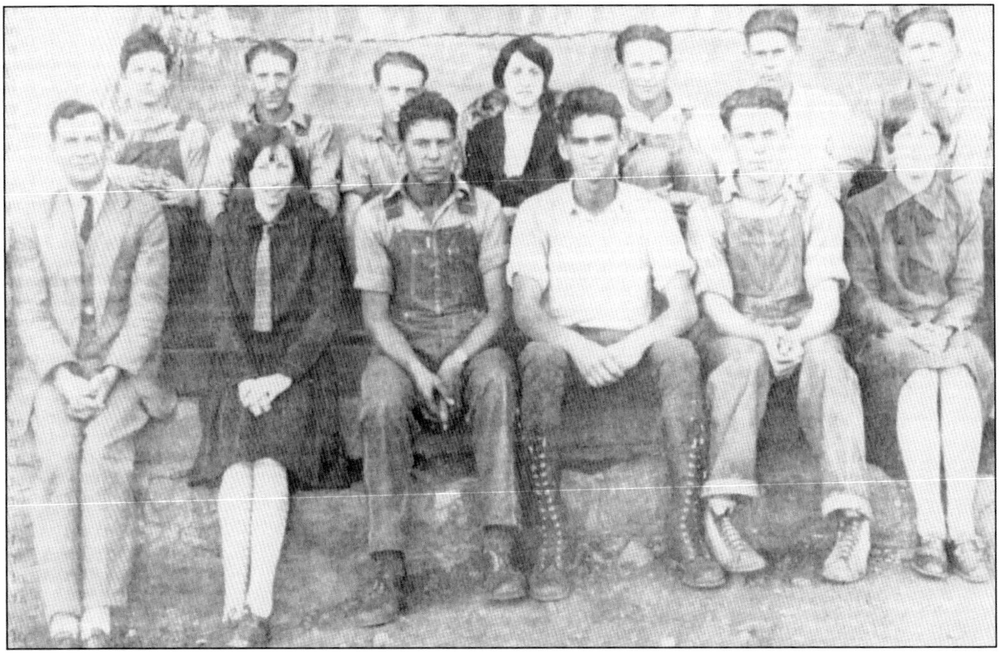

The 1926 graduating class of Winslow School are seen in front of the brick school. From left to right are as follows: (front row) Professor Jim Osborn, Juanita Land, Glenn Innis, Ernest Standley, Carson Duncan, and Cleo Smith; (back row) Clayton Grube, Ralph Terry, George Dockery, Pauline Nickell, Emery Phillips, Paul Land, and Nolie Riddle. Very few teachers in the rural schools had much more than an eighth-grade education; some taught students older than themselves. Winslow was one of the few that offered high school education.

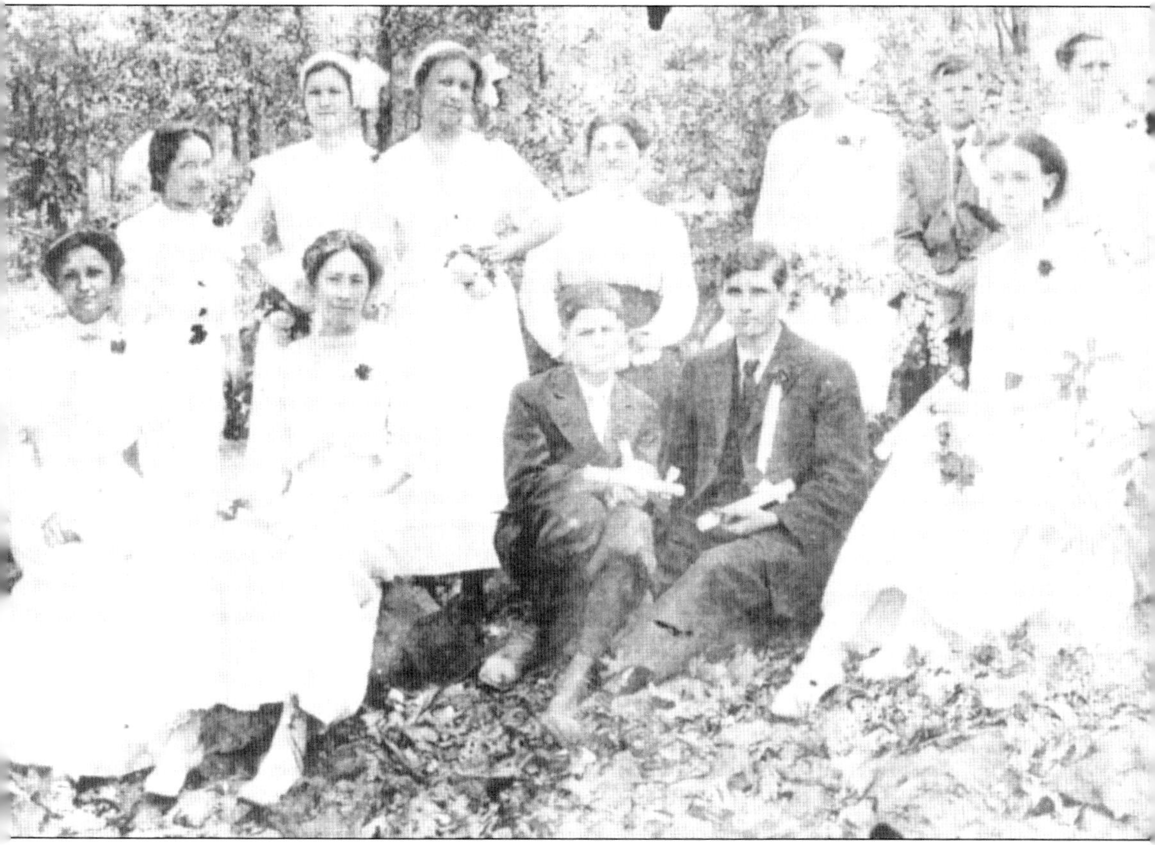

Unlike previous photographs, this 1912 graduating class of Winslow is almost all girls. From left to right are as follows: (seated) Jewell McClendon, Viva McHenry, David Grammar, Lyndell Deatherage, and Stella Winn; (standing) Ferrol Adkins, Jenny Grammar, Bess Guinn, teacher Mary Craig (seated), Bess Thompson, Estin Parks, and Alice Kelly. Legend has it that when the frame school building these students attended burned, the bell in the tower fell to the ground and rolled down the hill, coming to rest in the exact spot where the brick school would be built. Students in this photograph are grouped around a pile of firewood left over from the winter's fuel supply. Most schools of this era were heated by wood that was burned in a centrally located, pot-bellied, cast-iron heating stove. It was the teacher's duty to arrive early enough to build the fire and sweep the floor. Water was supplied to almost all of these schools, either by a well or spring. Usually, two students were assigned the task of fetching a bucket of drinking water each morning. This gave students a chance to escape from class for a while, and most welcomed the chore.

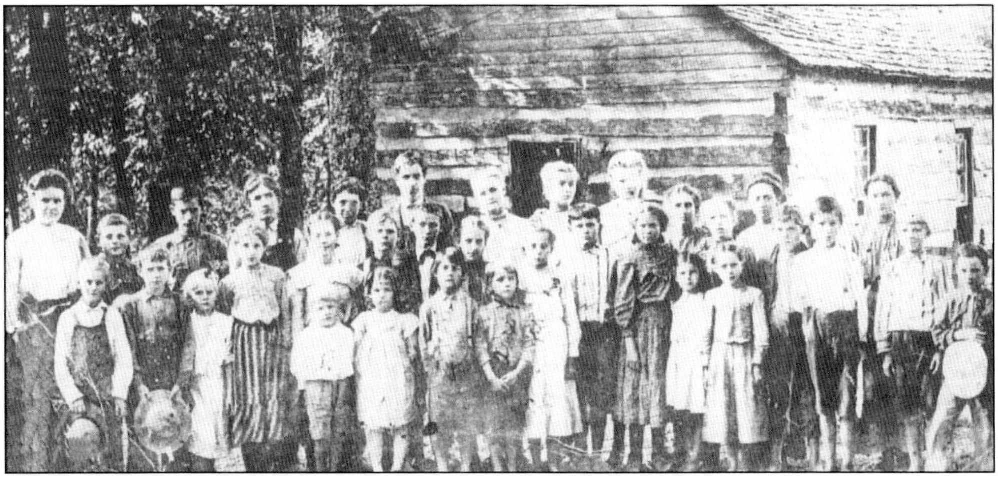

This much larger class of students attended Oak Grove some time before 1904, when this log school burned. From left to right are as follows: (front row) Virgil Smith, Lydia Fox, Billie Bird, and Forrest Bird; (second row) Joe Phillips, Cecil Talley, Lola Phillips, Josey Kittret, Ruth Reese, Argile Johnston, Fred Epley, Maud Smith, Effie Bird, Clifford Newman, Nora McClain, Bertha Smith, Hazel Talley, unidentified, Charley Newman, and Lester Reese; (third row) Dolly Smith (teacher), Guy Purser, Edgar Reese, Doyle Adkins, Renner Talley, Carl Adkins, Ethel Phillips, Grace Hunter, Ada McClain, Maud Armour, Myrtle Talley, Josey Epley, and Ruth Epley.

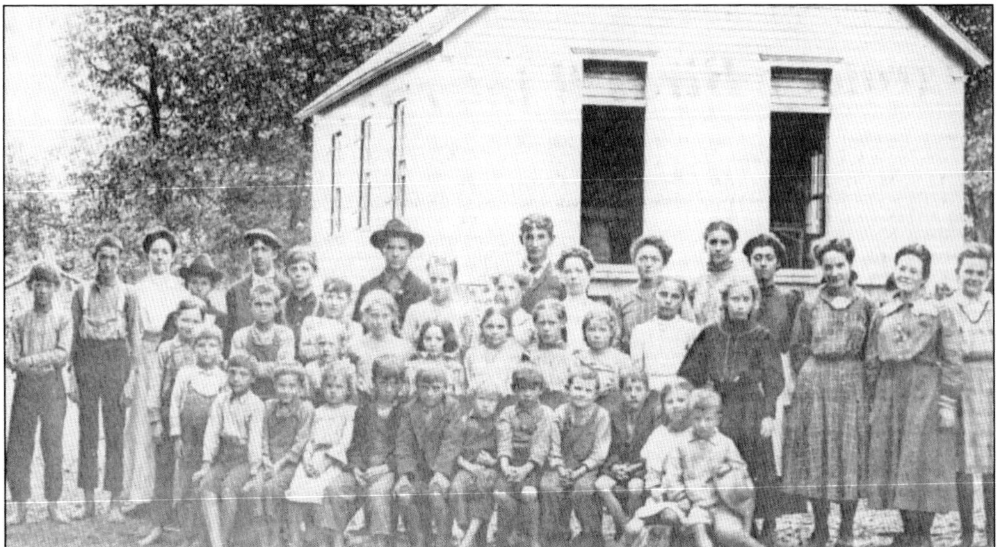

In September 1908, this large class gathered in front of the Oak Grove frame school house that replaced the earlier log structure. From left to right are as follows: (front row) Bill Bird, Izaac Caudle, Sarah Caudle, Lester Caudle, Forrest Bird, Carl Smith, unidentified, Raymond Brock, Virgil Smith, Horace Smith, Bertha Smith, and Floyd Smith; (middle row) Lester Reese, Virgil Smith, Jess Brock, Emma Caudle, Margaret Reese, Grace Brock, Hazel Talley, Martha Caudle, Effie Bird, and Elsie Purser; (back row) Hick Sutton, Ed Epley, Grace Reese (teacher), Guy Purser, Renner Talley, Argile Johnston, Cecil Talley, Milton Johnston, Maude Smith, Josie Kittrell, Doyle Adkins, Myrtle Talley, Ruth Epley, Maud Armour, Josie Epley, Farrell Adkins, Ruth Reese, and Alta Brock.

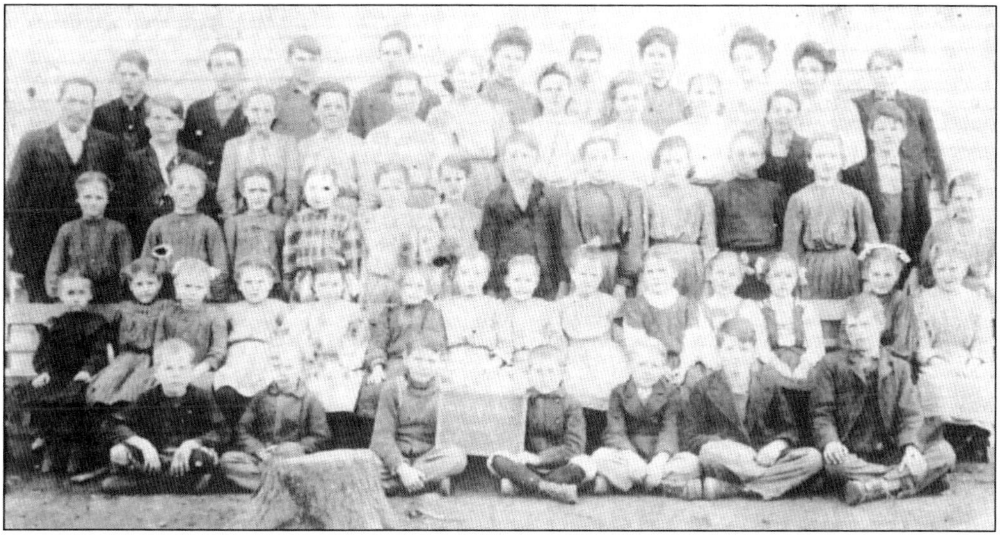

Liberty "86" School was known by both its name and its district number. Registered as a district in 1882, the school was located approximately 15 miles southwest of West Fork. This photo was taken January 26, 1909. While identification of students is available, those pictured are too numerous to name here. J. Frank Thrasher taught grades 1–8 during this school term.

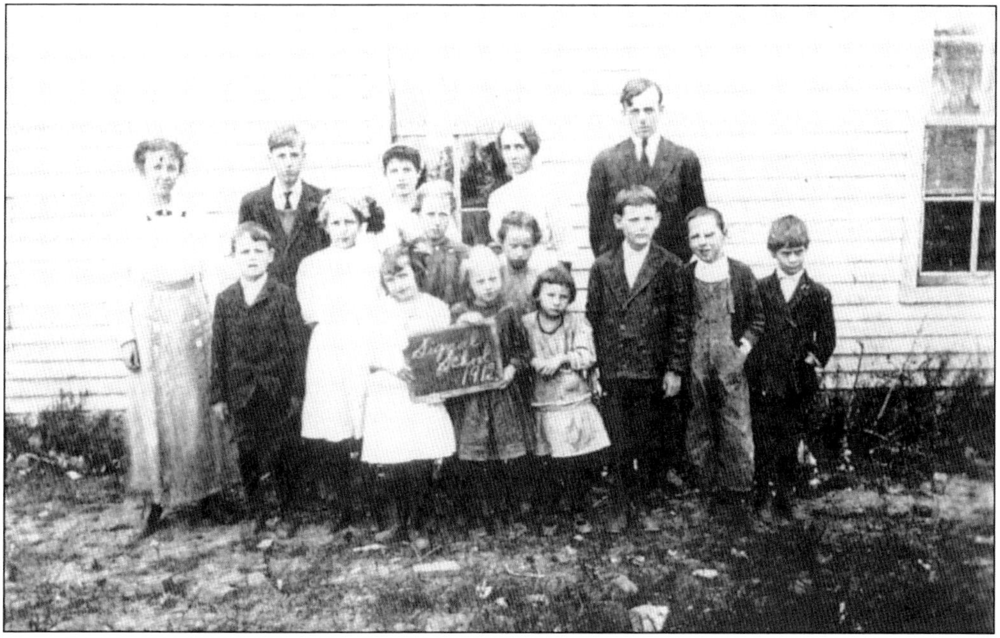

The date 1912 can be seen on the slate of this photo of Signal Hill School. This was the first year the school existed. It became district #167 of 169. From left to right are as follows: (front row) Gladys Caughman, Muriel Lyons, and Lillie Hill; (middle row) Roosevelt Center, May Caughman, Essie Lyons, Mabel Lyons, Gilbert Center, Idas Hill, and Wille Hughes; (back row) Bess Guinn (teacher), Sherman Caughman, Pearl Aday, Toni Caughman, and James Caughman (not a student). A small portion of the new, white-frame building is visible.

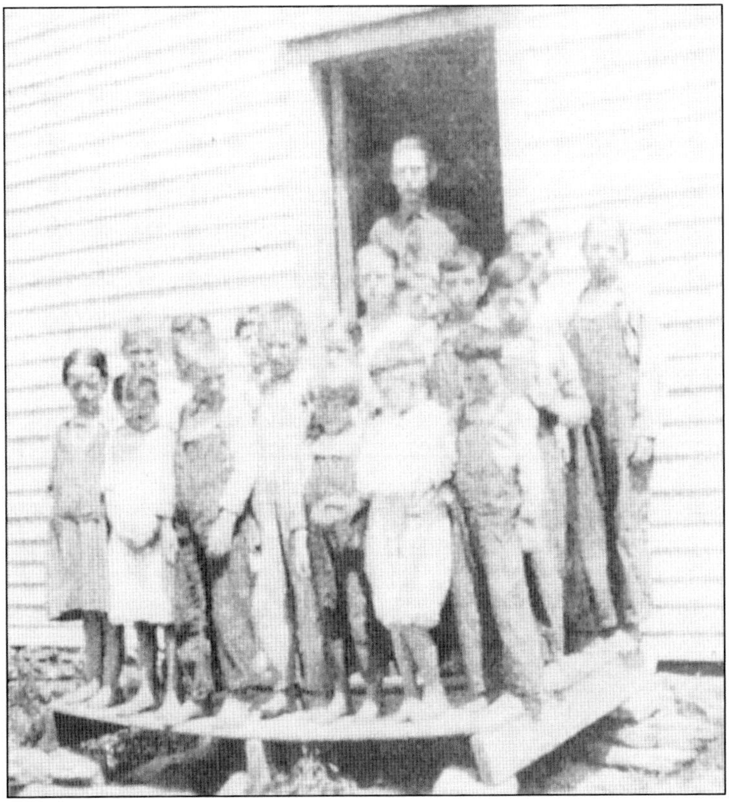

Signal Hill School probably existed a shorter length of time than any other district in the county. Located west of Winslow on top of a mountain, it was the highest-situated school in the state. A stage stop for the Butterfield Stage Line was located nearby. This 1921 picture features students from four well-known families: Faubus, Lyons, Mattingly and Westfall. Robert Winn is the teacher. After the children of these families grew up, there was no more need for the school.

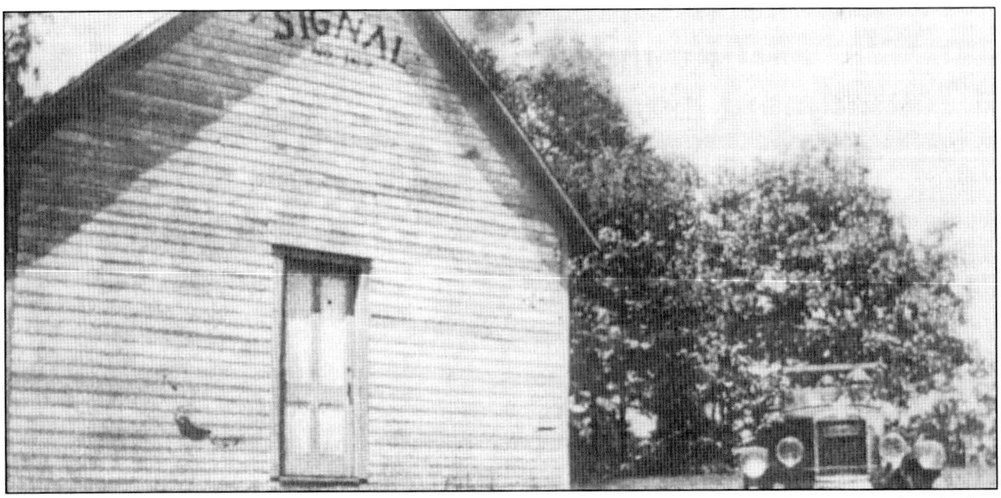

Taken after the school bell was silenced forever with the consolidation of Signal School, this photo depicts the fate of most one-room schools. The children of Sumner and Betsy Smith were the only students in the area, and they attended Winslow School. The people in the car are unidentified.

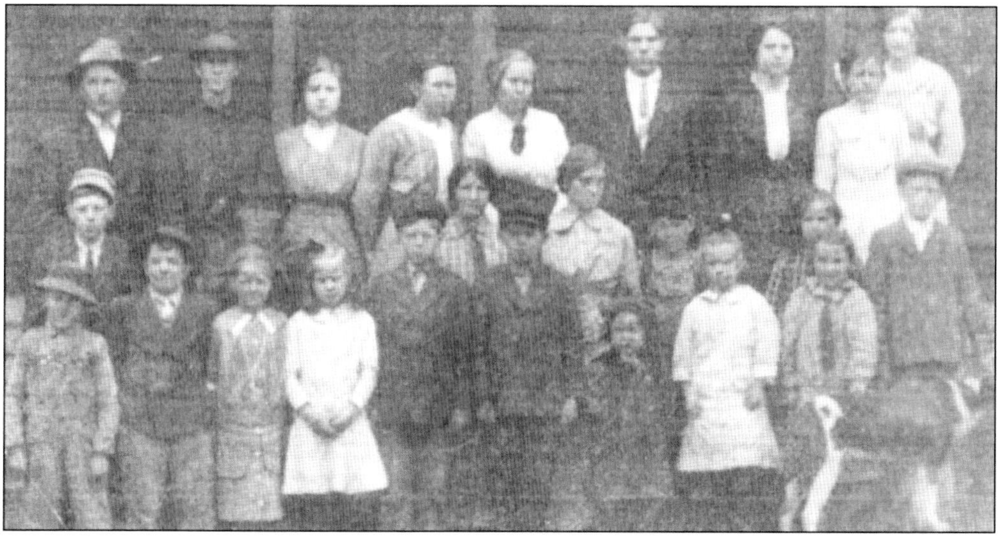

Old Red School was displaced c. 1920, when Blackburn school was built. Until that time, at least 65 children learned their three "Rs" there. The photographer, Philip Reid, arrived in a horse-drawn buggy. From left to right are as follows: (front row) Carl Parrish, Claude Southern, Agnes Bogan, Ophelia Reid, Luther Parrish, Clifford Parrish, Wanda Bogan (visitor), Blanche Lyons, Flora Southern, Clarence Bogan with his dog, Dick; (middle row) Marvin Parrish, Floyd Southern, Ora Southern, Lucretia Mannon, Burl Lyons, and Fanny Southern; (back row) Dewey Southern, Clifton Mannon, Pearl Davis, Mrs. Ethel Bogan (visitor), Sally Jones (teacher), and Everett Rucker (visitor).

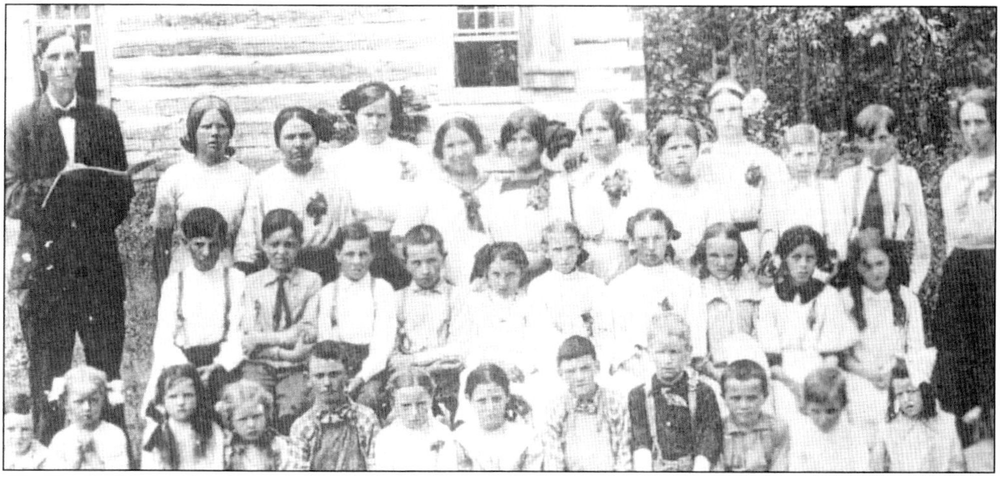

This log structure, Sassafras Pond School, replaced a subscription school known as Papa Gimme Nickel. When the log building burned c. 1925, a frame structure was built in its place. Pictured in this 1912 view, from left to right, are as follows: (front row) Dillard Clifton, Doris Poor or Lela Rush, Roenna Ridenoure or Edna Poor, George Ridenoure, Hanna Ridenoure, Stella Clifton or Martha Scott, Roy Ridenoure, Marion Poor, Henry Ridenoure, Virgil Kissinger, ? Devore or Mary Arnold or Ealine Harvey, Mary Lane or Ruth Smith; (middle row) Everett Ridenoure, Leonard Jenus or John Scott, Elmer Lane or Phoenix Kissinger, Clarence Ridenoure, and Veda Woods; (back row) Bet Poor, Annie Ridenoure, Ode Harvey, Effie Ridenoure, Myrtle Canady or Ethel Kennedy, Clara Ridenoure, Tish Poor or Lute Poor, Myrtle Ridenoure, Ervin Kissinger, Phoenix Kissinger or Henry Rush. The teacher is Walter Caughman.

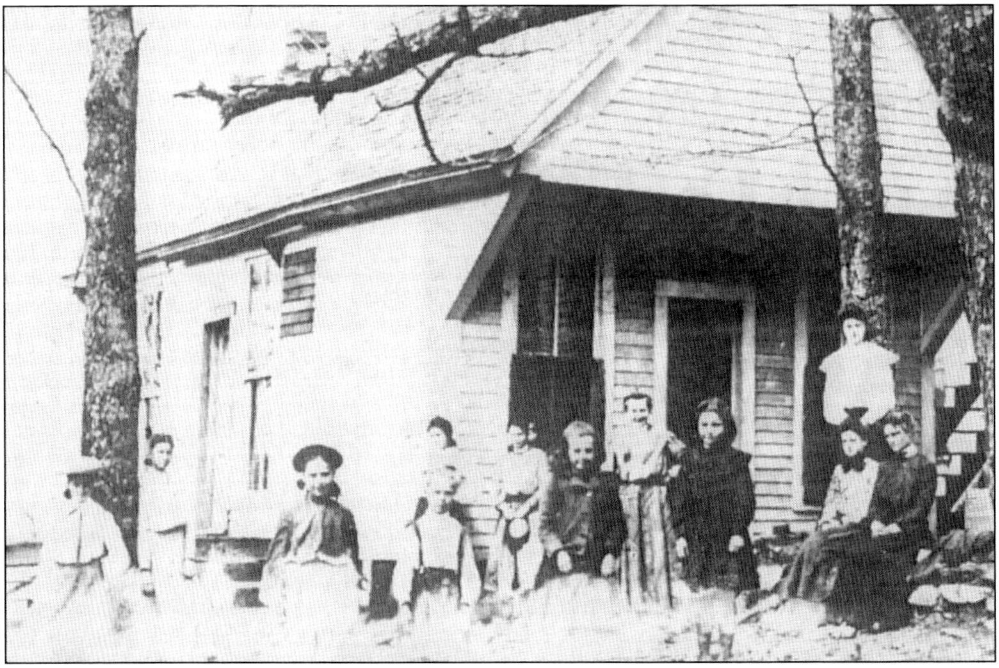

Boston Heights (the Helen Dunlap Memorial School) was established by Dr. Albert and his wife, Virginia C. Dunlap. It was a school expressly for young mountain girls who would otherwise have received no formal education. Boys attended at first, but it was later restricted to girls, many of whom boarded at the school. It was run under the auspices of the Episcopal Church.

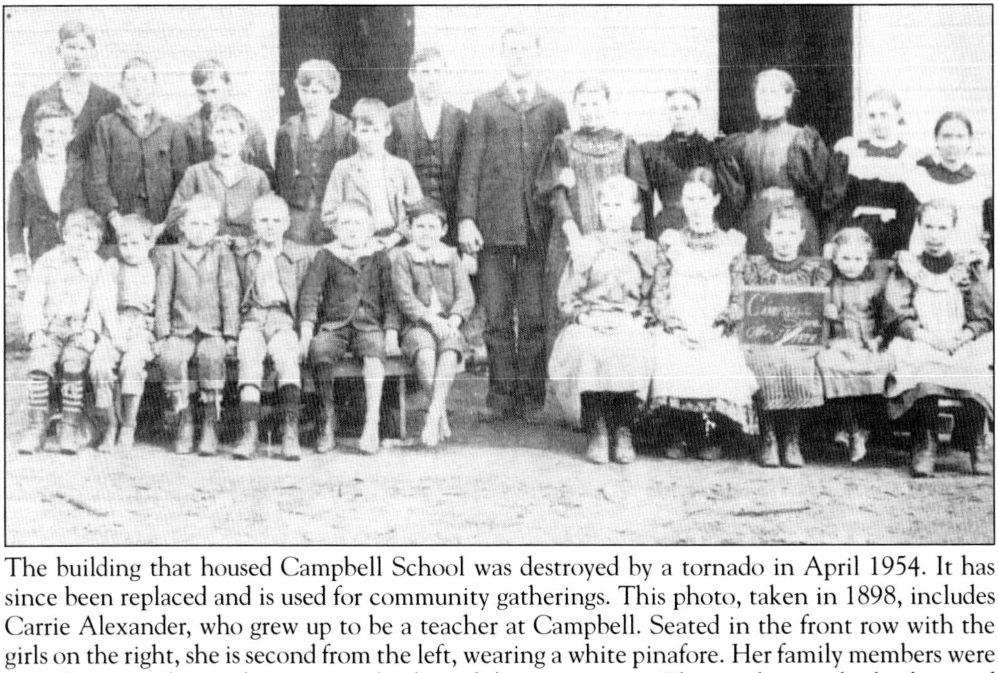

The building that housed Campbell School was destroyed by a tornado in April 1954. It has since been replaced and is used for community gatherings. This photo, taken in 1898, includes Carrie Alexander, who grew up to be a teacher at Campbell. Seated in the front row with the girls on the right, she is second from the left, wearing a white pinafore. Her family members were early homesteaders and prominent leaders of the community. The teacher in the background (center) is John E. Jones.

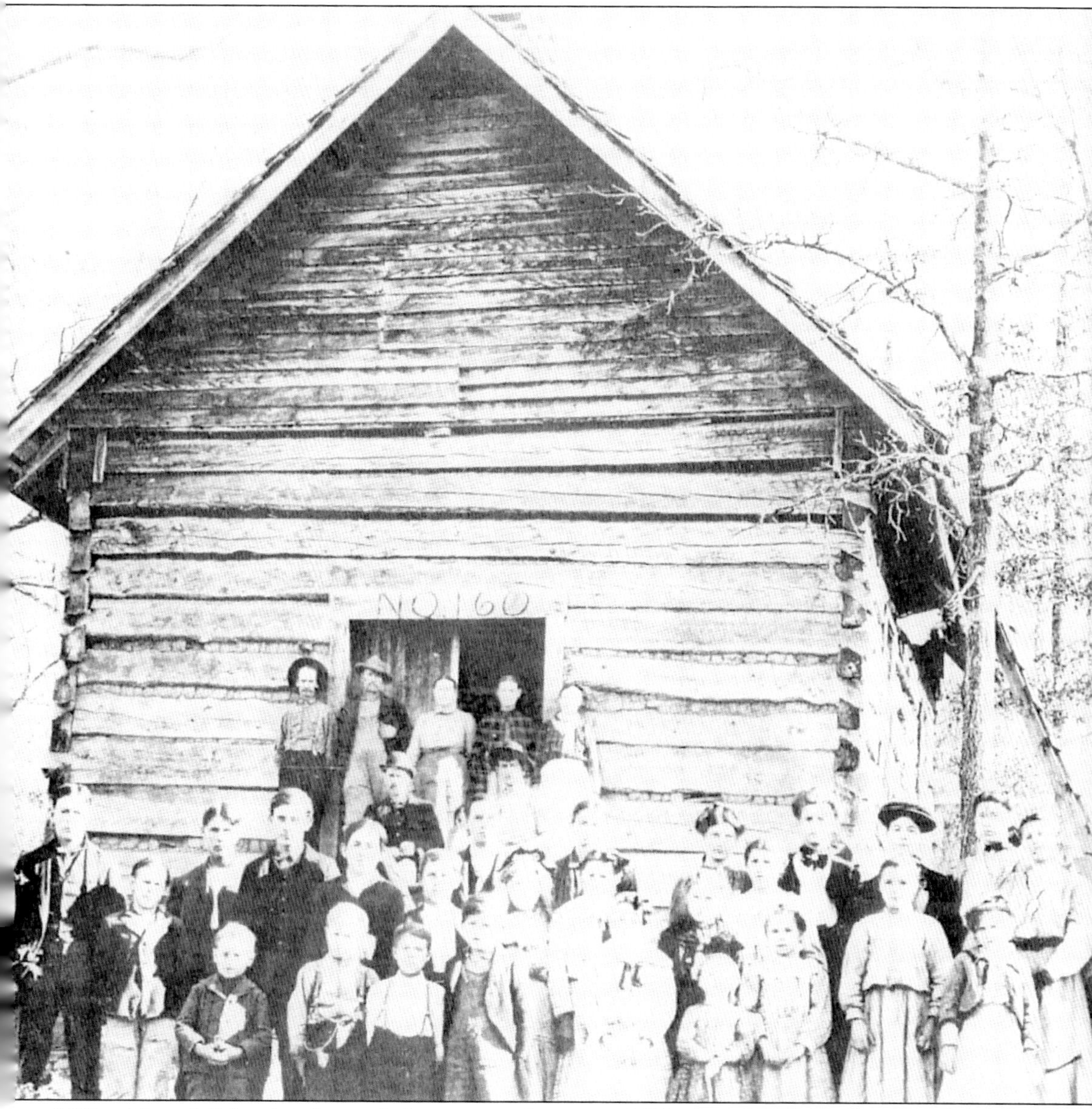

Miller Chapel School is located about six miles east of Winslow. Land for the school was purchased from Frank Miller *c.* 1887. The school became district #160 in 1888. From left to right are as follows: (front row) unidentified, Dovie Henson, Joe Mann, ? Hunter, ? Henson, unidentified, Mary Henson, Bessie Henson, Mary Wilckie, Cynthia Hampton, Marie Tanner, and Grace Henson; (second row) Frankie Providence, Bill Luper, ? Henson, Rolie Luper, Lchal, ? Henson, Lewis Sebourn, unidentified, Sitha Luper, Matilda Caughman, Mahalie Henson, ? Brashears; (third row) John Miller, ? Sebourn; (fourth row, standing on the porch) Frank Miller, Sam Preston, Mary Miller, Lily Preston, and Alta Shackelford.

Most of the families lived down in "The Chapel," along either side of a multiple branch creek. One Sunday night in 1924, a church service was held in the building. The teacher arrived the next morning to begin the new school term, but there was no schoolhouse. It had burned during the night. The new building, constructed of raw-cut, green lumber, remains at this site next to a large cemetery.

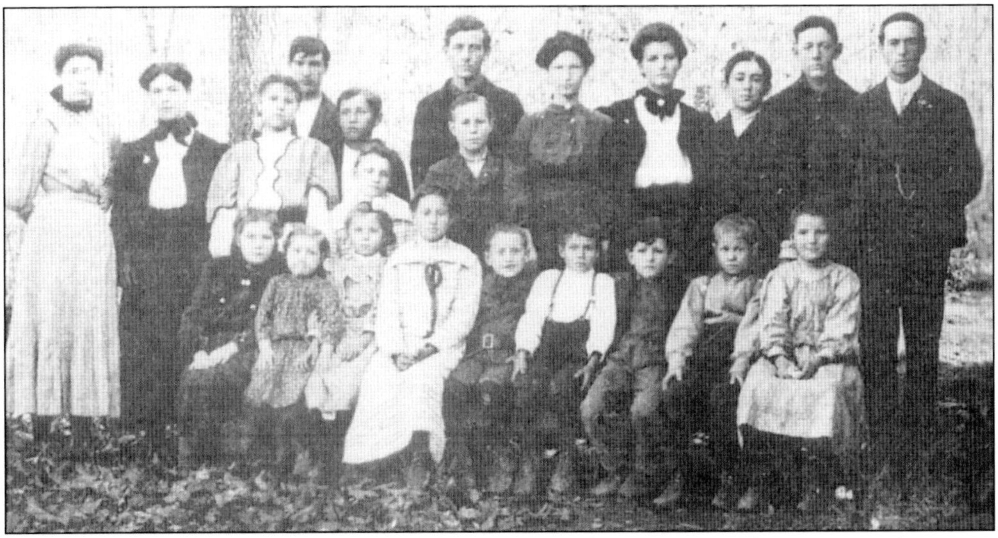

Today, Miller Chapel School is used for class reunions, decorations, and community functions. This c. 1910 photo includes both students and alumni. From left to right are as follows: (front row) Bertha Brashears, Ike Henson, John Broadie, Beulah Easter, Goldie Vaught, unidentified, Mary Henson, Bessie Henson, Dovey Henson, ? Hunter, Joe Henson, Joe Mann, and Marie Tanner; (Back row) Erma Dethridge, unidentified, Frank Providence, Rolie Luper, Litha Luper, Mathilda Caughman, Lee Paschal, Billie Luper, and Jim Luper.

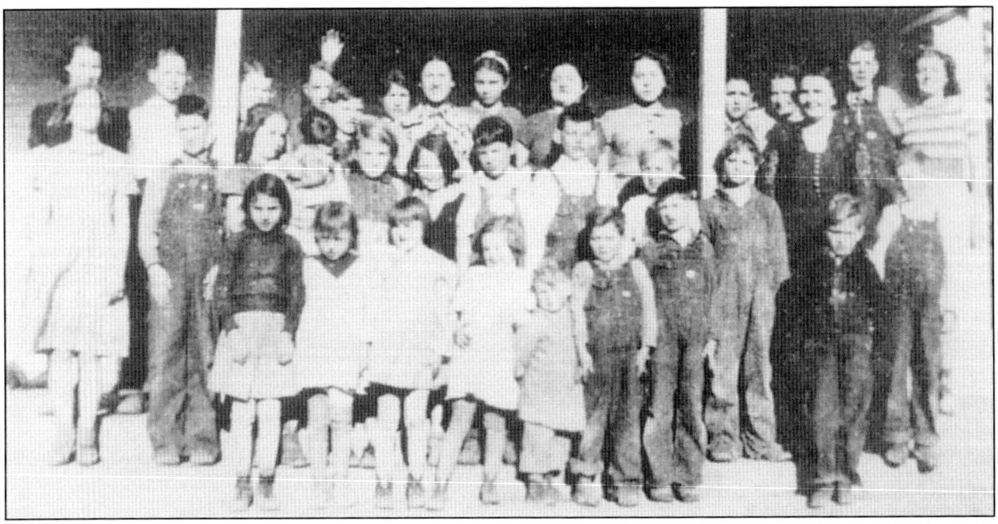

Black Oak School is about seven miles east of Winslow. There are three Black Oak Communities in the county. The one shown is in a community settled c. 1850; there was probably a subscription school there prior to this one. From left to right are as follows: (front row) Louise Lawless, unidentified, unidentified, Inalene Skelton, unidentified, unidentified, Dale Ramey, and Roscoe King (visitor);(middle row) Adrian Hutchins, Arvin Bradley, Rose Skelton, unidentified, Ruthie King (visitor), Violet Skelton, George Hardcastle, Buddy Fry, unidentified, Lester Hutchins, and Lawrence Skelton; (back row) Helen Hardcastle, Dayton Hardcastle, Dean Skelton, Oran Parrish, Billy Ramey, Robert Bradley, Ivalene Bradley, Louise Skelton, Bernice Ramey (grad), Ilora Parrish, M.C. Parrish (grad), Ruth Skelton, Geneva Price (teacher), Roger King (visitor), and Naomi Skelton (grad).

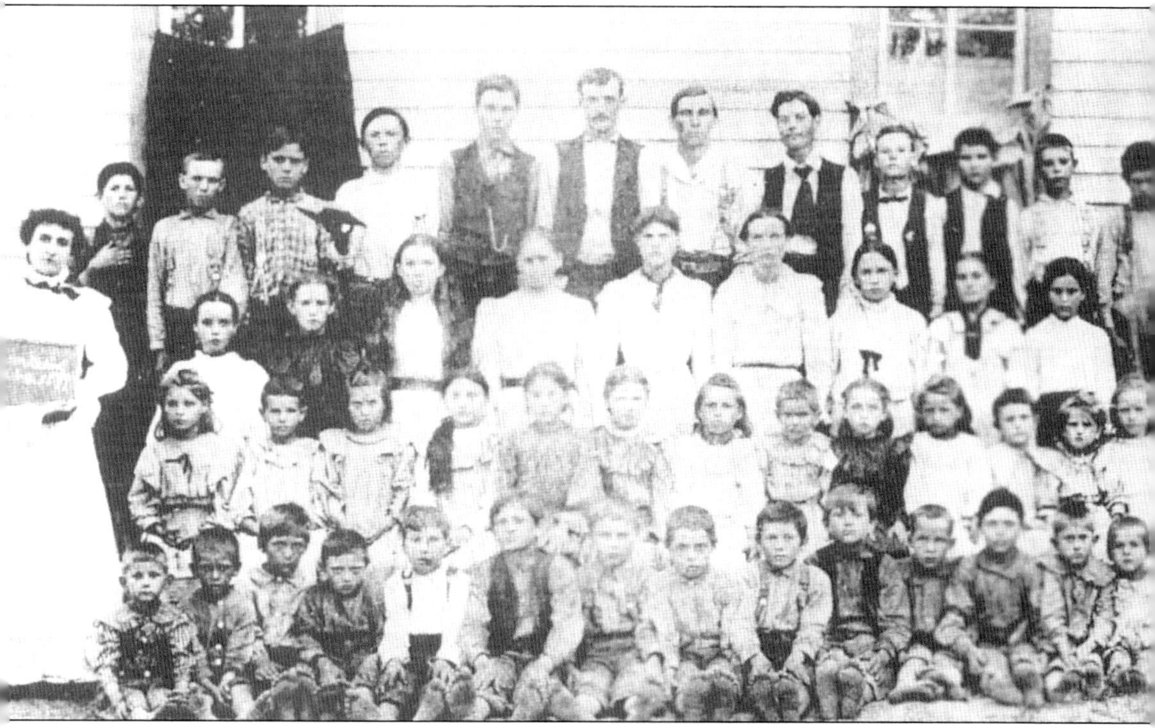

Boston School had a large attendance when this photo was taken in 1899. The teacher was Mollie Campbell. From left to right are as follows: (front row) Johnny Tackett, Jess Riggs, Willia Riggs, Floyd Logue, Jessie Terry, Louis H. Osburn, Oren Horn, Seth Horn, Frank Osburn, Charlie Osburn, Melvin Horn, Forrest Logue, William H. Tackett, Roy Horn, and Bob Dockery; (second row) Mattie Butts, Easter Dockery, Ethel Owens, Ellie Osburn, Hallie Osburn, Mollie Butts, Myrtle Terry, Missouri Osburn, and Lula Elliott; (third row) Alice Calhoun, Mary Elliott, Tennie Blevins, Mable Logue, Lula Osburn, Mida Dockery, Victoria Osburn, Lydia Elliott, Cora Dockery, Cora Osburn, Nina Elliott, Clarcy Osburn, and Rosie Butts; (fourth row) Henry Osburn, John Dockery, William H. Dockery, Sherman Terry, Asa Horn, David Condra, George Hindrickson, Osby Butts, Monroe Doss, Carwin Horn, Pleasant Terry, and Tommy Osburn. This school was first established as a subscription school in 1873. It burned in 1909 and was rebuilt near the same site as Sunset School. The new, two-story school was made of pine lumber. It had windows with screens, blackboards, a globe, and desks. On February 12, 1909, a fund-raiser was held and $15.75 was raised to buy a set of lamps for the school and an outside post lamp.

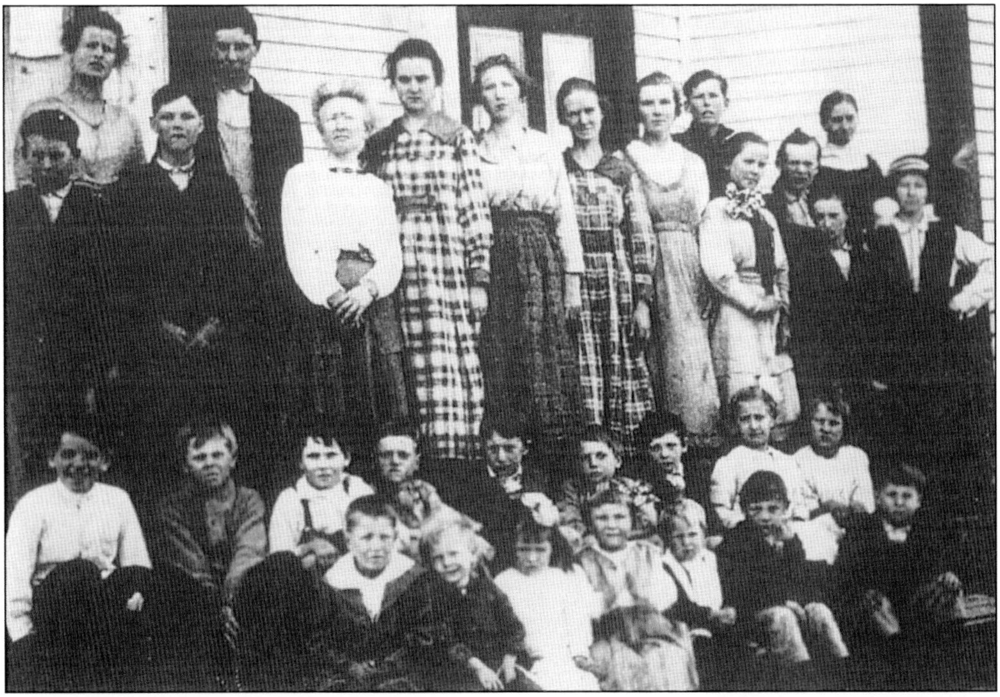

These students attended Sunset School in 1918–1919, in the building that replaced the original Boston School. From left to right are as follows: (front row) Clifford Doss, unidentified, unidentified, and ? Terry; (middle row) Lee Terry, Oliver Terry, Maud Hart (teacher), ? Dockery, Anna Brown, ? Dockery, unidentified, unidentified, Lily Doss, Clint Skelton, ? Dockery, Florie Terry, and Mellie Terry; (back row) Grace Skelton and Frank Terry.

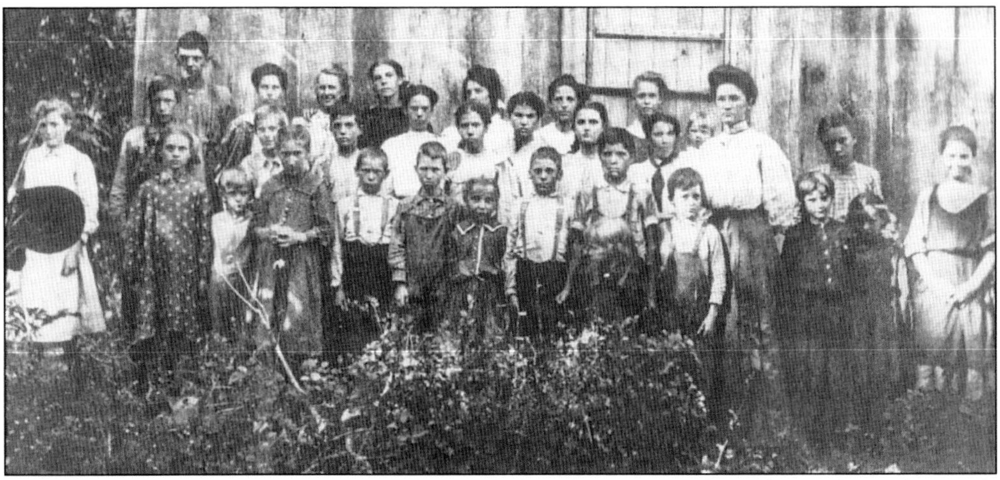

"Old" Valley Grove school was located directly below the Frisco Railroad line, a few miles north of Winslow. The earliest known existence for this school is 1881. Identification is not made individually, but the following are pictured in this 1905 view: Addison Day, Kay Foster, Lou Foster, Ollie Nickell, Mollie Nickell, Florence Nickell, Tom Nickell, Bill Waterfield, Dora Smith, Leo Waterfield, Ed Waterfield, Bessie Smith, Myrtle Watts, Alma Smith, Jim Gunnells, Pate Gunnells, Nannie Gunnells, Dick Gunnells, Barbara Notestein, Clarence Notestein, Will Notestein, Ella Reed, and Jeff Foster.

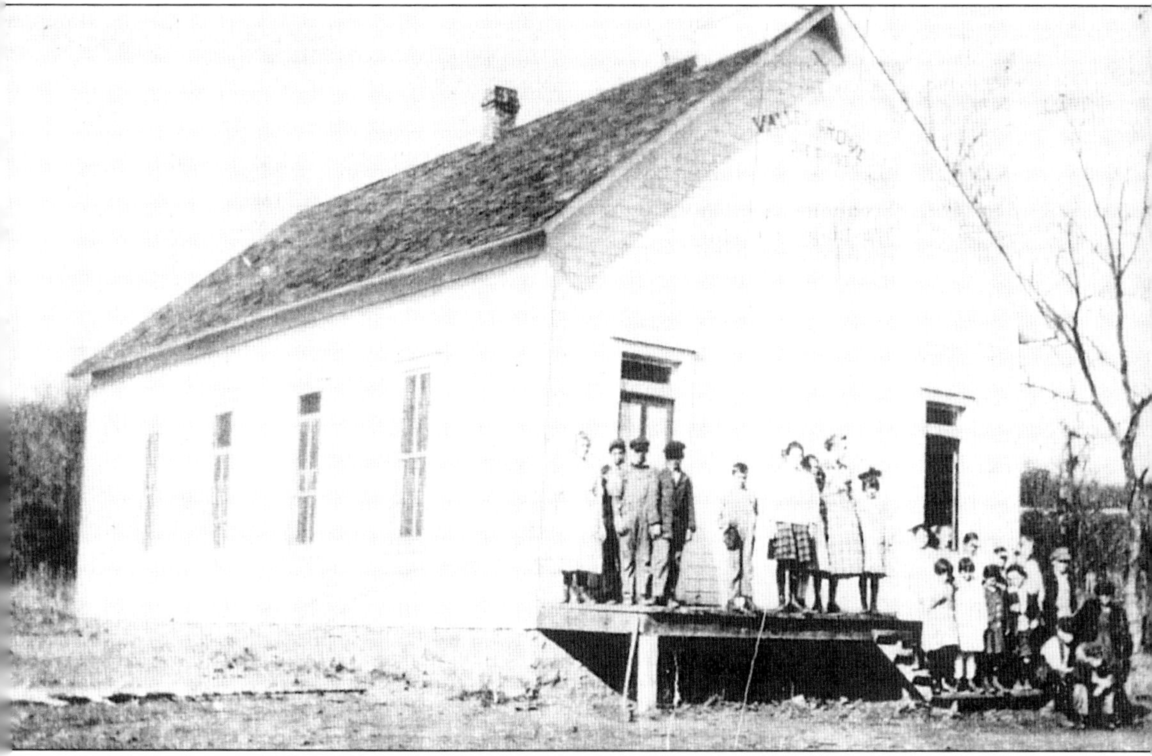

This white frame building was erected for Valley Grove School District 153, south of its original location c. 1887. The photo was taken in 1919. Students are, from left to right, as follows: Byrd Sebourn, Roy Guinn, two Gunnells boys, Toni Caughman, Glenn Anderson (teacher), Roy Anderson, Jewell ?, Ruby and Hazel Lehn, Hazel and Willie Langston, Wanda Bogan, Gladys ?, Ruby and Louise Guinn, Clyde and Lyda Smith, Miles and Jim Sebourn, and Elsie and Ethel Shackelford. Behind the building, on the right, are the tracks of the Frisco Railroad. This building, remodeled after consolidation closed the school in 1923, remains standing alongside U.S. Highway 71. For a time, it housed the Adam Reed Real Estate company, but it is now a private home. Across the highway is Slicker Swimming Hole, a favorite gathering place for youth in the area.

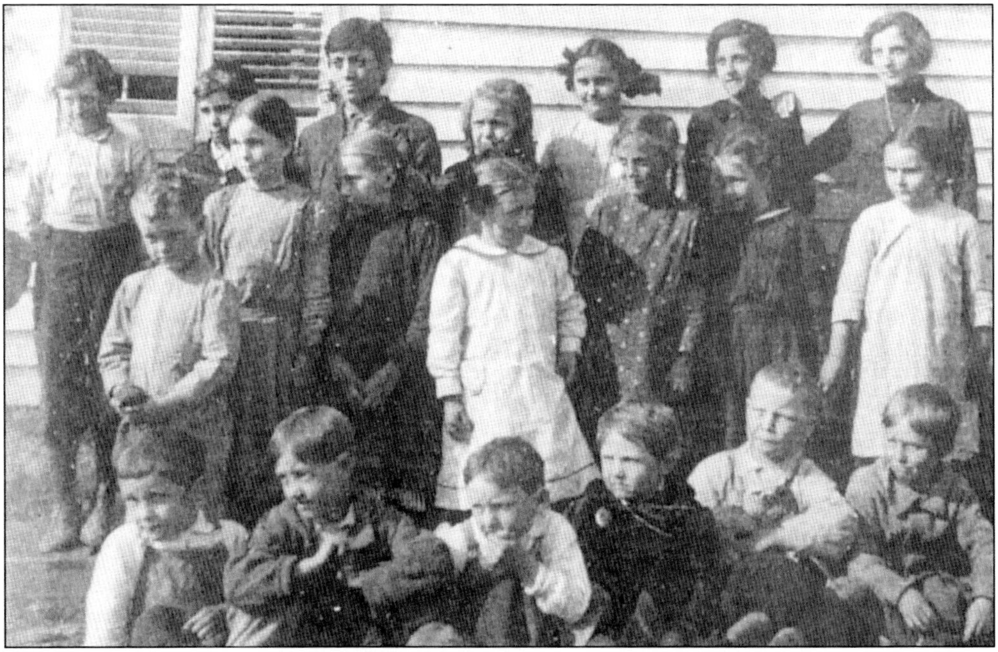

Formed in 1883, Brentwood School was located in the center of what is now U.S. Highway 71. Four years after this picture was taken, in 1913, the classroom was divided by a curtain and two teachers were hired. Nearby Dog Town School was consolidated with Brentwood in 1889. From left to right are as follows: (front row) Hugh Jett, Tillman McKenzie, Jack Hutchens, Willis Wright, Roy Day, and Lawrence Wright; (middle row) ? Ellerton, Cecilia Bell, Lillian Crossno, Nellie McKenzie, Lena Parker, Bonnie Bell, and Alta May; (back row) Aubrey McKenzie, Wendell May, Raymond McKenzie, ? Ellerton, Hazel May, Hazel Jeffrey, and Annie Parker (teacher).

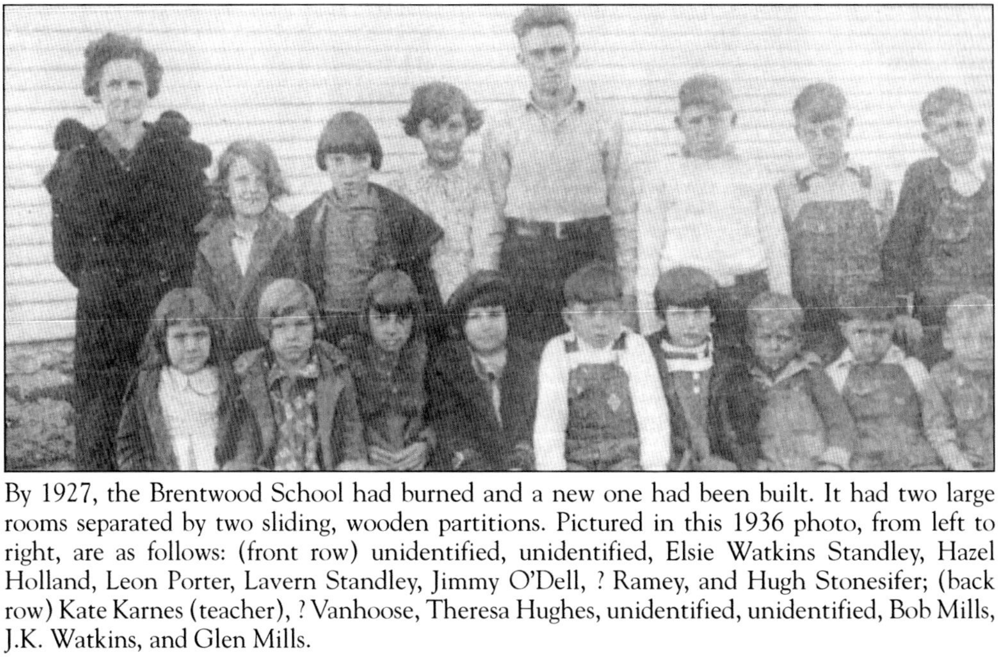

By 1927, the Brentwood School had burned and a new one had been built. It had two large rooms separated by two sliding, wooden partitions. Pictured in this 1936 photo, from left to right, are as follows: (front row) unidentified, unidentified, Elsie Watkins Standley, Hazel Holland, Leon Porter, Lavern Standley, Jimmy O'Dell, ? Ramey, and Hugh Stonesifer; (back row) Kate Karnes (teacher), ? Vanhoose, Theresa Hughes, unidentified, unidentified, Bob Mills, J.K. Watkins, and Glen Mills.

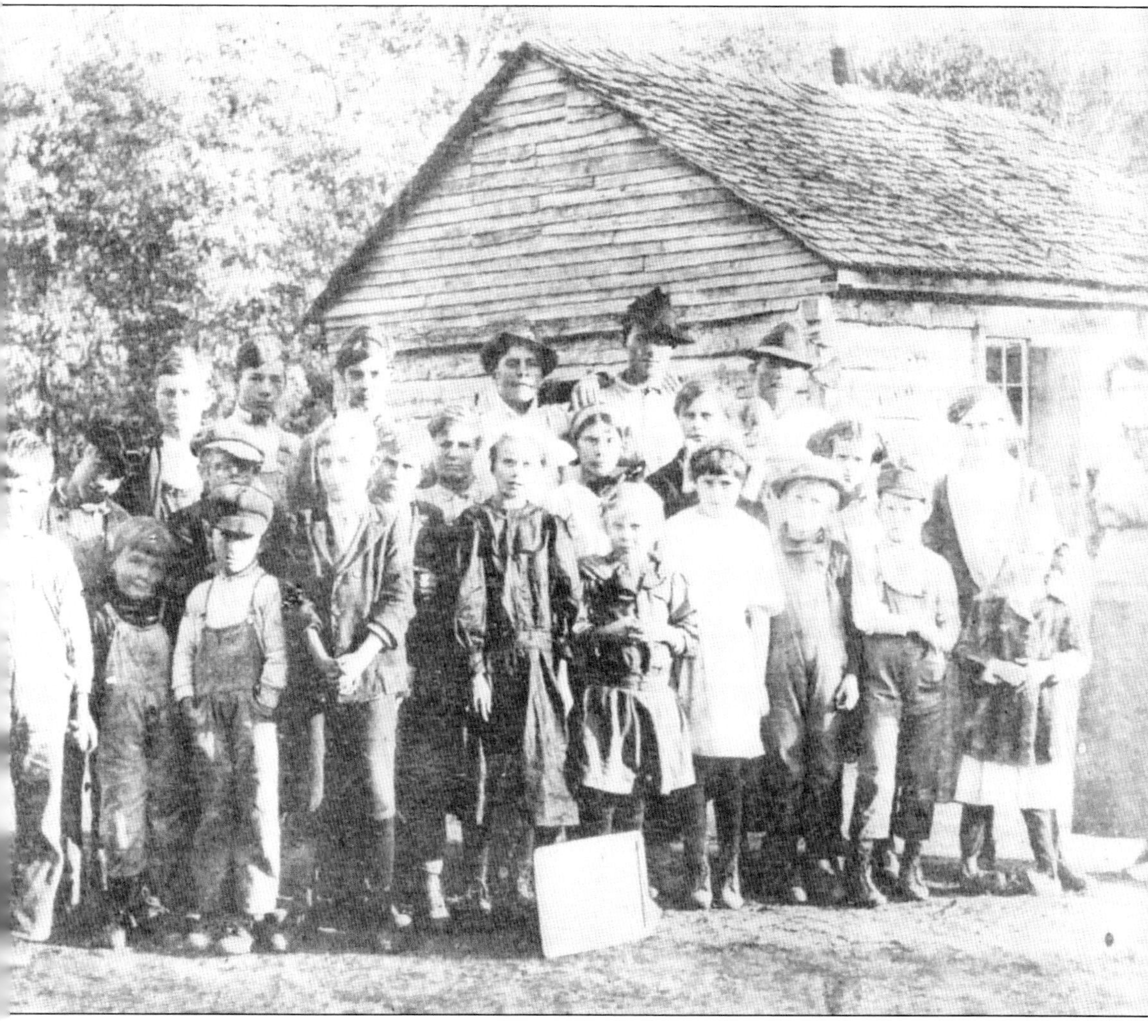

McDaniel School bears the distinction of having served the first hot lunches in the area. Across the road, on top of the mountain, was a thriving sawmill. Each day, the wife of the sawyer cooked over an open fire for the men who worked there. She often sent hot soup down to the school. The students in this picture attended McDaniel in 1912. They are, from left to right, as follows: Glen Anderson, Jessie Davidson, Edd Dillard, Earnest Weaver, Marvin Davidson, Paul Dudley, Marvin Anderson, Anzie Tomlinson, Odis Hutchens, Wayne Davidson, Paul Davidson, Sylvia Tomlinson, Martha Tomlinson, Pet Foster, Maggie Tomlinson, Jack Hutchens, Joe Davidson, Harvey Barnhill, Marry Dillard, Marie Weaver, Mable Nott, Arthur Davidson, Roy Anderson, Ethel Foster, and Pink Dillard (teacher). The building is typical of the first log schools built in the county. Note the shutters; many buildings of this type did not have window glass. For the most part, school was held through the late summer and let out for the year at Christmas so the children wouldn't have to walk in bitter cold weather.

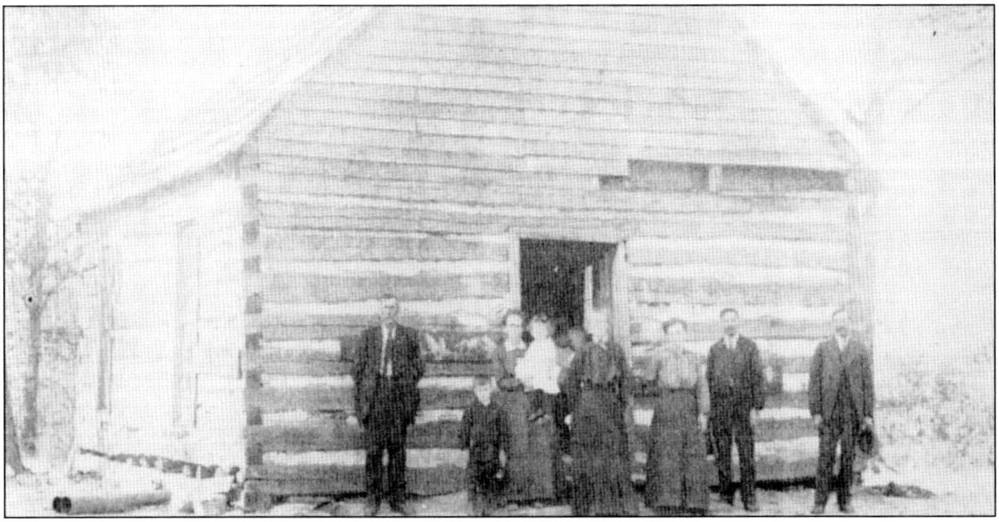

The original Mineral Springs School was established in 1885, one full year after the first request was made to build a new school from families whose children walked much too far to attend Round Mountain. This photo is a view of the celebration of the first Christmas in the new school building. The tradition of the Christmas tree was not widespread in the Ozarks at that time; early Ozark pioneers were of Dutch or German descent.

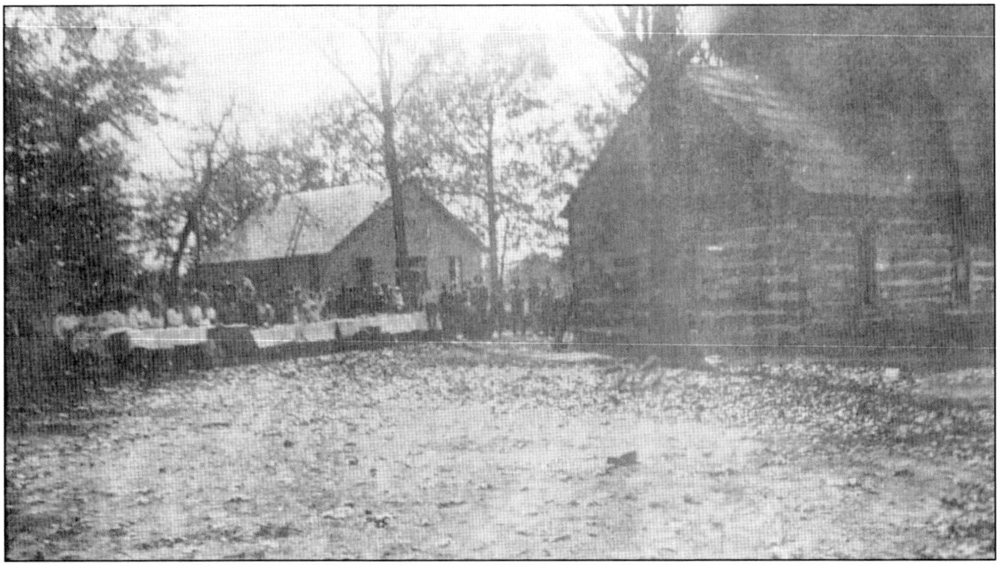

In the background, a huge gathering celebrates the building of a new schoolhouse at Mineral Springs in November 1915. The original log building is seen in the foreground. This one-room school building was recently added to the National List of Historic Places. It is also listed by the Arkansas Historic Preservation.

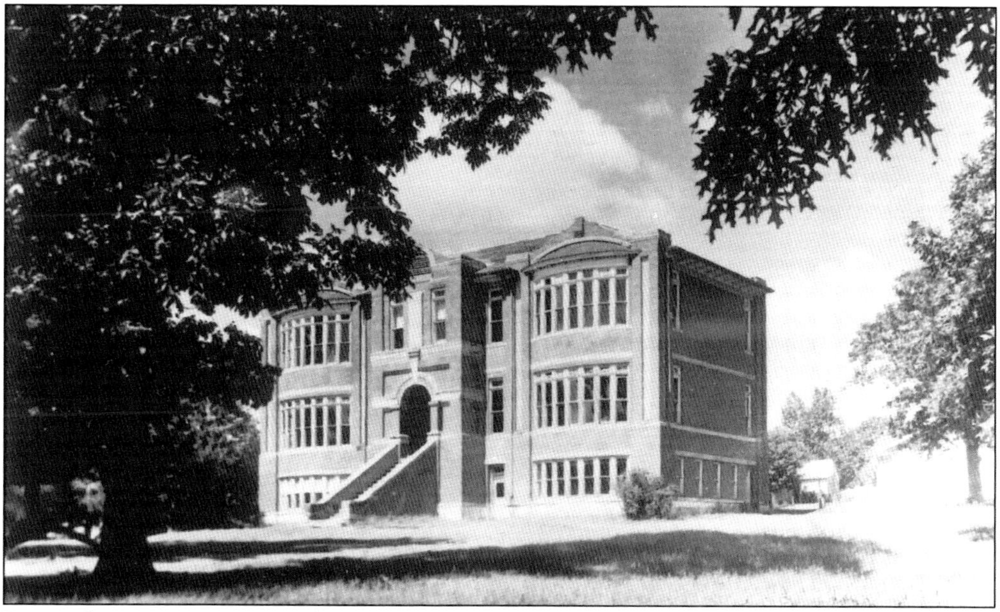

Pictured is Prairie Grove School in 1911. Though the city had various schools begun by churches, its first public high school was opened in 1883 in a two-story brick building, with several teachers involved in the project. There was no running water or electricity, no school lunch programs or athletics, and everyone walked to and from school. The first graduating class was in 1905. Graduates included Porter Pittman, Manard Dorman, Amy Blakemore, Dorothea Campbell, and Emily Maupin. (Photo courtesy of Roy Nixon and Shiloh Museum of Ozark History, Springdale.)

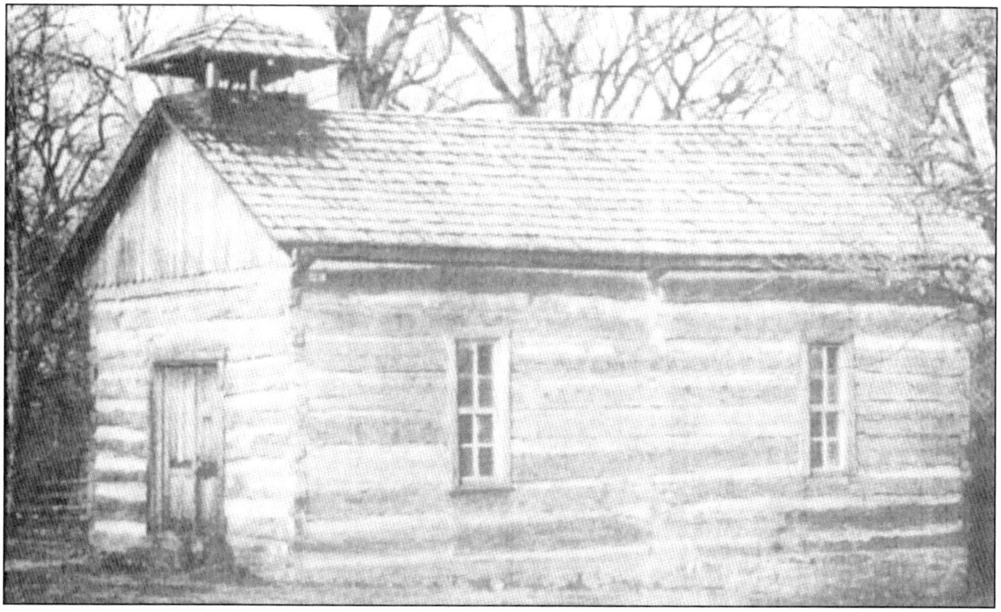

Garrett Creek (Garrett Hollow) School was located about 20 miles south of Prairie Grove, on Cove Creek Road. It was opened in 1889 as a district, but classes were probably held there much earlier. The building has been preserved and moved to the grounds of Battlefield Park in Prairie Grove.

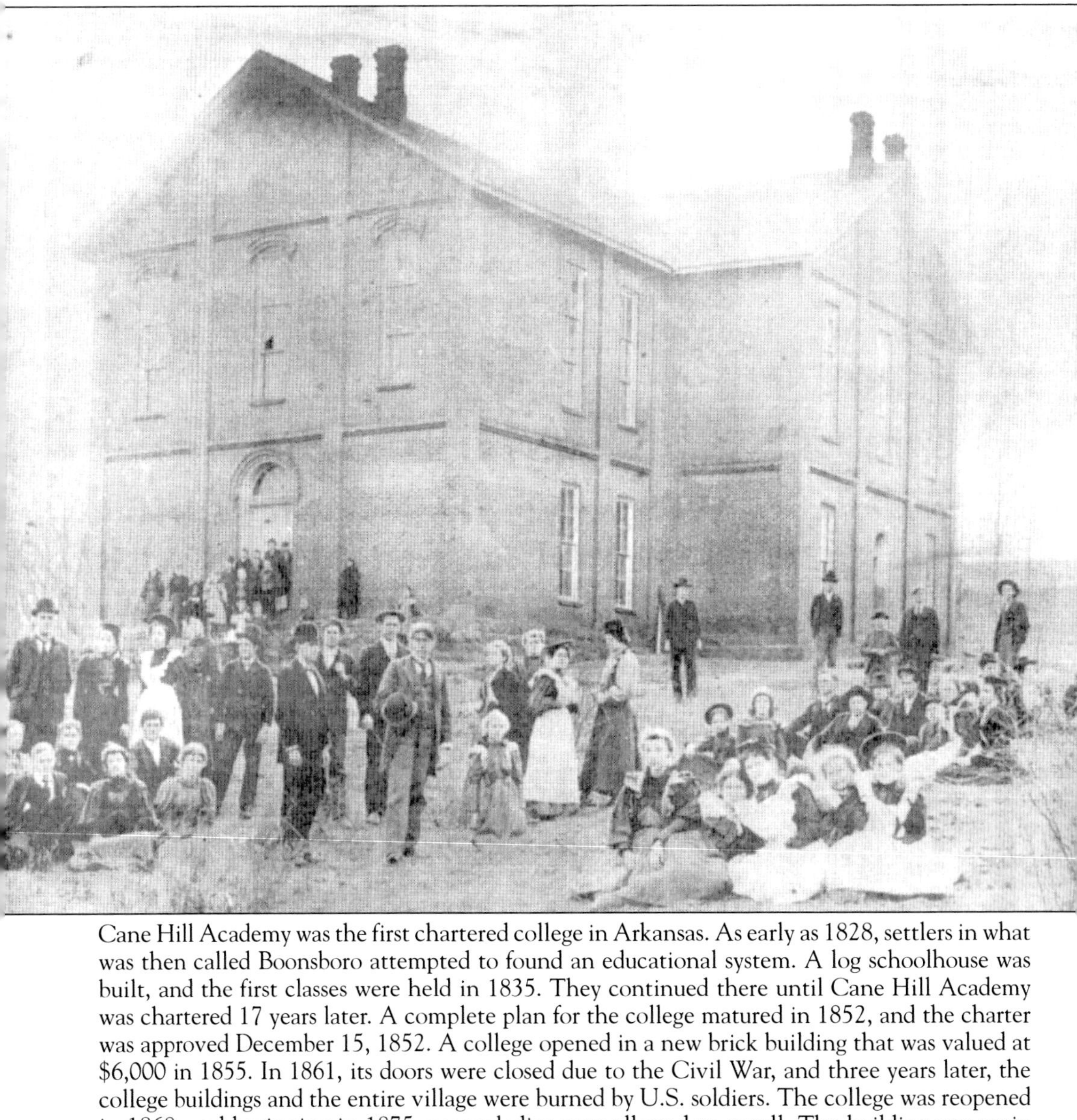

Cane Hill Academy was the first chartered college in Arkansas. As early as 1828, settlers in what was then called Boonsboro attempted to found an educational system. A log schoolhouse was built, and the first classes were held in 1835. They continued there until Cane Hill Academy was chartered 17 years later. A complete plan for the college matured in 1852, and the charter was approved December 15, 1852. A college opened in a new brick building that was valued at $6,000 in 1855. In 1861, its doors were closed due to the Civil War, and three years later, the college buildings and the entire village were burned by U.S. soldiers. The college was reopened in 1868, and beginning in 1875, young ladies were allowed to enroll. The building was again destroyed in 1885, this time by accident. The building shown here, a two-story brick structure, was erected in 1887. The state university (University of Arkansas) in Fayetteville, founded in 1871, soon overshadowed the academy, and its doors were closed for good in 1891. One building remains standing; it is presently used as a museum.

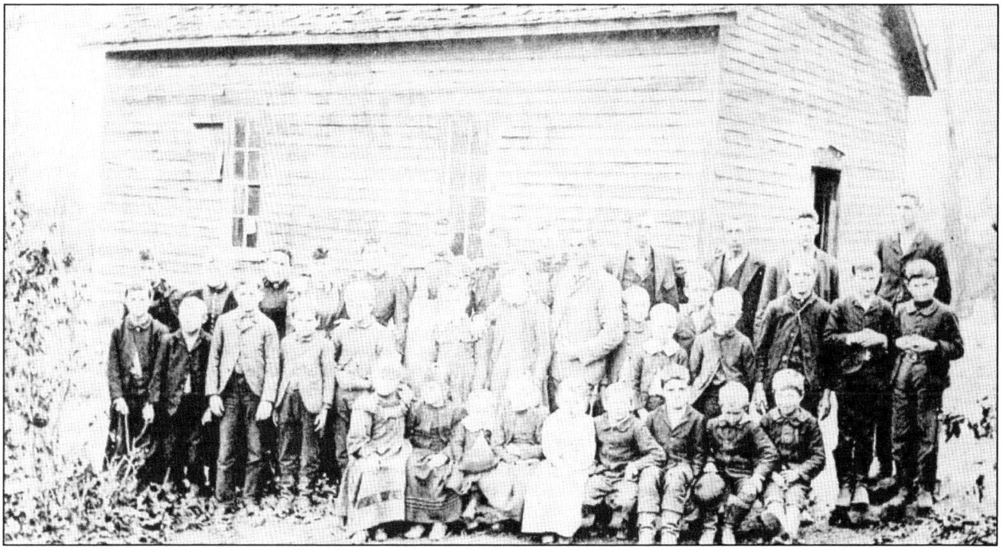

Constructed in 1880, Round Mountain was the sixteenth school district in the county. This building replaced a private (subscription) school in Owl Holler known as Shanghai. Very short terms were held at the school because parents couldn't afford to pay for longer sessions. There were ten families in the community, and between them, there were 100 school-age children. When fire destroyed Shanghai, it was imperative that a new school was built to replace it. The photo is not dated, and the students shown are unidentified.

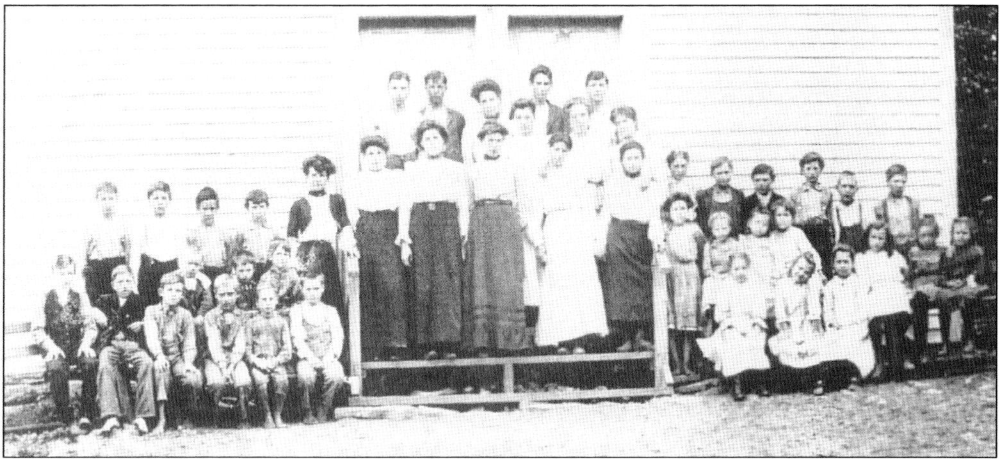

Commonly known as Low Gap School, district 89 was officially Fairview School. Shown here in 1904, students are, from left to right, as follows: (front row, left of steps) Jessie Pridemore, Roy Brown, Roy Fine, Frank Wiles, Arthur Wiles, and Fieldon Chandler; (middle row, left of steps) Thomas Chandler, Earl Brown, and Nealie Fine: (back row, left of steps) Jess Morgan, Weaver Mann, Archie Lathrop, Earl Shook, and Millie Robb; (front row, center) Ina Morgan, Annie Morgan, Ida Morgan, Maudie Mann, and Alice Smith; (middle row, center) Myrtle Burris, Eva Burris, and Nellie Lathrop; (back row, center) Clarence Chandler, Martin Brown, Oma Stockburger (teacher), Archie Smith, and Bryan Mann; (front row, right of steps) Madge Morgan, Hattie Williams, Anna Williams, unidentified, Minnie Howell, and Grade Pridemore; (middle row, right of steps) Nola Foutch, May Hooten, Maudie Williams, and Rosie Foutch; (back row, right of steps) Clemma Howell, Virgil Lathrop, Jim Robb, Clint Shook, Ellis Burris, and Jim Morgan.

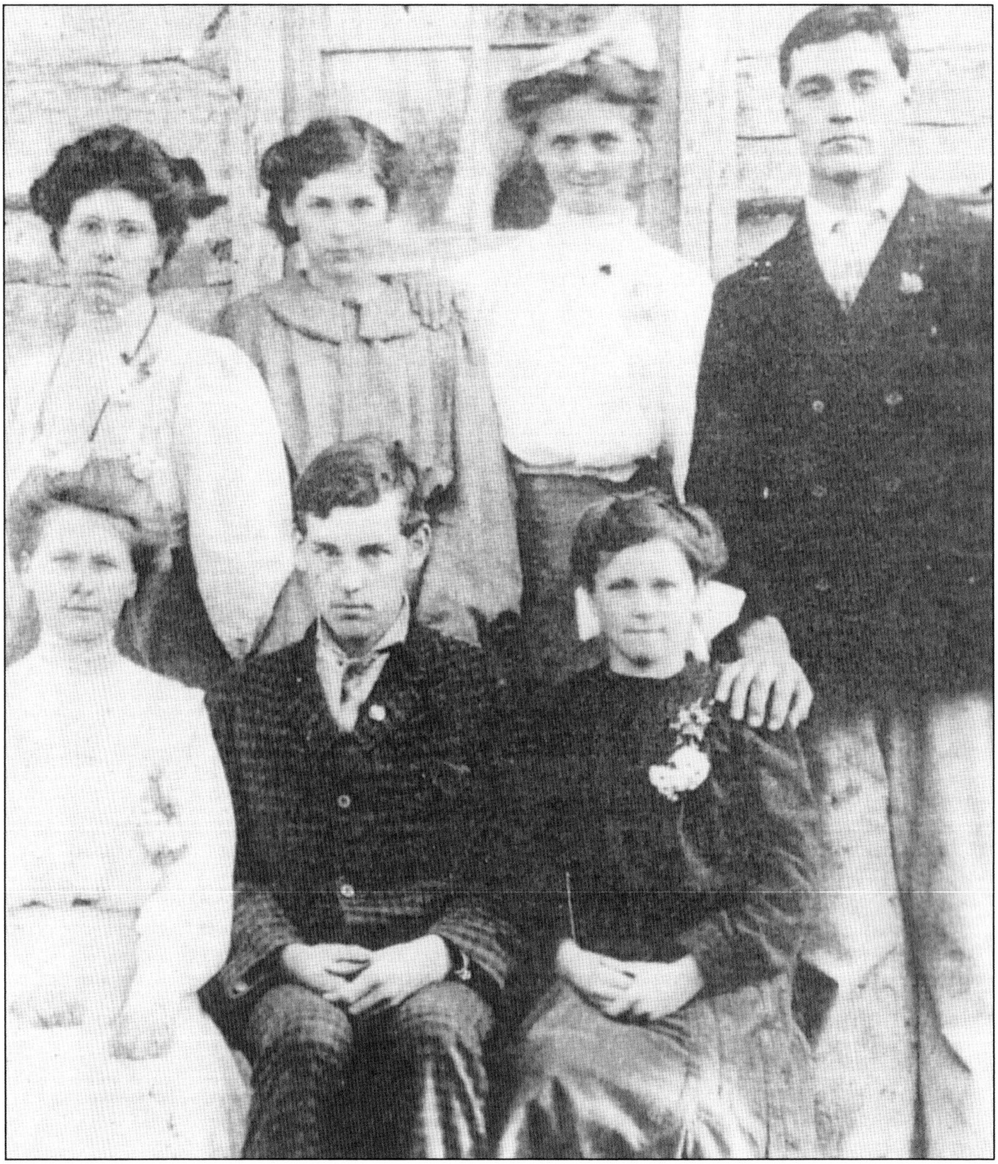

Records show that Mt. Olive School was in existence in 1880. This picture is dated 1907. From left to right are as follows: (front row) Ellen Johnston Arnold, Elisha Johnston, and Tilda Redfern Ridenoure; (back row) Erma Deathridge (teacher), Lou Johnston Brady, Pearl Johnston Hays, and Austin Mannon. The school became district 30 and was located on a steep, crooked road leading into what is now Devil's Den State Park, near Winslow. In the late 1930s, boys with the Civilian Conservation Corps, who were building the park, cut wood for the school so it could be heated. During that time, the teacher, Retha Woods, rode to school on horseback; she kept her horse in a nearby pasture. The school was nicknamed "Possum Knob College." It merged with Blackburn in 1937, after mail service to the area was discontinued. This made it necessary for folks to travel to the post office in Blackburn for their mail. Since the residents had to travel to the area to receive their mail, the transition of sending their children to the school was easily made. Students were thrilled one day to receive movie passes from the park superintendent and be allowed to hear and see Kate Smith singing on the screen.

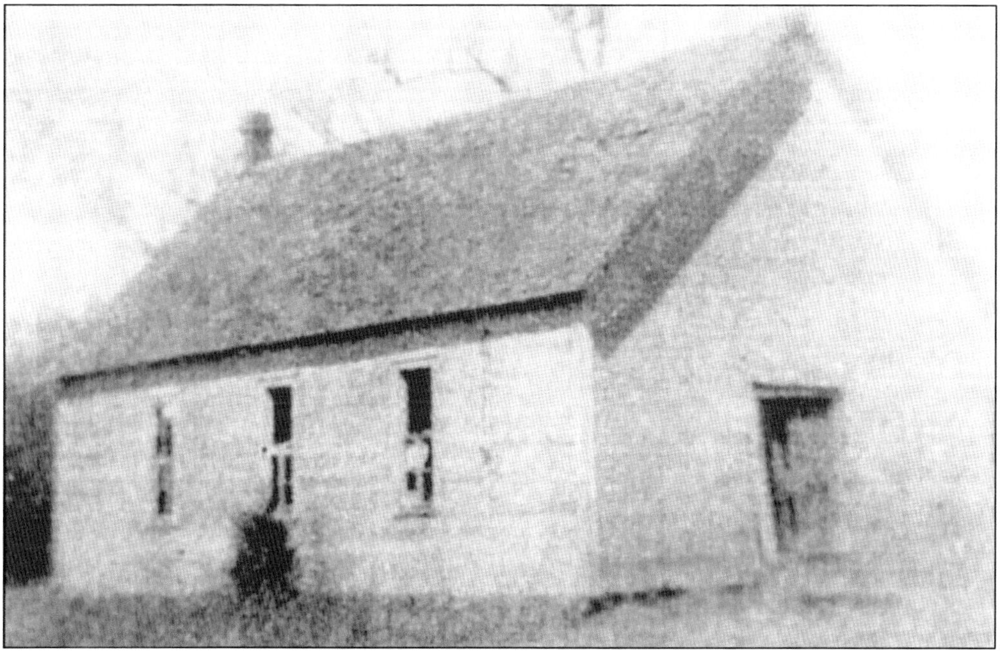

This is the last picture taken of Shady Grove School, which was located near the community of Hog Eye (Hogeye). Directly south of this school was a school for black children, which was unusual because there were very few blacks in Washington County outside Fayetteville. A teacher at Shady Grove during the early 1900s rode a mule to class every day from her home at Dripping Springs.

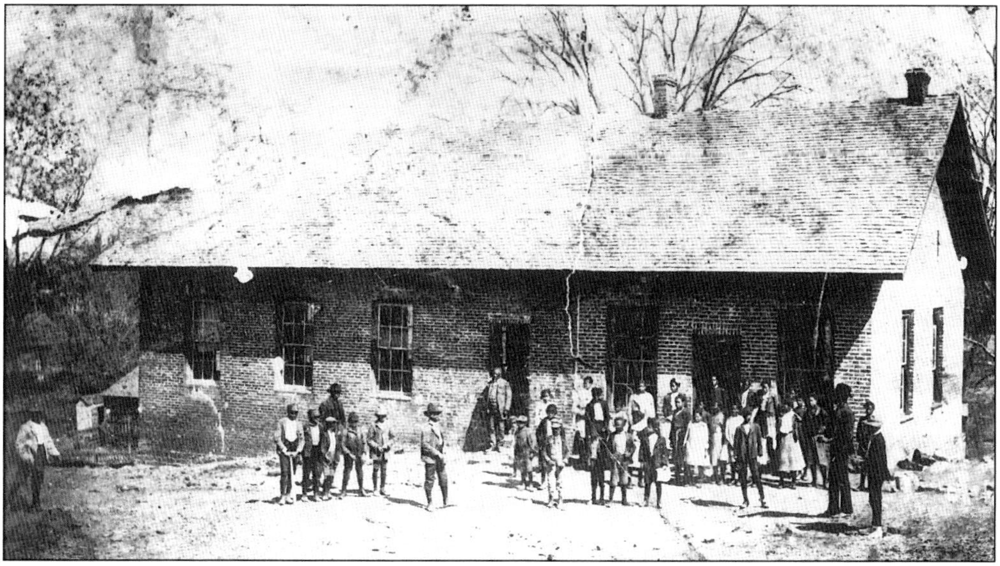

From 1870 through 1890, the county was favorable to black growth. Though subscription schools were common at the time, Henderson School (pictured), was probably the first free school in Fayetteville. It was built in 1868. Another black school existed south of Shady Grove, which is in the Hog Eye area. Most students were the children of migrant workers and ex-slaves who followed the crop harvests. (Photo courtesy of Robert G. Winn and Shiloh Museum of Ozark History, Springdale.)

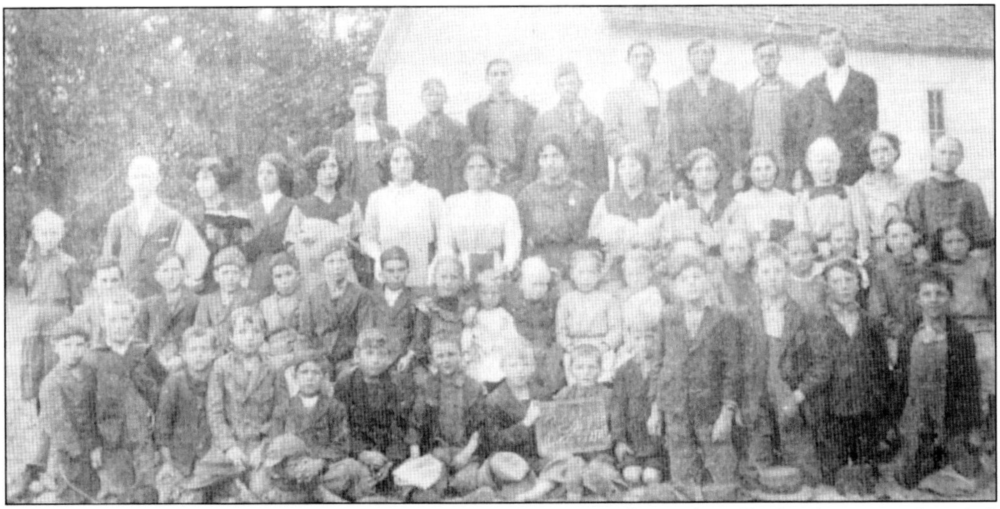

In 1912, Zinnamon School had a huge enrollment for one teacher to handle. Students are, from left to right, as follows: (first row) Clarence McBride, Leo McKnight, Thomas Steward, Floyd Dotson, Joe Montgomery, Otto Dotson, Pete Caviness, Sam McGarrah, Sam Richardson, Floyd Cobb, Jake Hall, Frank McGarrah, Frank Cobb, and Joe Caviness; (second row) Susie Treece, Oscar Strickler, Grace McBride, Lucy Montgomery, Ethel McBride, Fannie Dotson, Mae Miller, Lona Strickler (teacher), Mae McBride, Alice Montgomery, Ethel Miller, Pearl Strickler, Bettie Caviness, and Zelma Stewart; (third row) Ralph Hayes, Everett Richardson, Charley McBride, Claud Miller, Glenn McBride, Ivan Wilson, Mae Stewart, Flora Smallwood, Ruby Strickler, Nora Miller, Dorthea McGarrah, Alice Rieff, Ola Caviness, Ruby Wilson, Lillie Smallwood, Zona Richardson, Ella Hall; (fourth row) Earl Strickler, John Treece, Everett Miller, Clair McGarrah, Rufus Deaton, Frank McBride, Oscar Miller, and Lewis Treece.

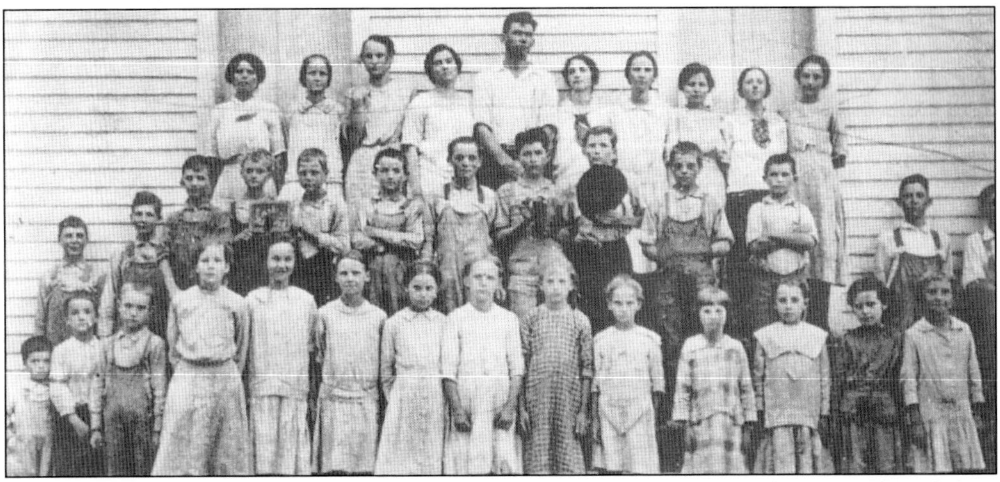

By 1916, Zinnamon School's enrollment had dropped considerably. Students are, from left to right, as follows: (front row) Jeff Miller, Burl Dotson, Delford Rieff, Florence Treece, Hazel Bayless, Alice Rieff, Nora Miller, Mae Steward, Lillian Dotson, Gladys Hall, Alice Richardson, Nettie Cobb, Eva Miller, and Bessie Rieff; (middle row) Frank Cobb, Charlie McBride, Sam Richardson, Earl Smallwood, Tom Steward, Roy Dotson, Floyd Dotson, Mike Ford, Glenn McBride, Elmer Wright, Clarence McBride, Ivan Kennedy, and Everett Richardson; (back row) Mae Miller, Susie Treece, Zelma Stewart, Mary Ford, Joe Copeland (teacher), Ethel McBride, Zona Richardson, Ethel Miller, Ruby Kennedy, and Nettie Easom.

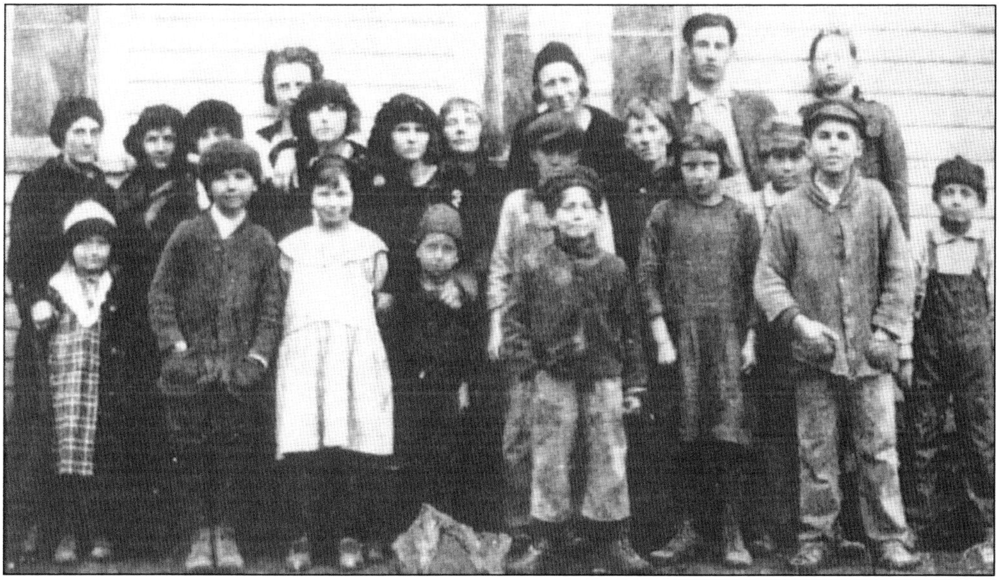

The year after this photo was taken in 1921, Old Sycamore School was moved and renamed Winn's Creek School. The students are, from left to right, as follows: (front row) Iva Smith-Kennedy, Elmer Garrett, Edith Roberts, Alvin Roberts, Eugene Richardson, ? Roberts, Orville Garrett, and Roy Davis; (middle row) Jewell Caudle (teacher), Irene Harp, Velma Brock, unidentified, Ethel Harp, Eura Roberts, Emory Brock, Fred Doyle, and Howard Davis; (back row) Effie Smith Hays, Bertha Doyle, Argil Brock, and Frank Richardson.

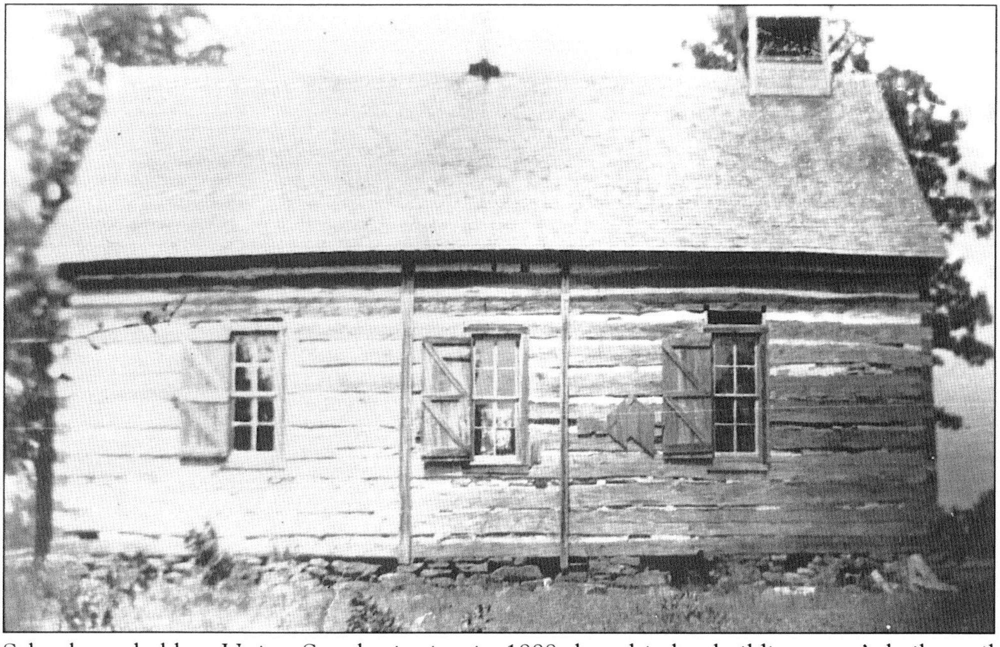

School was held at Union Star beginning in 1888, but this log building wasn't built until 1895. Three years later, the district was enlarged to include Shady Grove and Longview (Holcomb). The building was destroyed by fire soon after consolidation with West Fork in 1949. (Photo courtesy of Shiloh Museum of the Ozarks, Springdale, from the Bernice Karnes and Rae Smith collection.)

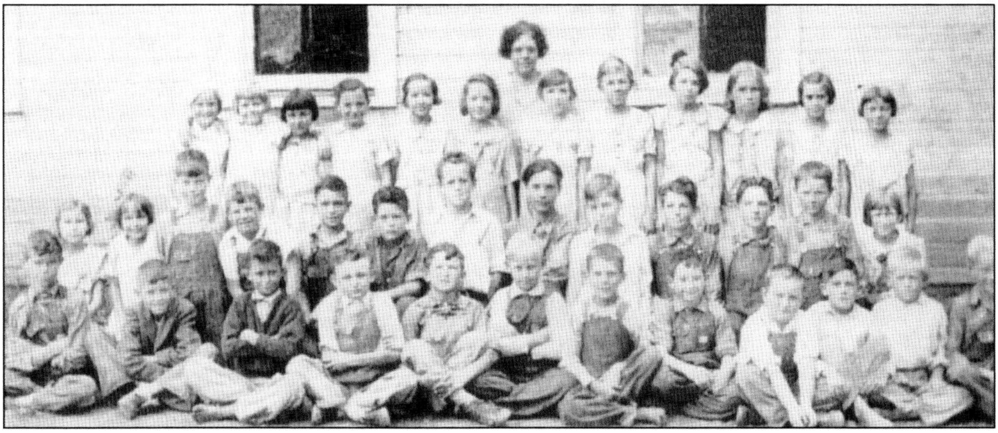

By 1934, one teacher at West Fork taught fourth, fifth, and sixth grades. Students pictured are, from left to right, as follows: (front row) unidentified, Marvin Winn, Kenny Bell, Wendell Caughman, Roy Webber, Rex Harrison, Ray Roseberry, J.C. Jay Webber, Charles Stearns, Calvin Curtis, Bobby Curtis, and David Roseberry; (middle row) Clara Jean Noel, unidentified, Glen Hudson, Howard Lipson, Floyd Drybread, Ben H. Noel, Dale Drybread, Loyd Drybread, O.D. Little, and Louise Baker; (back row) Jean Dameron, Mildred Earp, Betty Underhill, Ruth Lofton, Mildred Donald, unidentified, Muriel Ray, Rozene Hobbs, Jessie Ruth Winn, Myrtle Hutton, Emma Ruth Phillips, and Marjorie Lee.

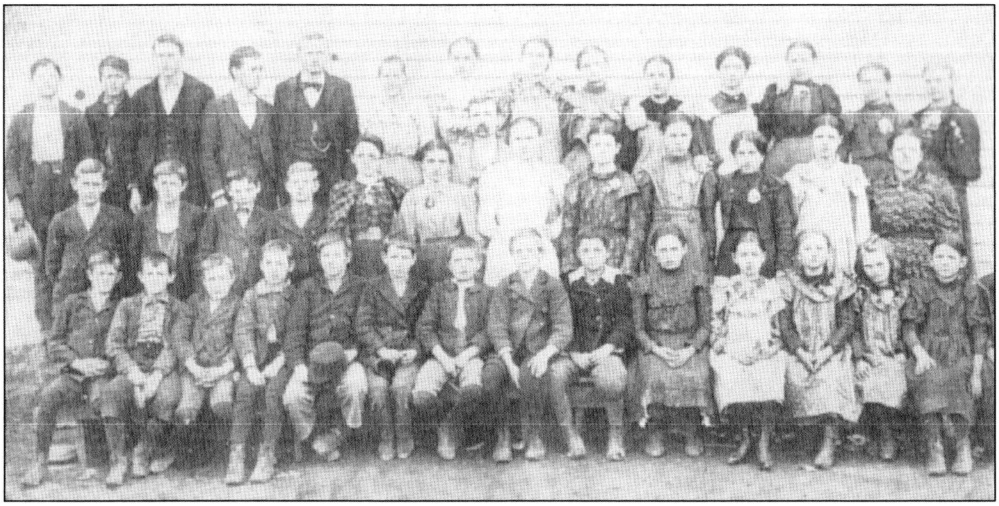

Pictured is West Fork School in 1898. Students are, from left to right, as follows: (front row) Jim Hughes, Roy Robinson, Jim Gilstrap, Roy Karnes, Jake Winn, Hugh Karnes, Arlie Height, Argile Langston, Tillman Bell, Maud Hughes, Allie McKnight, Stella Gilbreath, Ollie Gilbreath, Nora Robinson, and Maud Little; (middle row) Charley Gilstrap, Will Little, Jake Gilstrap, Everett Luther, Lillie Langston, Ola Everett, J.S. Thompson (teacher), Rose Gilstrap, Grace Bloyed, Jessie Little, Nora Baker, Ethel Jones, a "hand" girl; (back row) Earl Brown, Claburn Bloyed, Garland Bloyed, Austin Langston, Charley Luther, Elsie Robinson, Lucy Gilstrap, Dora Hughes, Mary Gilstrap, Rose Robinson, Edna Belle, Mayme Little, Bessie Steel, and Mattie Brown.

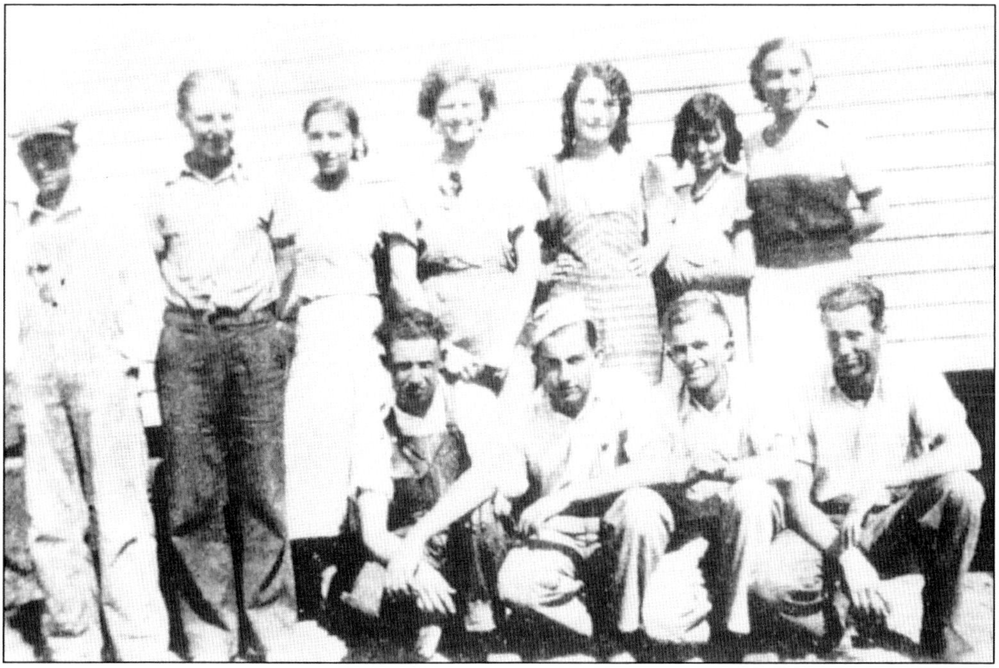

This 1933 photo of the graduating seniors of West Fork High School shows all but two students: George Meason and Brant Dillard. The senior motto that year was "Launched but not anchored." Graduates are, from left to right, as follows: (sitting) Conrad Harp, Harold Hutcheson, Donald Hobbs, and LeRoy Burris; (standing) John Donald, Andrew Lofton, Delois Gulley, Edith Dearing, Pauline Walker, Mary Ann Arnold, and Thelma Gulley.

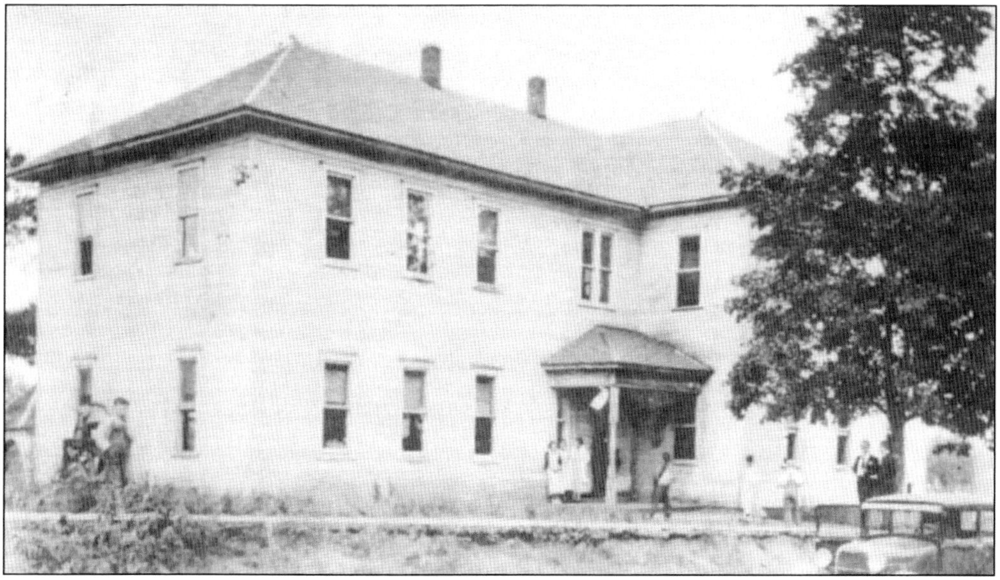

Pictured is the West Fork School building in 1935. It was torn down in 1936 and replaced with a rock building that still stands today. The boy standing by the bell is identified as Custard Pie Baker. The girls near the door are Lois Hobbs, Aileen Arnold, and Lilabel Curtis. Superintendent Eugene Brewster, who was originally from Cane Hill, is seen on the right.

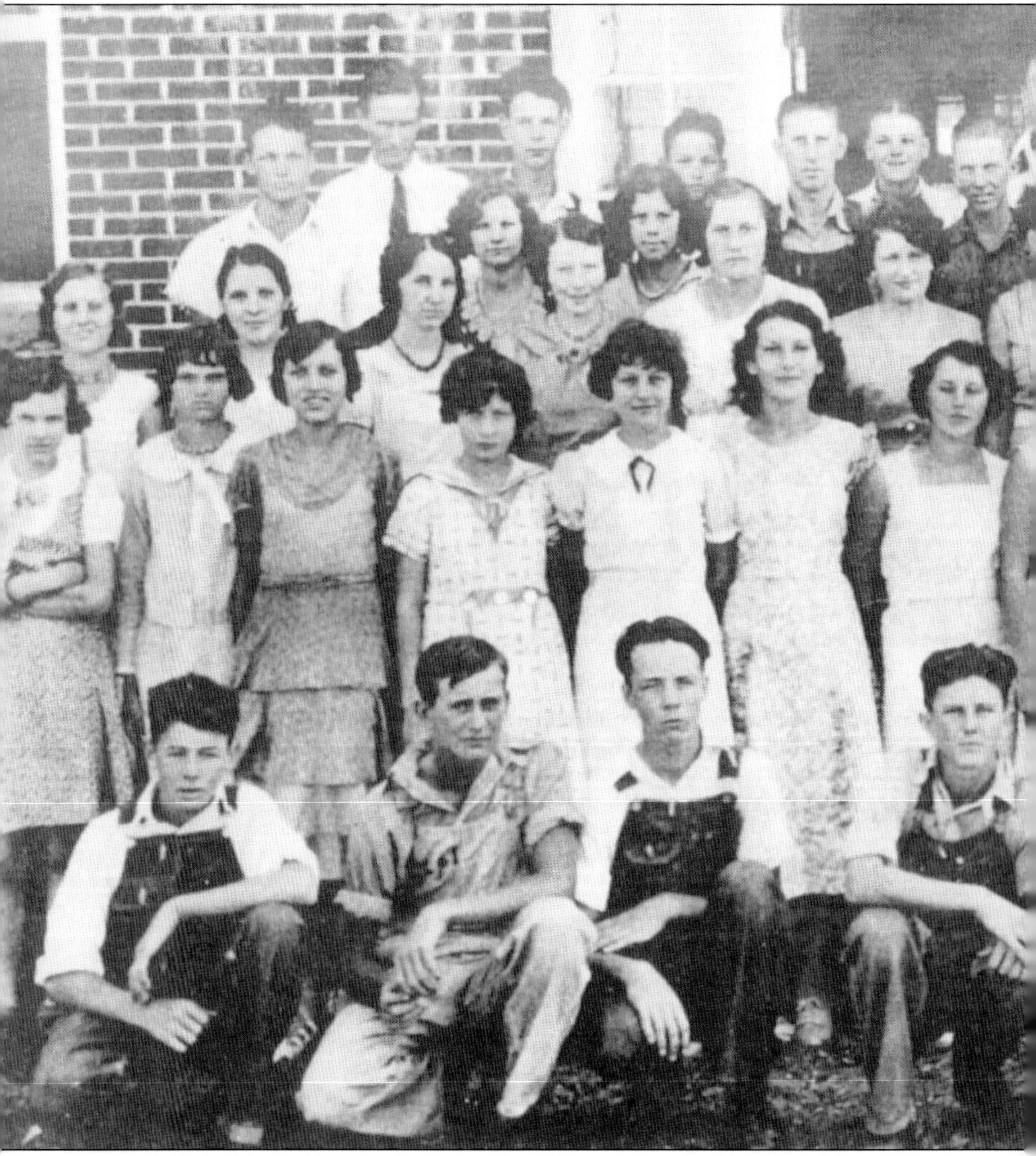

The brick school building behind these students was constructed in the mid-1920s in Greenland. Students pictured, from left to right, are as follows: (front row) Joe Laney, Floyd Thomas, James Malone, Jack Kerley, Howard Haas, Bob Jones, Guy Davis, and Raymond Taylor; (second row) Eileen Cate, Mary Collins, Marie Shaffer, unidentified, Evelyn Hembree, Thelma Davis, Ruby Williams, Lydia Jane Williams, Clara Leimser, Loretta Marshall, Frances Harp, Beatrice Peachee, Opal Epply, Venna Alexander, and Laura Bradshaw; (third row) unidentified, Loretta Toombs, Alma Thomas, Jane Turner, Juanita Davis, Anita Reetus, Hazel Hall, Mary Arrington, Irene Webb, Billie Owen, Helen Crider, Carolyn Marshall, Audrey Owen, Lexie Dill, and Thelma Burlingame; (back row) Richard Milsap, E.B. Brewster (teacher),

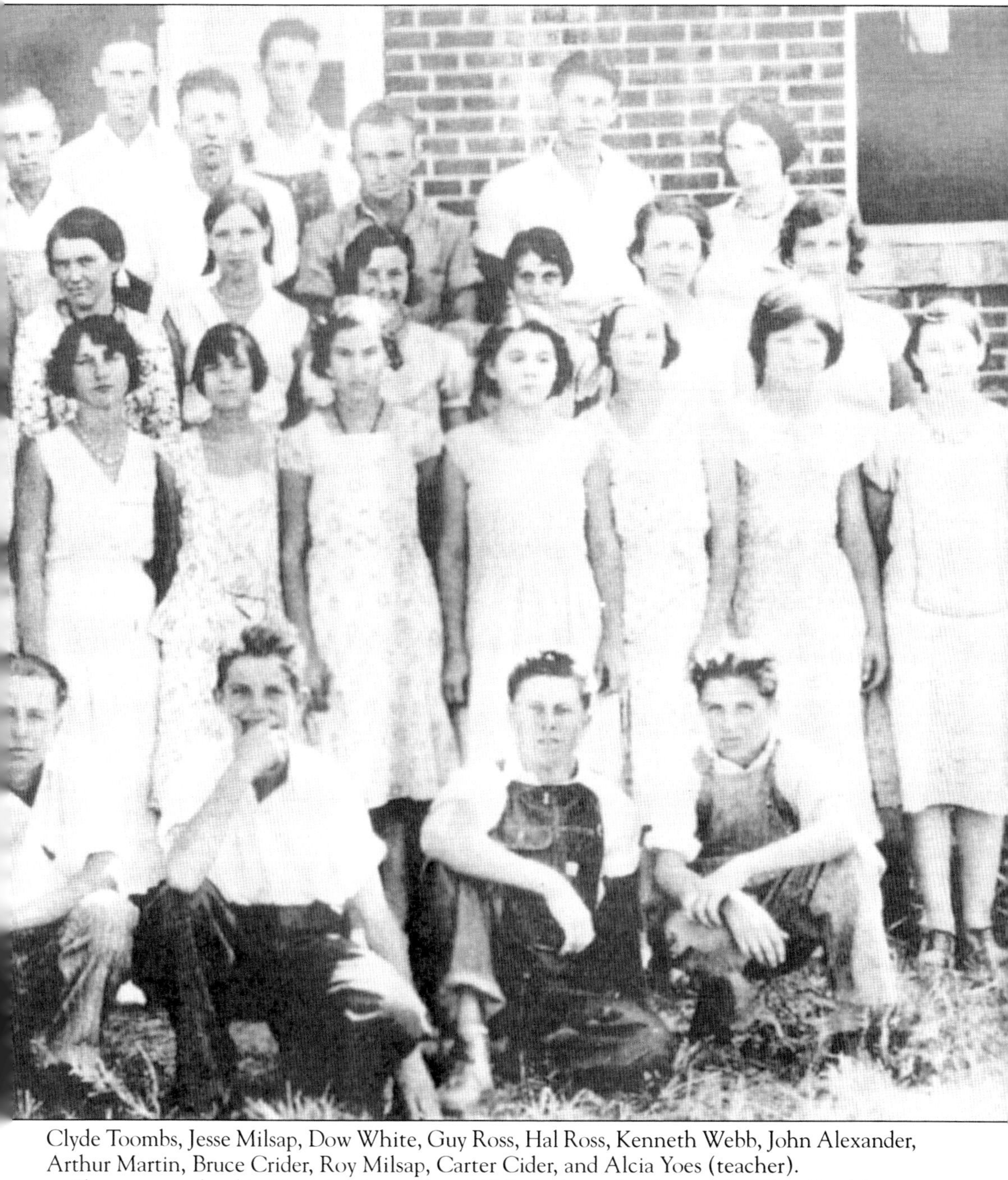

Clyde Toombs, Jesse Milsap, Dow White, Guy Ross, Hal Ross, Kenneth Webb, John Alexander, Arthur Martin, Bruce Crider, Roy Milsap, Carter Cider, and Alcia Yoes (teacher).

There was a school in Greenland as early as 1877; the first school was called Frog Pond. It was located on the property that is now Drake Field, Fayetteville's airport. Four buildings were used for schools in the area before this one was built. Many outlying schools have been consolidated with Greenland, which is still a district.

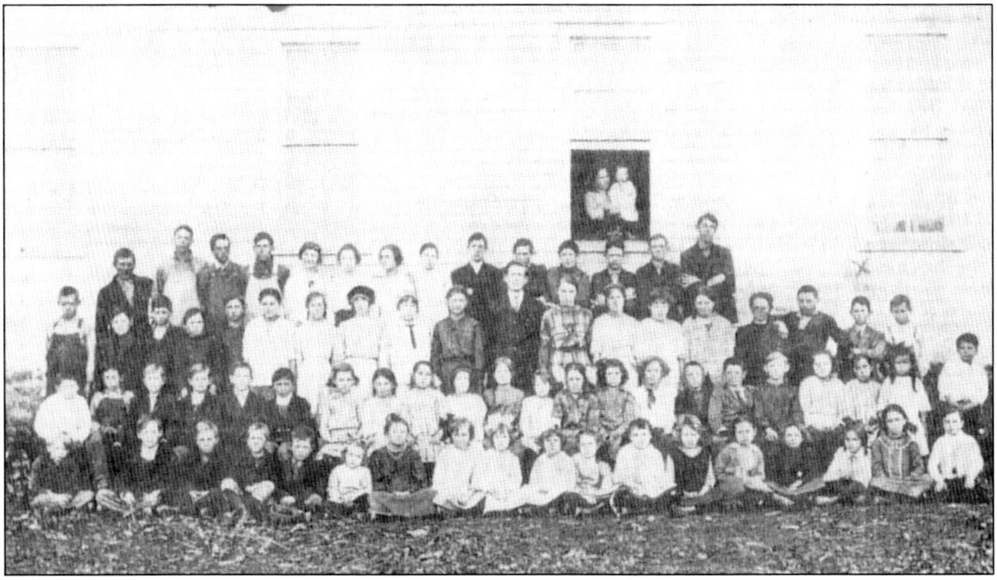

Hazel Valley, originally Bogan School, was started in 1886. As seen in this 1916 view, the school had quite a large enrollment. Only a few of the students are identified. Pictured, in no particular order, are the following: Euell Napier, Roy Osburn, Strib Brown, Oren Osborn, May Carter, Alfred Shackelford, Carl Osborn, Hearl Hammonds, J.P. Brown, Bill Nickell, Clarence Hammonds, Everett Skelton, Jewell Nickell, Prof. James Osborn, Grace Long, Gladys Mack, Sid Jarell, Vernon Polly, Herb Shackelford, Hugh Shackelford, Raymond Mack, Ansel W. Polly, and Berl Hight.

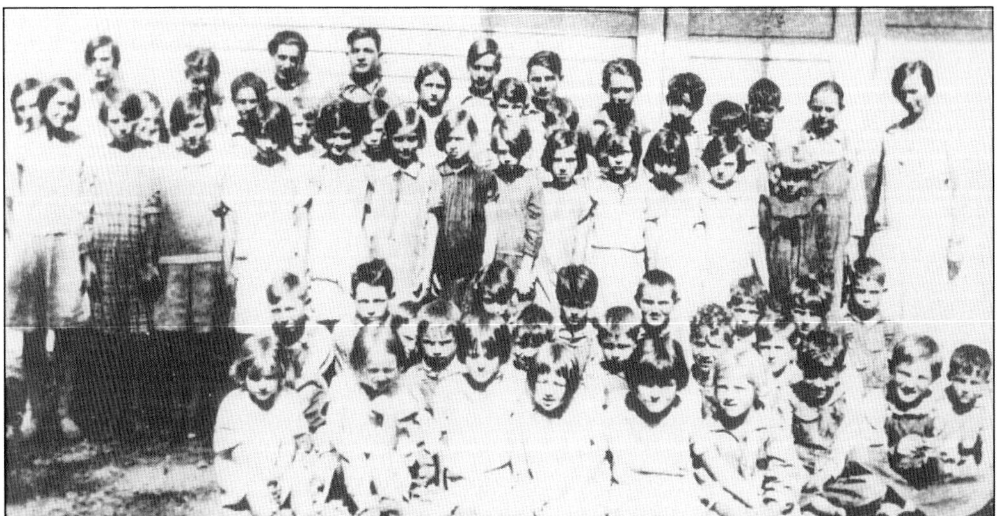

In 1828, Hazel Valley School had an enrollment of 80 students. Fifty-five were present when this photo was taken. In 1927, a third room was added, and in 1948, the high school was moved to Elkins. The Methodist Church built the building in 1877 and later sold it to the school district.

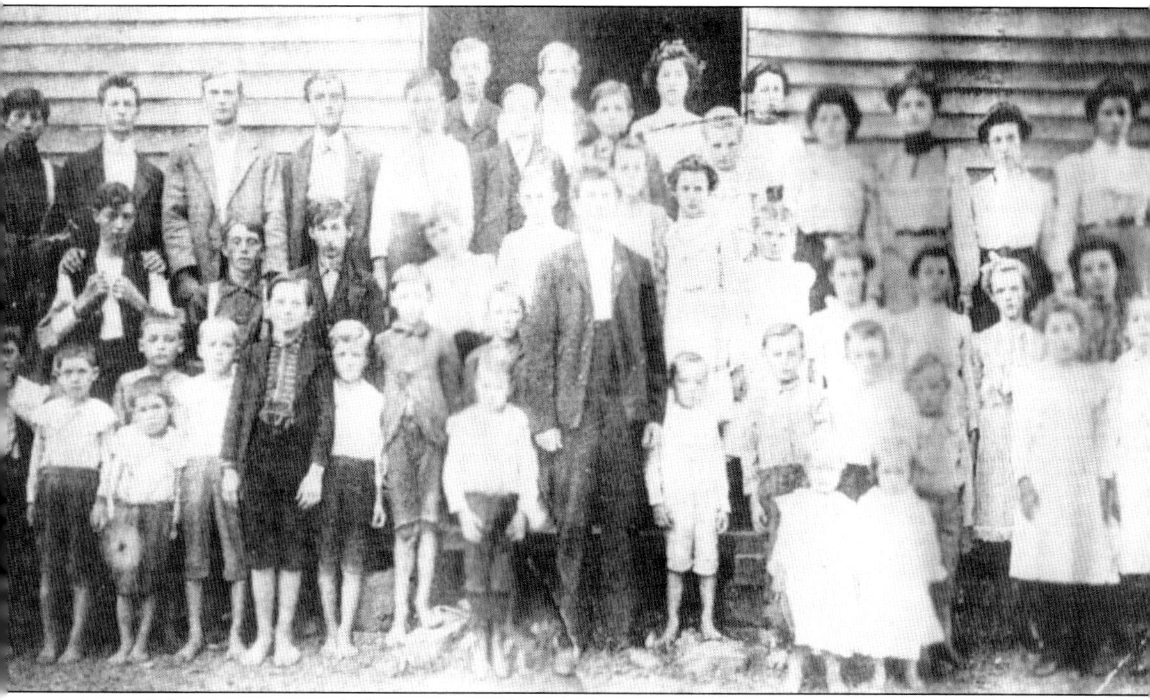

Osburn School was named for Henry Osburn, who donated land to the district. Students shown in this 1905 view are, from left to right, as follows: (front row) Johnny Browder, Roy Osburn, Orin Osburn, Strib Brown, Walter Lemasters, Hugh Curry, Grover Calhoun, Sam Calhoun, Jenny Brown, unidentified, Rachel Osburn, Addie Brown, and Walter Osburn; (middle row) Stant Fairchild, Henry Taylor, unidentified, Floyd Brown, Jim Osburn (teacher), Lydia Ratliff, Roxie Winkle, unidentified, Hala Osburn, Belle Curry, and unidentified; (back row) Manford Lemasters, Floyd Brown, Dean Smith, unidentified, Thurman Brown, Angus Hight, Ella Bogan, unidentified, Cinda Osburn, Maude Curry, Emily Wilson, and Ella Bogan (there were two). The two small girls in front, Hattie Osburn and a Winkle girl, were not yet old enough to attend school. The school building was located near Bogan (Hazel Valley) School and another school called Plum Orchard. Soon after the turn of the century, Osburn and Plum Orchard were closed and students went to Bogan. The log schoolhouse was replaced by a two-story frame structure, and another teacher was hired.

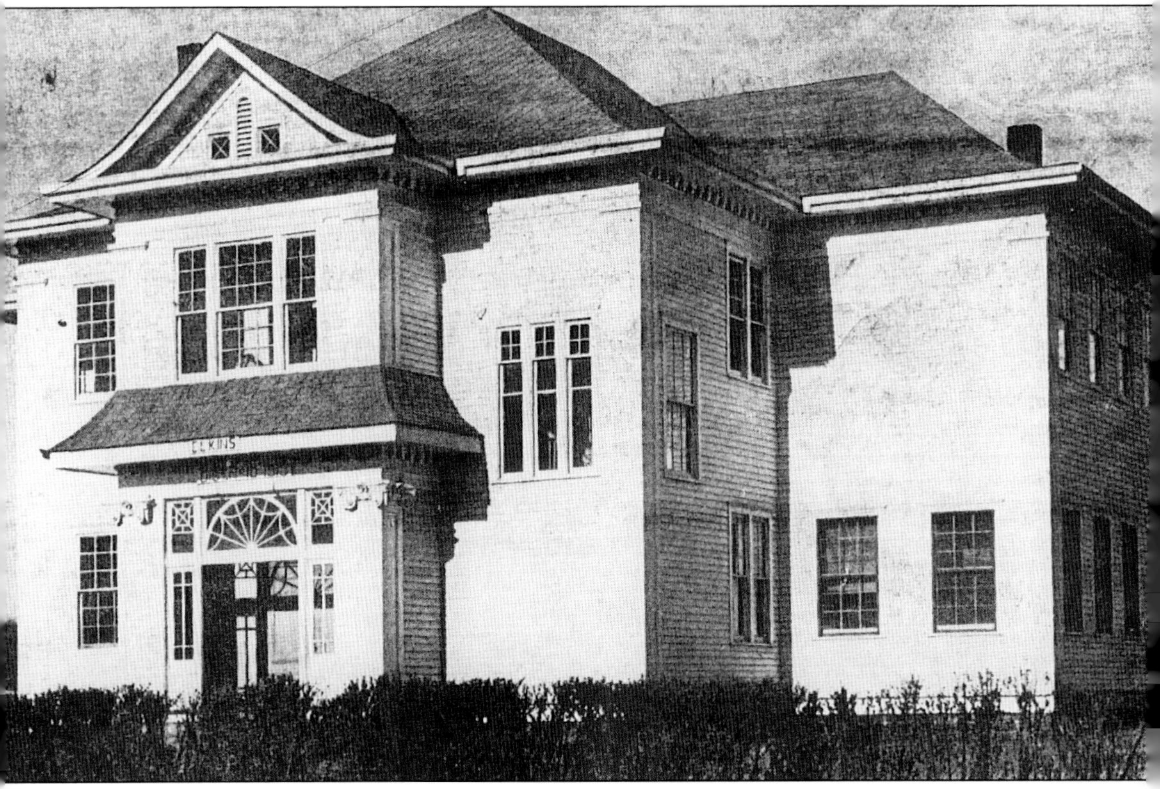

This two-story school at Elkins featured an impressive architectural front entrance. This popular photograph, once used on a calendar, is undated. Land for the school was bought from James F. Hood. The school existed as early at 1877 in the small town east of Fayetteville, but this building was probably built much later. Like most rural communities, the first schools were one-room buildings, and the classes ended after eighth grade. Elkins, once known as Hood, remains a booming town with a fast-growing school system. The old building shown here was demolished in the 1950s and, sadly, the sidewalk inscribed with all the seniors' names was removed. Original plans had been to extend the sidewalk into the downtown area. Many schools in the area were consolidated with Elkins in 1949. Rodolph Stokenberry was the first and only senior to graduate from this school in 1919.

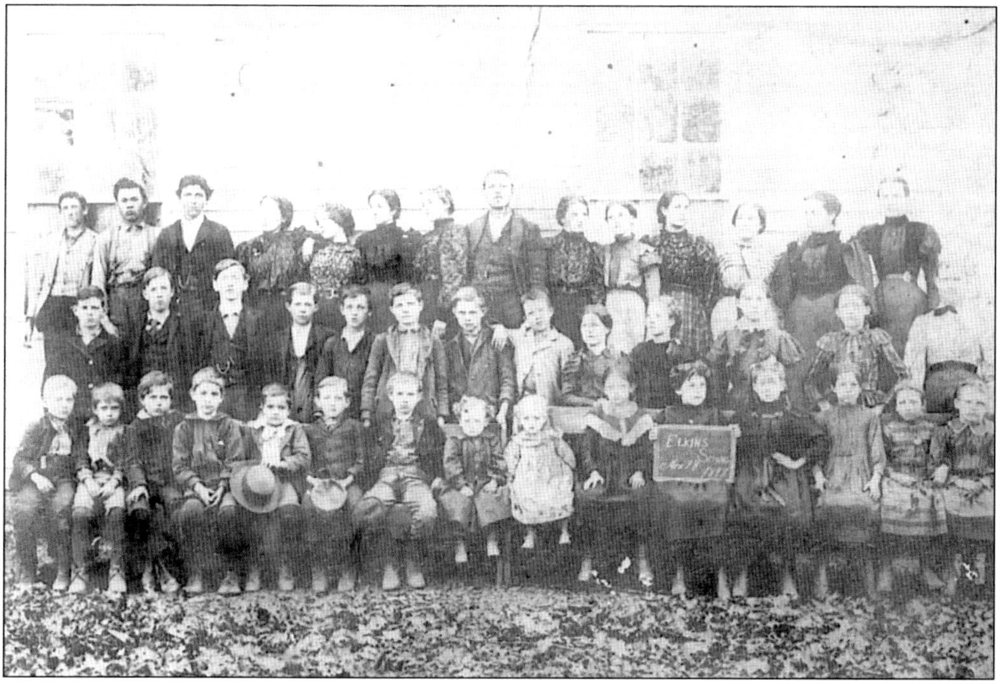

In 1898, Elkins grade school was quite large. The students in this view are unidentified, but the teacher is A.W. Mintun. Like many early grade school pictures, several adults visited on the day school photographs were made and were often included in the picture. The back row appears to be all adults.

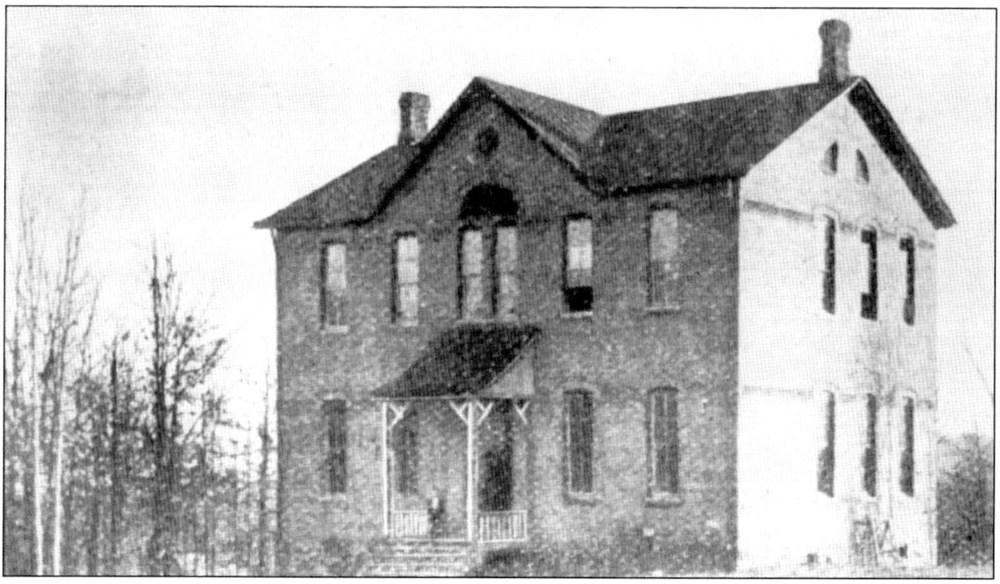

Fayetteville Public School is the identification on this photo. In 1833, the first school in Washington County was built in Fayetteville. It was located in a small building on what is now known as School Street. A high-rise apartment building now occupies the site. Since there is no date on this photo, it can not be established what year it was built or where it stood. (Photo courtesy of Peter Harkins and Shiloh Museum of Ozark History, Springdale.)

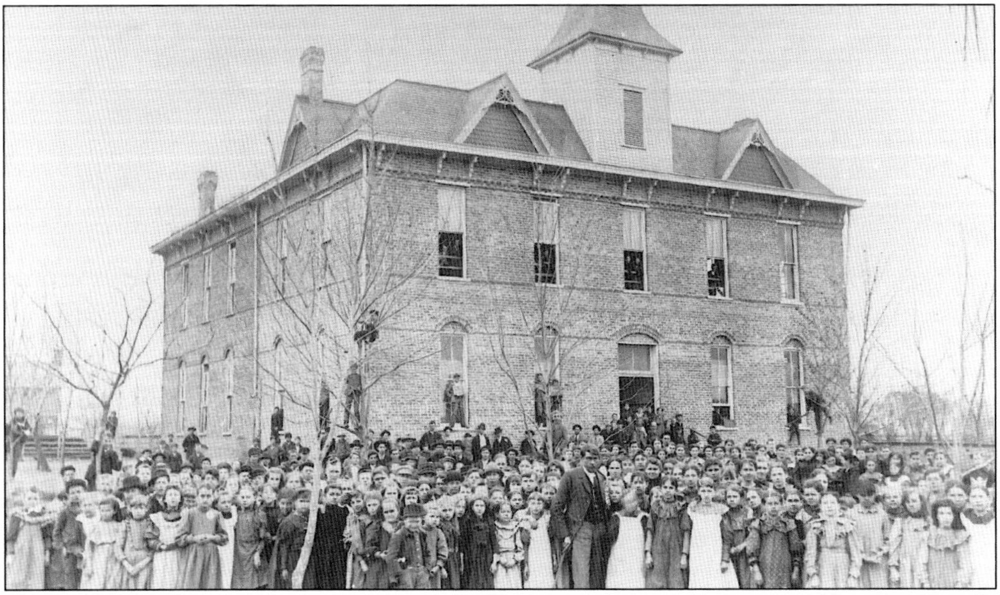

The first public school in Springdale was held in Shiloh Church. Springdale was originally known as Shiloh. Pictured is a c. 1913 view of the school known as Springdale Grammar School, district 50. Originally built in 1869, its size doubled some years later. It was used as a grammar school until 1929 and was dismantled in 1940. (Photo courtesy of W.G. Howard and Shiloh Museum of Ozark History, Springdale.)

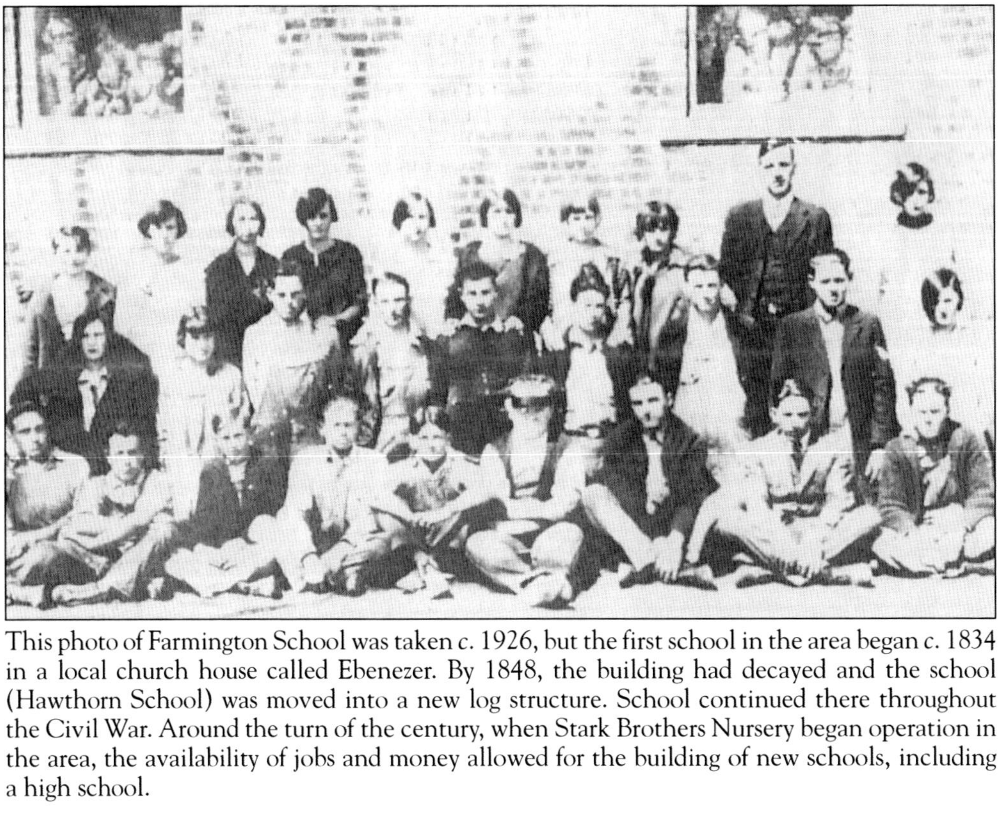

This photo of Farmington School was taken c. 1926, but the first school in the area began c. 1834 in a local church house called Ebenezer. By 1848, the building had decayed and the school (Hawthorn School) was moved into a new log structure. School continued there throughout the Civil War. Around the turn of the century, when Stark Brothers Nursery began operation in the area, the availability of jobs and money allowed for the building of new schools, including a high school.

Two

Gettin' Around

The early settlers found impassable roads through the rugged Ozarks that were little more than foot trails hacked from the wilderness. The terrain was rocky, some soil was clay, springs flowed from crevices and kept the earth wet in all but the hottest summer months. Mules or oxen were used to pull wagons, but horses were used more and more as civilization inched its way into the mountains. The automobile was slow to appear, but by 1882, the Frisco Railroad had hacked its way south from Fayetteville to Van Buren and the Arkansas River Valley. The railroad played a big part in transportation after that time. Those lucky enough to have settled along its route now had an easier way to travel. At the same time, roads were being laid in the remote areas of settlement. Small towns grew everywhere, a few families settled, and rural folks tended to stay home most of the time.

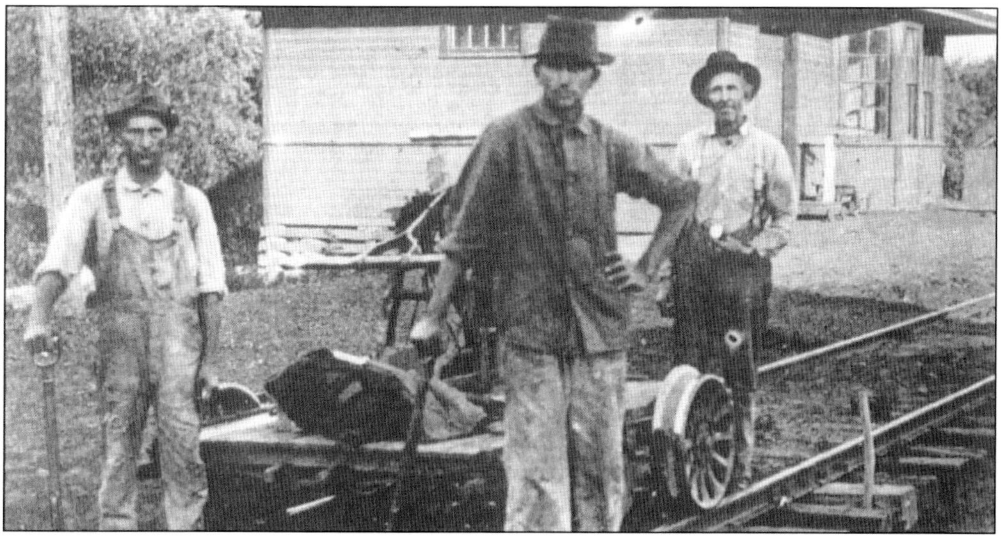

In 1916, one of the major modes of travel was by train. Railroads employed many workers to keep the tracks in repair. They were referred to as section crews. This crew worked out of Delaney on the St. Paul branch of the Frisco Railroad. Crew members, from left to right, are as follows: Toughe Tackett, Marvin Thomas, and Jerry Roberts. Note the railroad watch in Jerry Roberts's hand. He had just bought it and was happy to display it for the photographer.

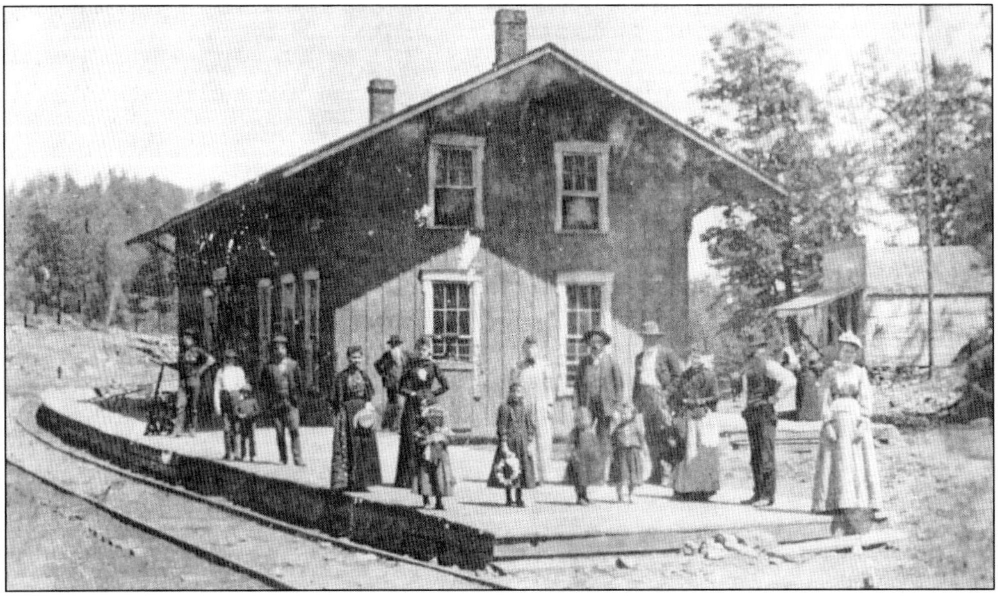

In 1892, when this photo was taken at the Winslow Depot, train time was one of the big events of the day The small girl holding a flower-crowned hat is Gertrude Gregg Yerton. The small frame building to the right was the drug store and office of Dr. Albert Dunlap.

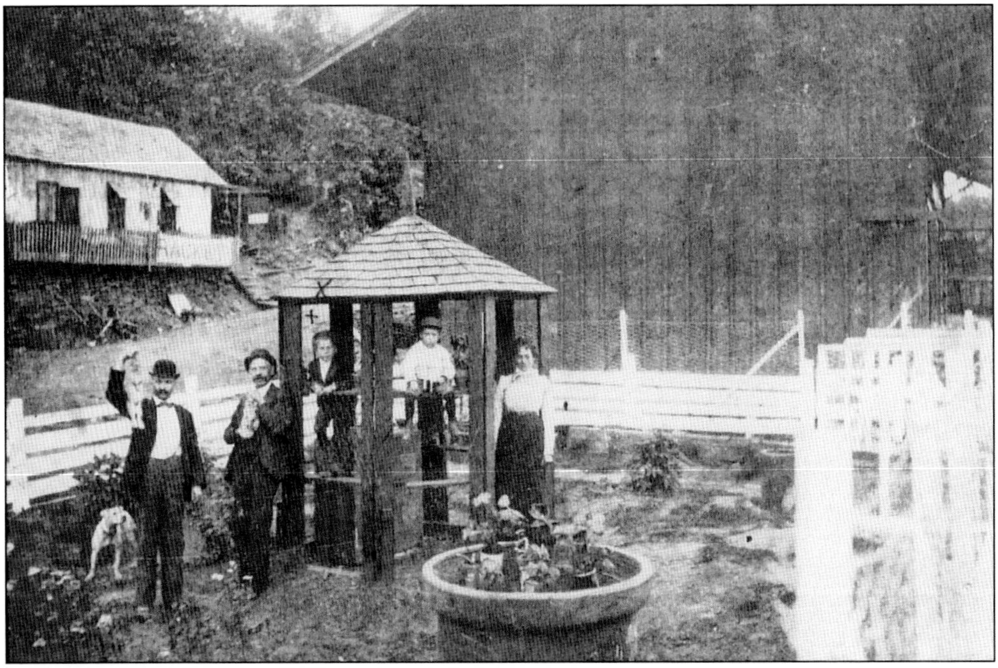

This 1900 view, made at the north end of the Winslow Depot, is the rose garden and park surrounded by white fencing. Belgian hares, such as the one in the foreground, were kept in the wire enclosure. Pictured are Mr. Williams and J.A. Winn, who served as agent and telegraph operator. The children are J.A.'s sons, Paul and Burl Winn. Their mother, Laura Winn, is on the right.

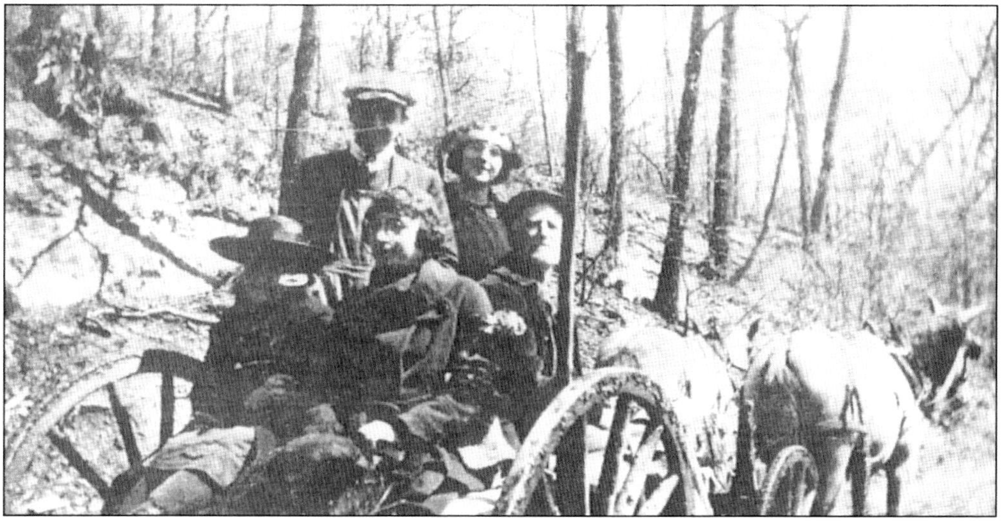

When traveling to town to catch a train, plenty of time was allowed for the trip over less than desirable roads. A grub box was a standard part of traveling gear. Here, two girls are being taken to the depot to return home to Monett, Missouri, after visiting with Will and Ida Southern. The Southerns raised a large family in a log house west of Winslow.

Soon after the tracks were laid by the Frisco Railroad, this tunnel at Winslow was built to save miles of steep grade. Completed in 1882, the brick-lined tunnel is 1,726 feet long It was restructured in 1969 to accommodate diesel engines. On Friday, Sept. 17, 1965, the last passenger train ran north from Fort Smith to Monett, Missouri, and the following day, it retraced the route south. At the age of 94, W.W. Swaney was aboard for that last ride, as he had been for the very first one on July 4, 1882.

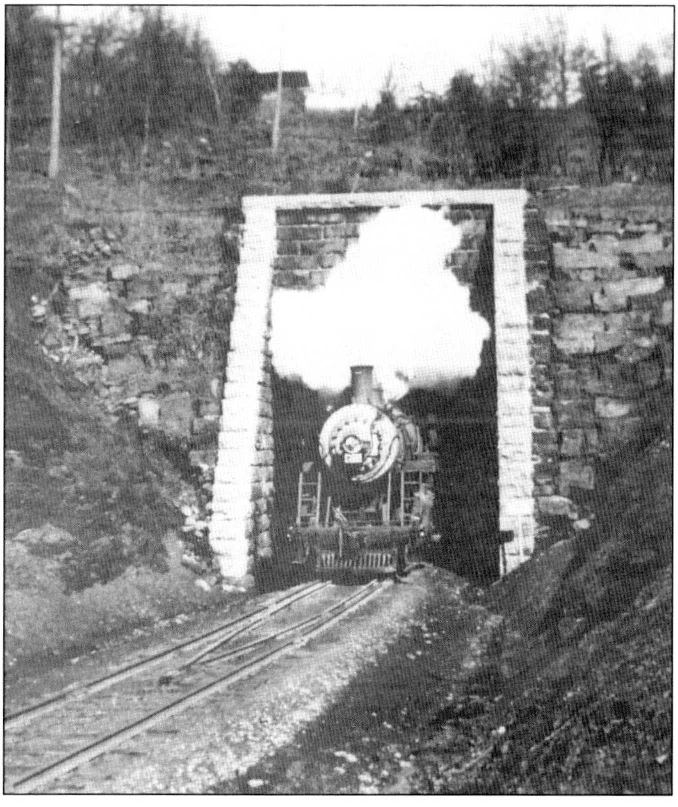

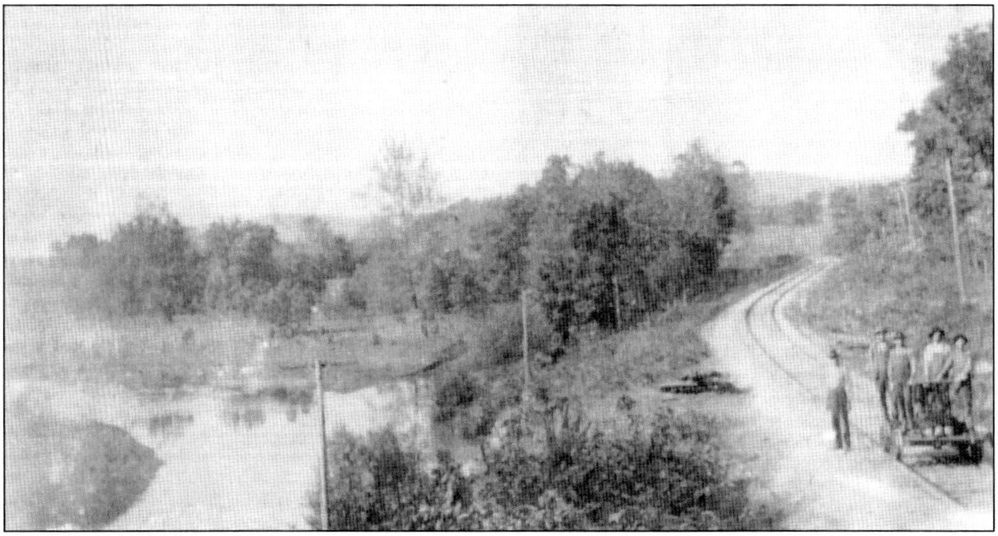

Members of the Frisco section crew pose on a hand-pumper, alongside what is known as the "Wreck Hole" just north of West Fork. Several trains have derailed there over the years. In this *c.* 1915 view, the following crew members are pictured on the car from left to right: Jack Karnes, Claude Epps, George Hope, and Oscar Malone.

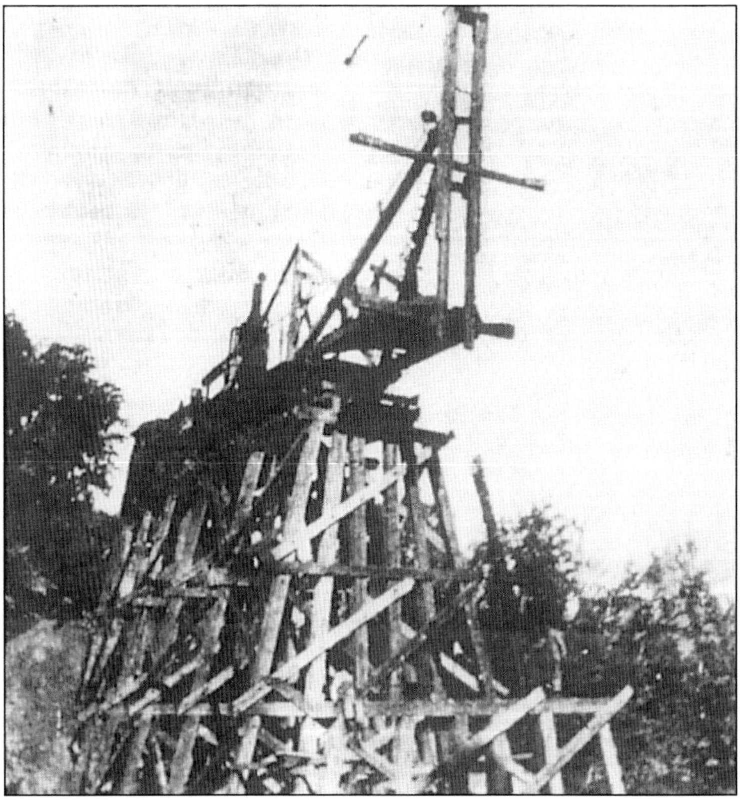

This photo of a bridge under construction on the Black Mountain Railroad illustrates the enormous feat of such an undertaking. The size of the timbers used can be gauged by finding the two men barely discernible, one sitting in the center and one standing to the far right of a cross timber about a quarter of the way up. At the top, a log is being hoisted. The 29 hazardous miles of this short line were built in 1915.

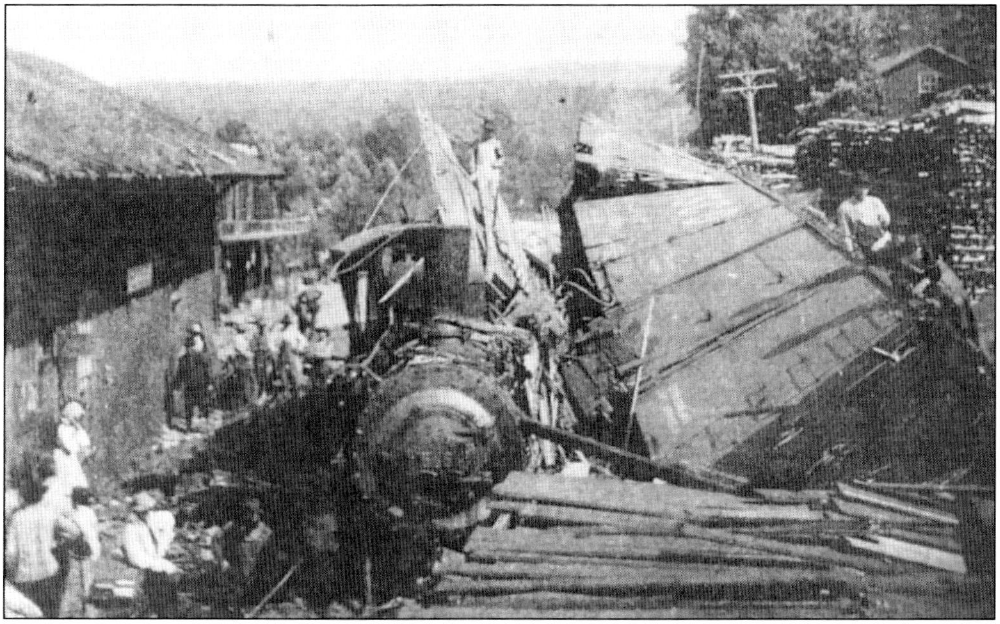

Wrecks along the railroad were not all that uncommon, and many have been documented. This engine left the rails in front of the Brentwood Depot. The only injury occurred when the station agent, John May, saw that the engine was headed straight into the depot and leapt out the back window, striking his head on a pile of wood. No date is available for the photo.

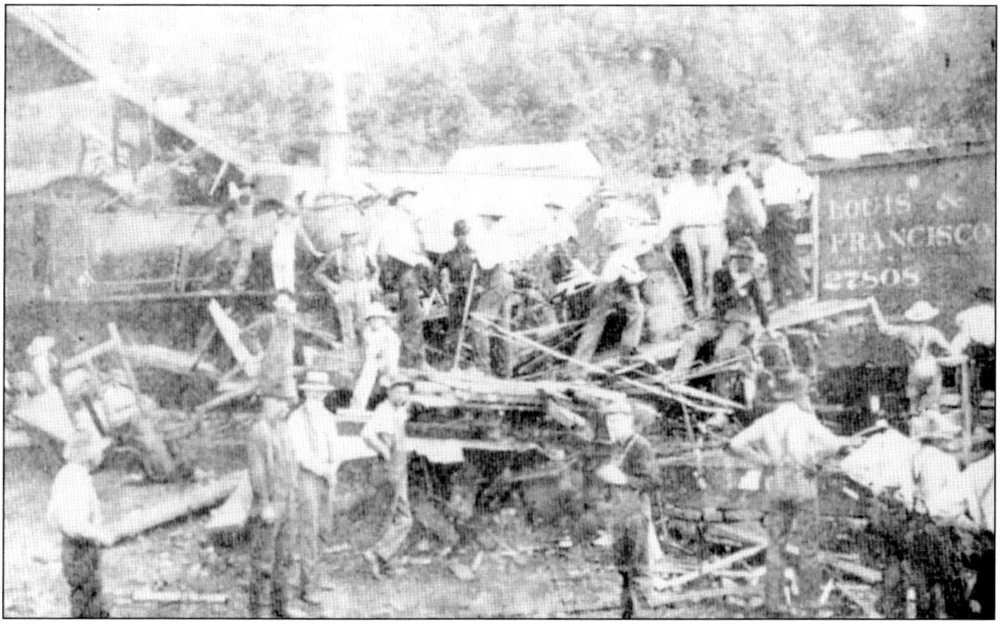

Just south of the Brentwood Depot, the tracks made such a sharp curve that approaching trains were not always visible. In 1912, two trains collided head-on there. No flag man had been sent up the line because the freight was waiting safely on the siding. For some reason, the engineer uncoupled the engine and pulled on to the main track just in time to be hit by the fast freight from the south.

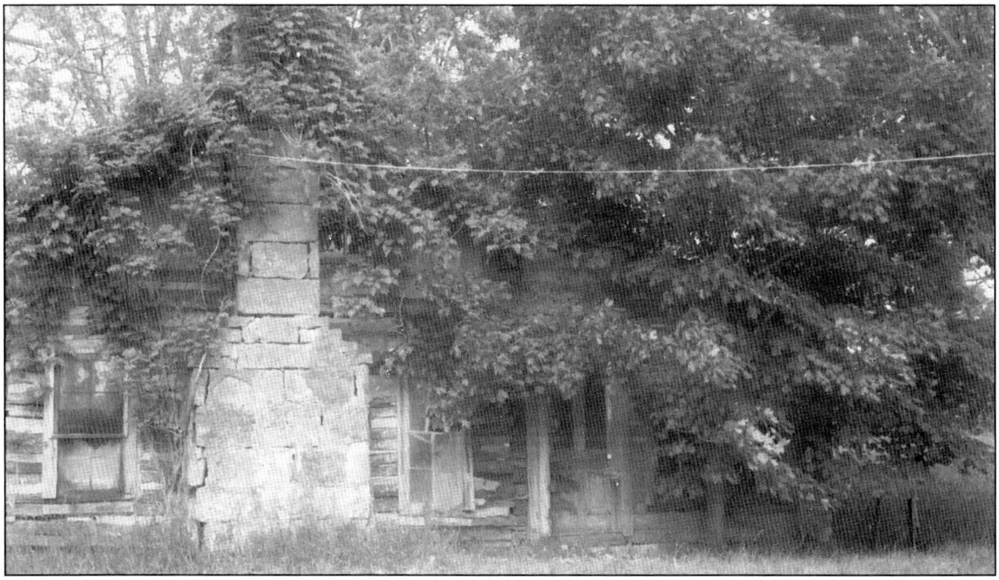

Before the railroad people arrived and filled in the deep gorge that would become Winslow, a branch line of the Butterfield Stage known as the Wollum or Woolem branch stopped here. This stage stop was still standing on the old Collier-Yoes place near Signal Mountain in the late 1970s. The stage went on to stop at Summit, at the top of the mountain, above what was to become the bustling town of Winslow.

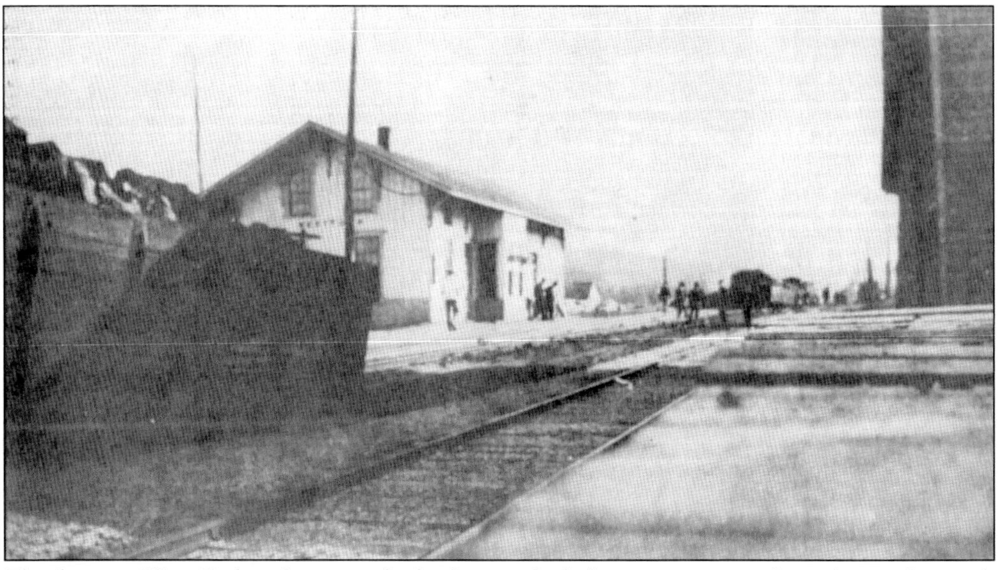

The depot at West Fork is shown in the background of what was meant to be a photo of a wreck involving coal cars, one of which can be seen in the foreground. No one knows when this wreck occurred or when the photo was taken. Train wrecks were apparently a common occurrence during the early days of the railroad.

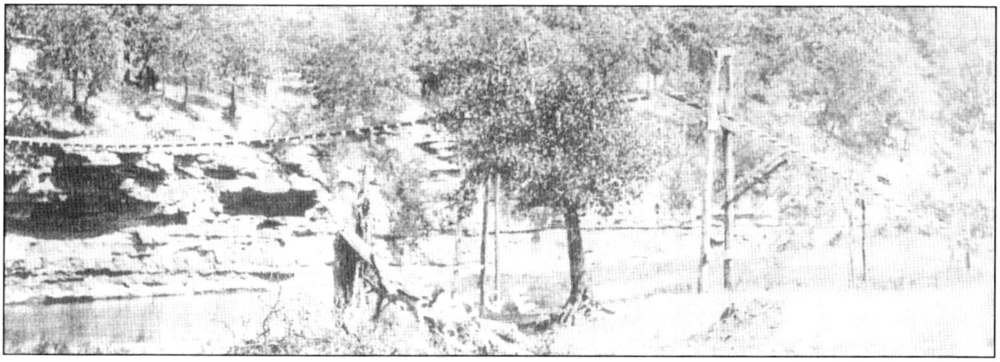

Most streams could not be crossed by stepping stones or a felled tree because the water rises too high during rainy weather. Swinging bridges became popular but were often quite unstable. This one, across the West Fork of the White River, went from the tower and bank (shown here) to a high bluff on the opposite side.

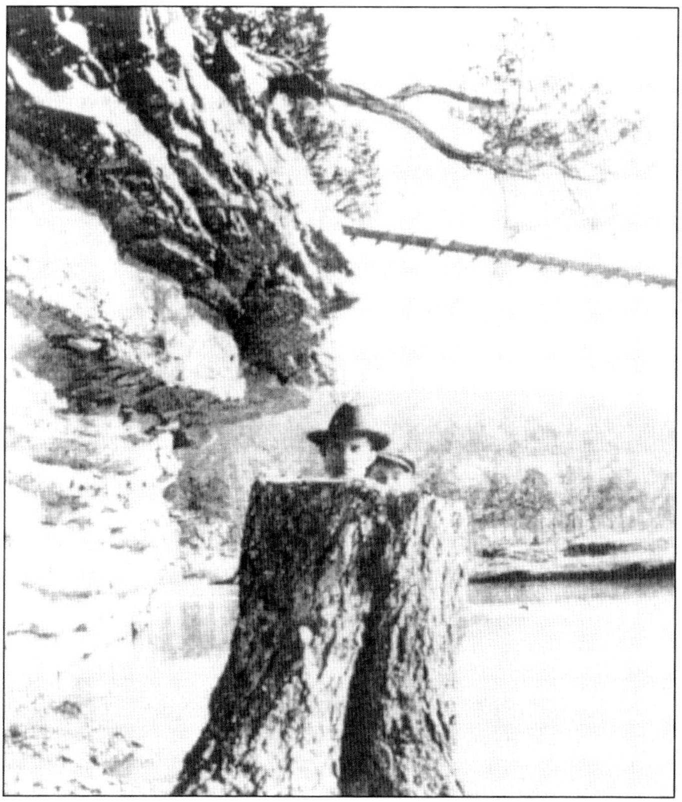

In the background of this early 1900s view is the swinging bridge at Fount Caudle that crosses Winn's Creek. The young man facing the camera is Ed Hutcheson. Today, Winn's Creek occasionally rises above its banks and completely floods the road beside it.

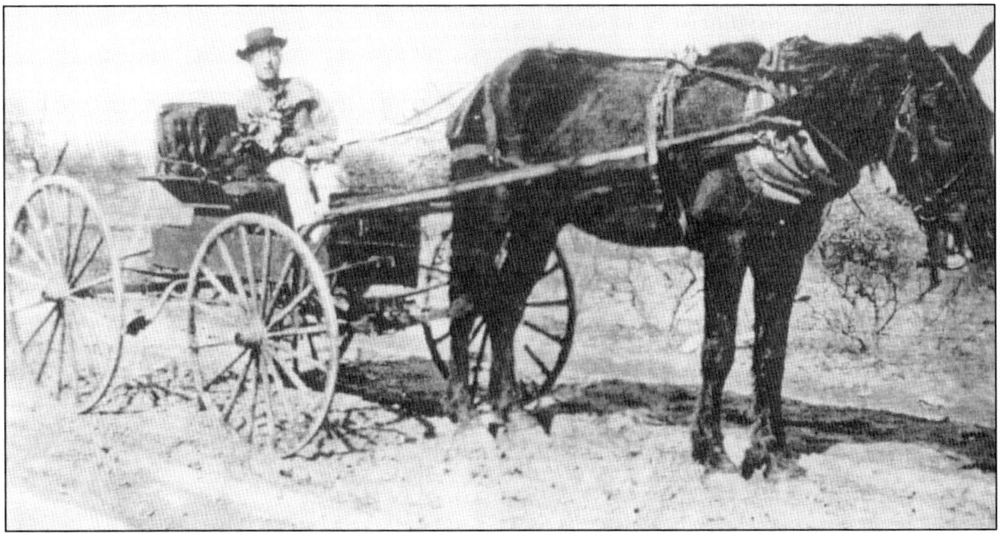

Goin' courtin' in the good old days was pretty simple. The options were horseback, buggy, or shanks mare (on foot). In this 1919 view, Clyde Jones of Winslow sits in his buggy with a bouquet of lilacs in his hand, ready to call on his best girl. The horse appears bored with it all and exhibits a wide yawn.

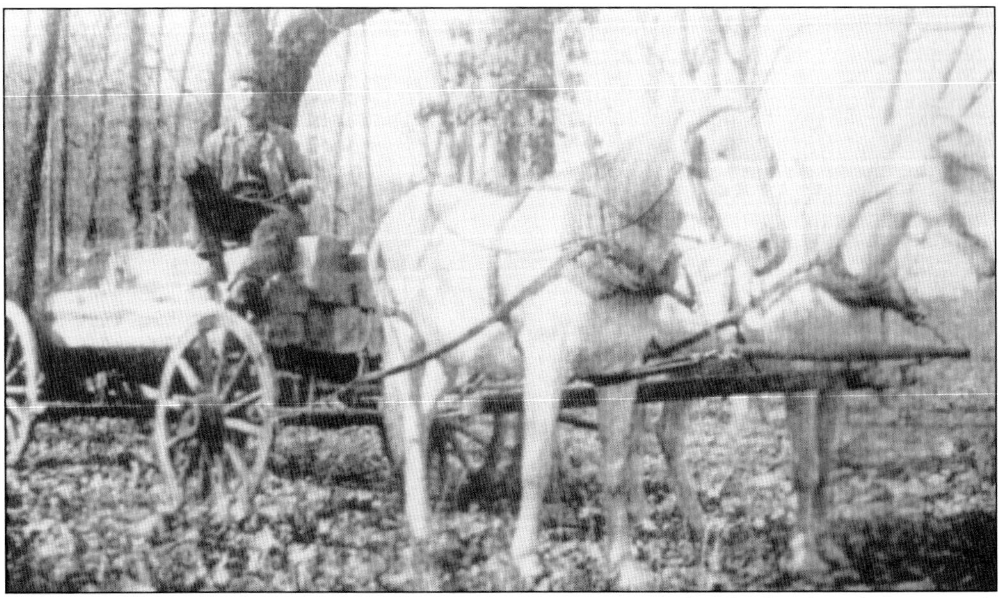

In 1911, horses did most of the hauling work. The slang term for the hard-working animals was "hayburners." All it took was a bit of hay and some grain to fuel them through the winter; there were no worries over buying gasoline or checking the oil. Note the load of 8-foot ties on the wagon. A sawyer could sell his "crop" at one of the numerous tie yards located along the railroad line.

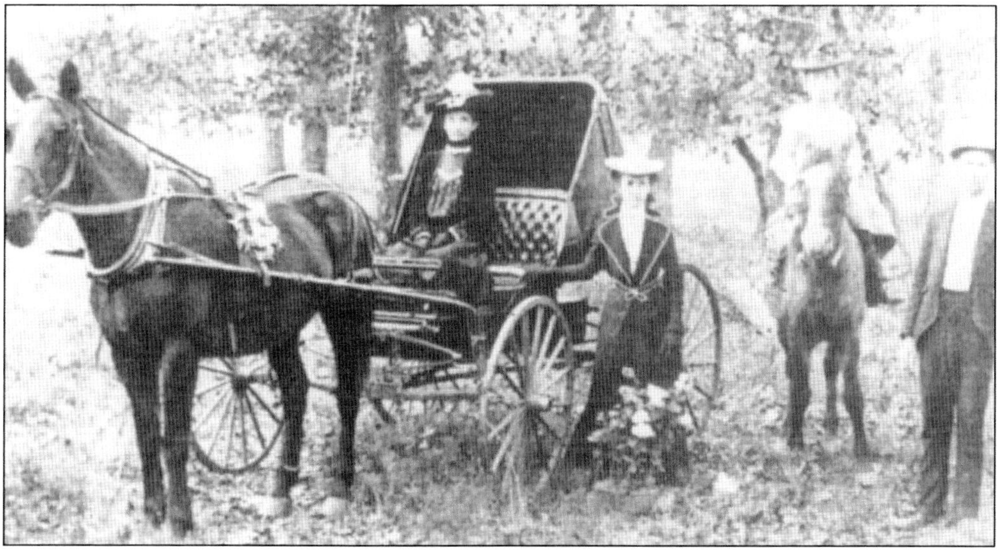

In this 1901 photo, Katy the mare is ready for an afternoon buggy ride. Elizabeth Dye is in the buggy, Mert is standing beside it, 13-year-old Icy is mounted sidesaddle on her pony, and Earl Dye is on the right. The buggy was upholstered in black, grained leather.

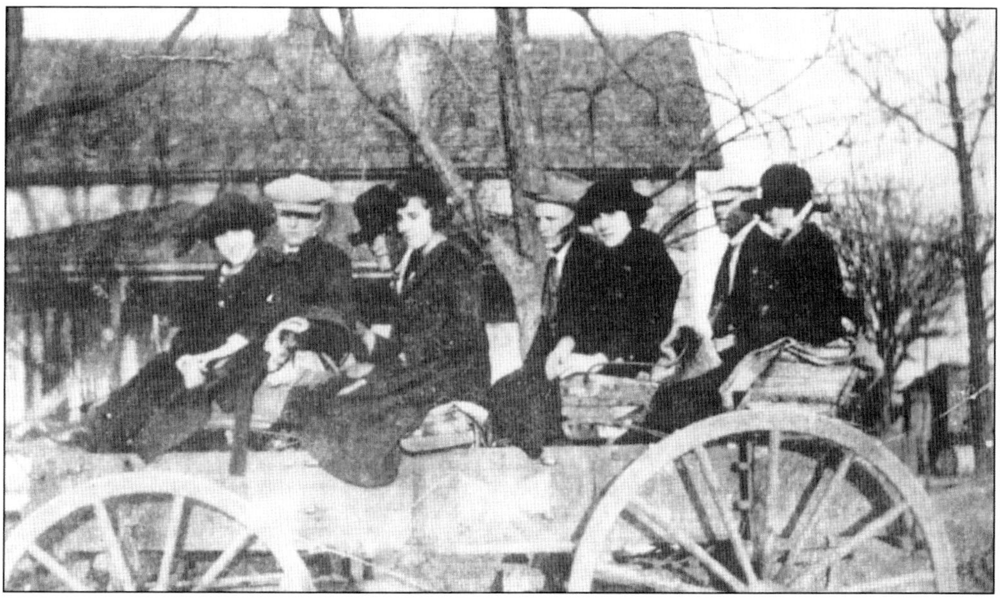

This wagon was not the latest model; only three spring seats were available, so the second couple from the front had to sit on a board. The picture was taken during the week of Christmas in 1921 in the Blackburn community as the couples were headed for a social at Manila School. From front seat to back, they are Albert Lofton, Gladys Johnson, Bertha Neil, Bill Winn, Jo Lofton, Mabel Johnson, Oscar Lofton, and Melvina Neil.

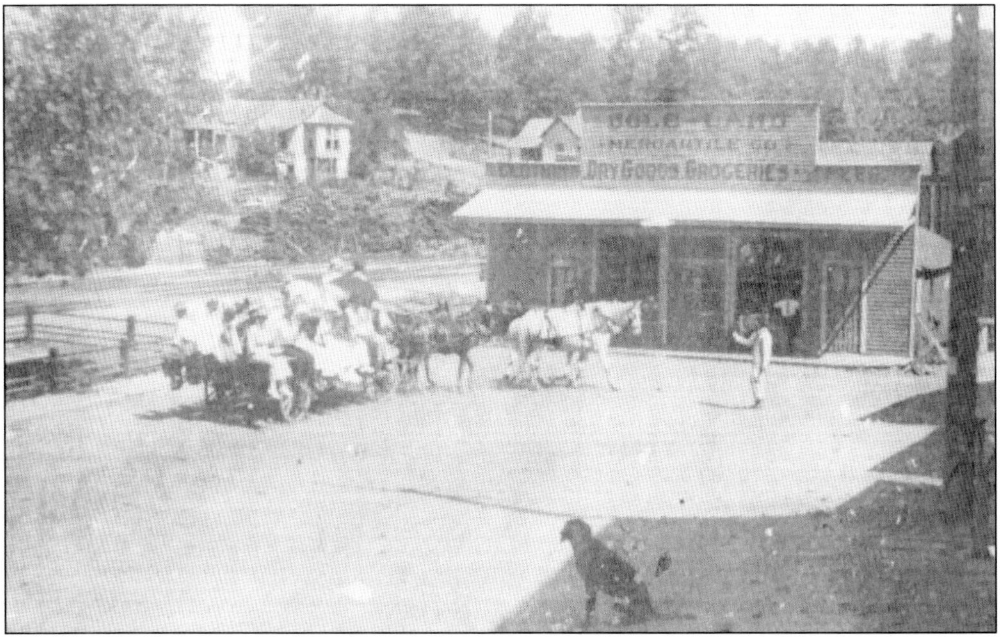

Hay rides were among the most popular diversions of young people in the early 1900s. This four-horsepower rig is loaded with a group of Winslow youth headed for a picnic. The store they are approaching is the Cole-Land Mercantile. On the hill above is the white, two-story lodge hall and below it is the Kelton home.

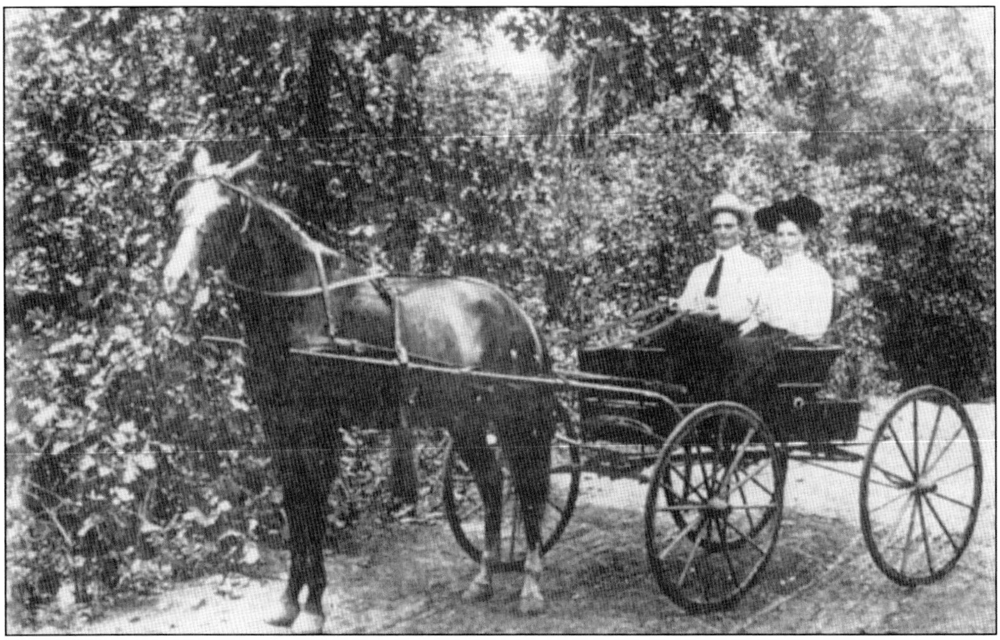

Maud Dunlap and Dr. T.E. Gray were once engaged but never married. Maud was the foster child of one of the most prominent families in Winslow at the turn of the century. One of the first women pharmacists in Arkansas at the time, she went on to become the editor of a local newspaper. She was elected mayor of the town in the 1920s. She and Dr. Gray remained close friends but never revealed why they didn't marry. He was murdered by a hitchhiker in 1938.

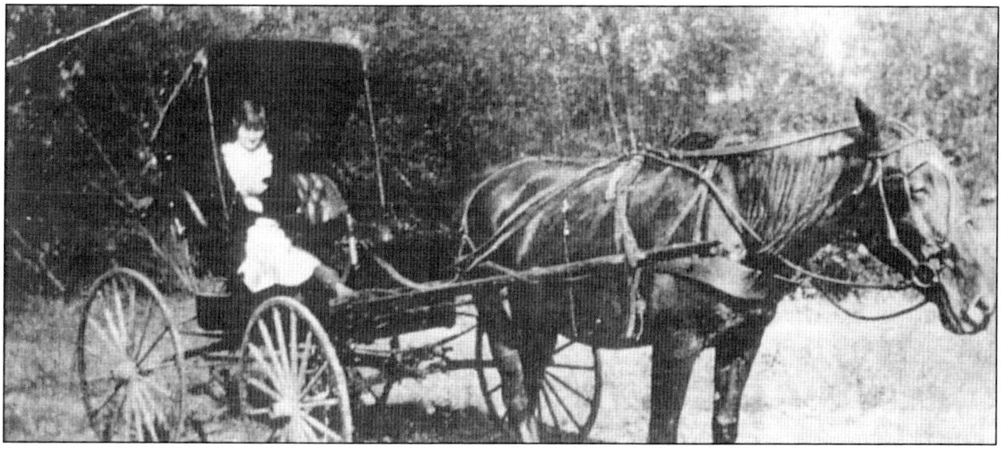

Mary Snow Winn is seen in the buggy in which she and her husband Adolph Webber, both of West Fork, courted prior to their wedding. After she snapped a picture of her intended in the same pose, the couple drove to the home of Alex Stockburger and were united in marriage, seated in this buggy .

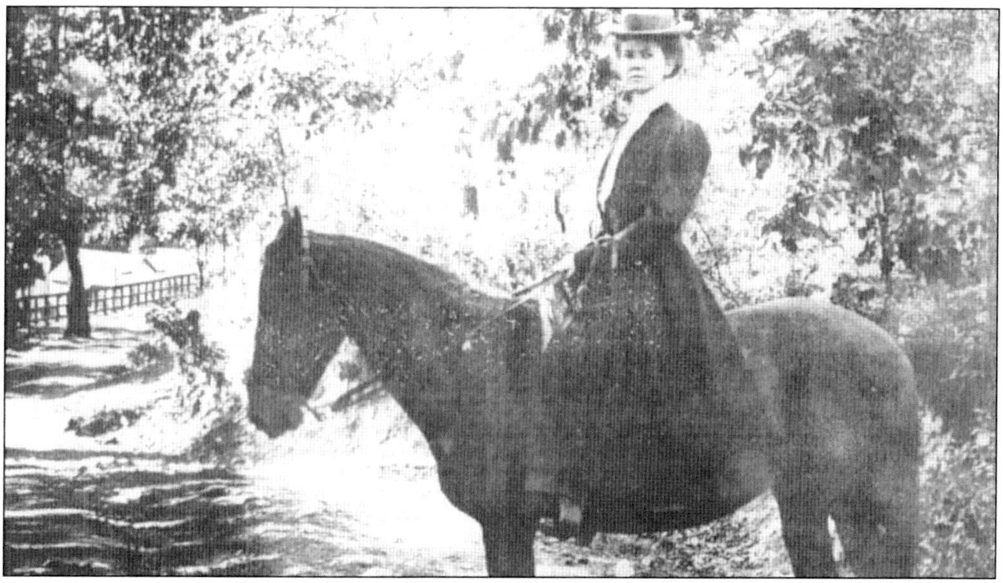

Only a few young ladies of the day would dare ride astride a horse in the early 1900s; Florence Young was one of them. Here she wears a divided skirt. Florence married J.P. Dunlap, the foster son of Dr. Albert and Virginia C. Dunlap. The road that curves out of sight was known as "the shoofly" because it was once the siding on which train cars were parked at the top of the divide to await being pulled over the steep mountain before the tunnel was completed.

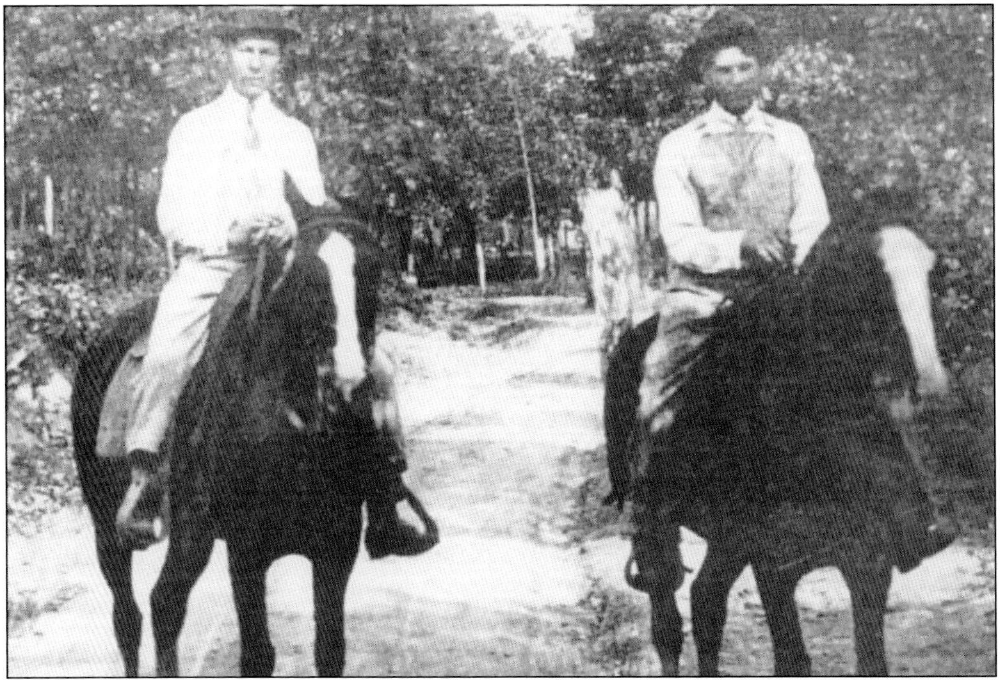

R.L. Maddox (left) and Lytton Deatherage, both of Winslow, were on their way to a semi-dress-up occasion shortly before World War I. The white shirts they are wearing with their overalls denote more than a casual occasion, and all young men wore hats or they weren't completely dressed. The occasion could have been calling on a couple of pretty ladies, an afternoon picnic, or a church social, possibly a decoration.

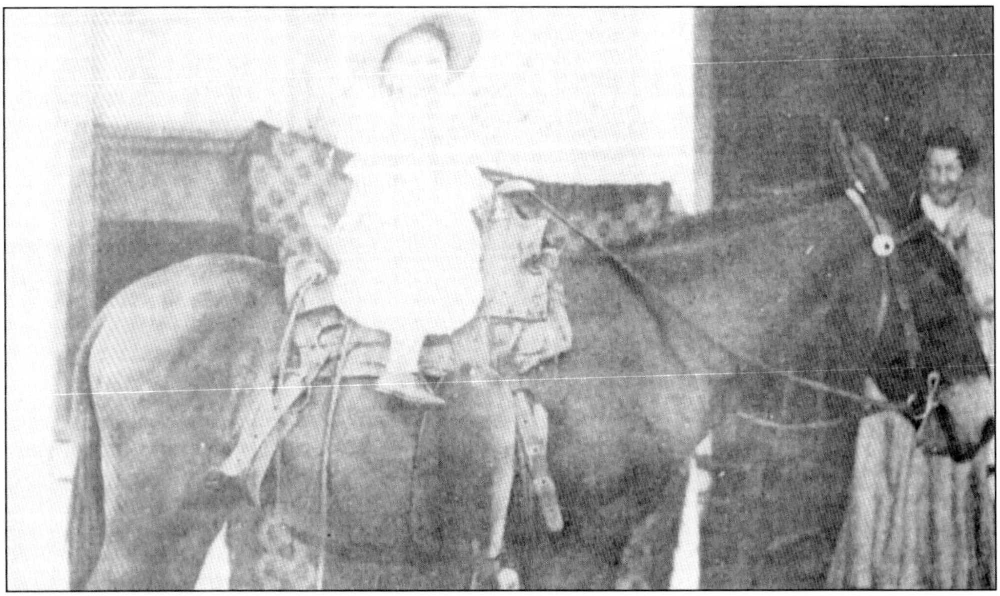

The custom of taking a young child's picture on horseback may have originated in the last century. In this *c.* 1908 photo, young Roy Guinn rides a mule at the home of his maternal grandparents, Mr. and Mrs. J.W. Nail of Winslow. Grandmother Nail is seen in the background on the right.

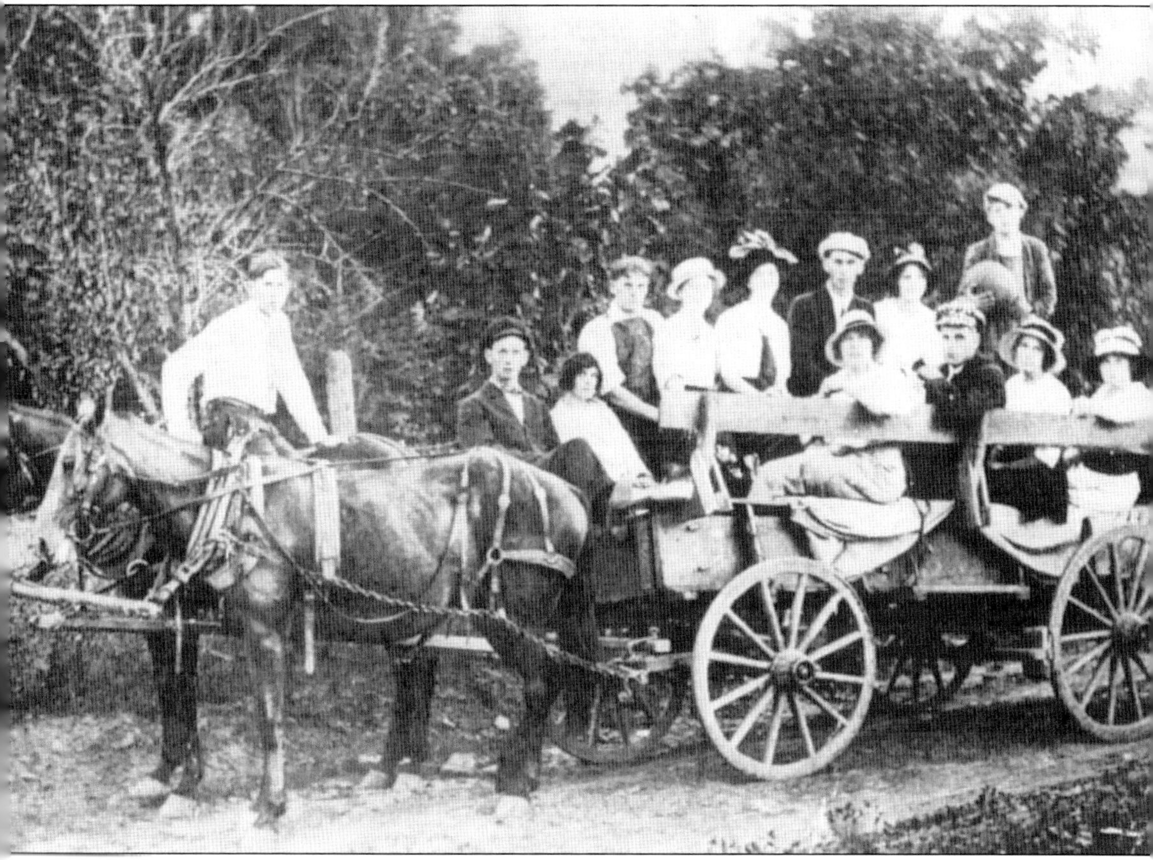

A Sunday afternoon ride always promised adventure to rural young people. This photo was taken near Slicker Swimmin' Hole, where this mixed crowd would not have dared to go as a group. In those days, young ladies did not "bathe" with young men. It would not be long before all that would change, but rural areas were the last to follow new trends, at least out in the open for all to see. Everyone here is dressed in "Sunday Go To Meeting Clothes." In the background is a pear tree, making this a popular fast-food stop for a snack. Pictured on the horse is Arthur Smith. Edgar Jones is the driver and owner of the rig. Myrtle Butts, Lytton Deatherage, Mollie Nickell, Laura Mannon, Arthur Jones, Florence Nickell, and Jonnie Kelton are standing in back of the wagon, and seated in front are Pearl Land, Guy Bradley, Faye Smith, Stella Smith, and Robert Humble. While the exact date of the photo is unknown, it was taken prior to World War I; Arthur Jones gave his life in that conflict.

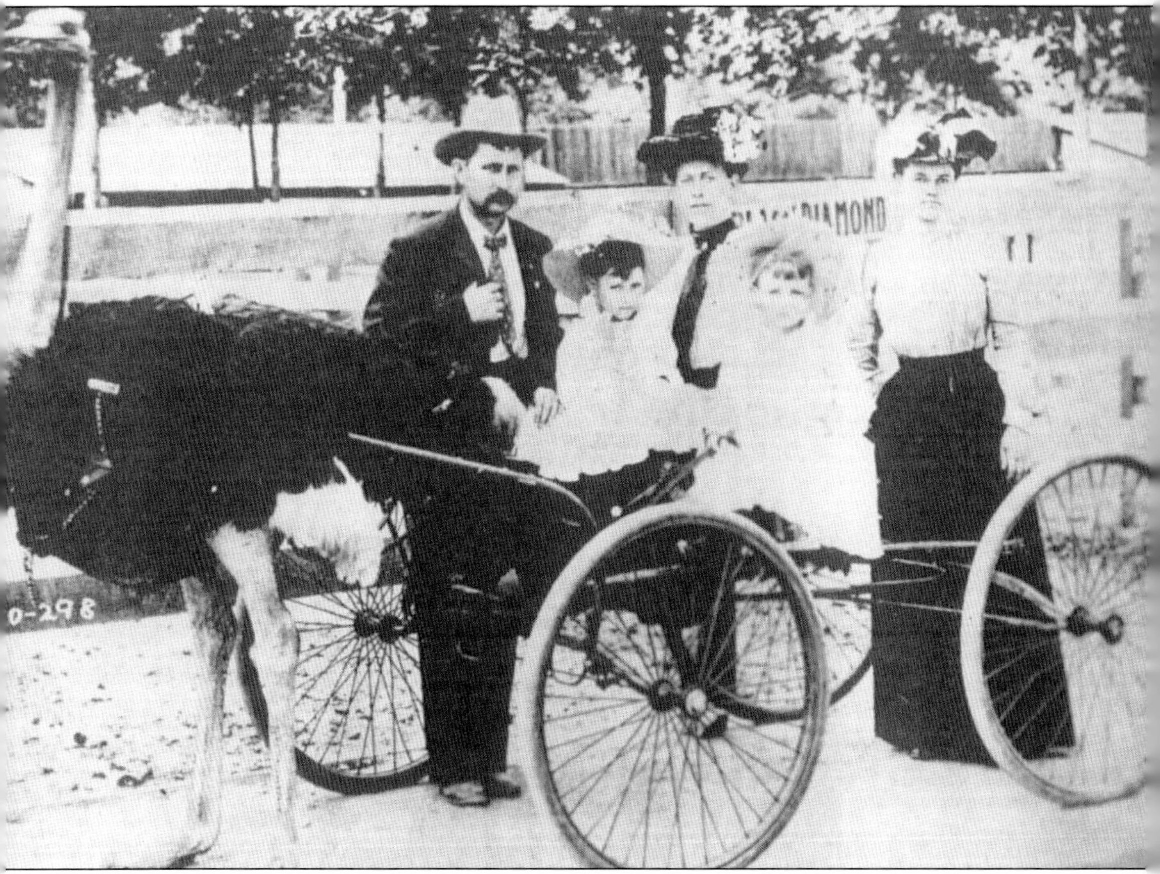

A trip to Hot Springs was a rare treat for families in Washington County, and everyone who went visited the ostrich farm. The bird in this c. 1902 photograph is the famous Black Diamond, the celebrated trotting ostrich. A.N. Cole and his wife, Addie Lee Land Cole, were partners in the Cole-Land Mercantile. They are shown here with an unidentified woman on the right, and their children are Fay and May. The ostrich farm and Black Diamond were so popular that many descendants of Washington County residents have found such pictures of their kin taken with the famous ostrich. Most visitors went to Hot Springs to enjoy the baths, which were believed to heal. In those days, Hot Springs was also known as Convention City.

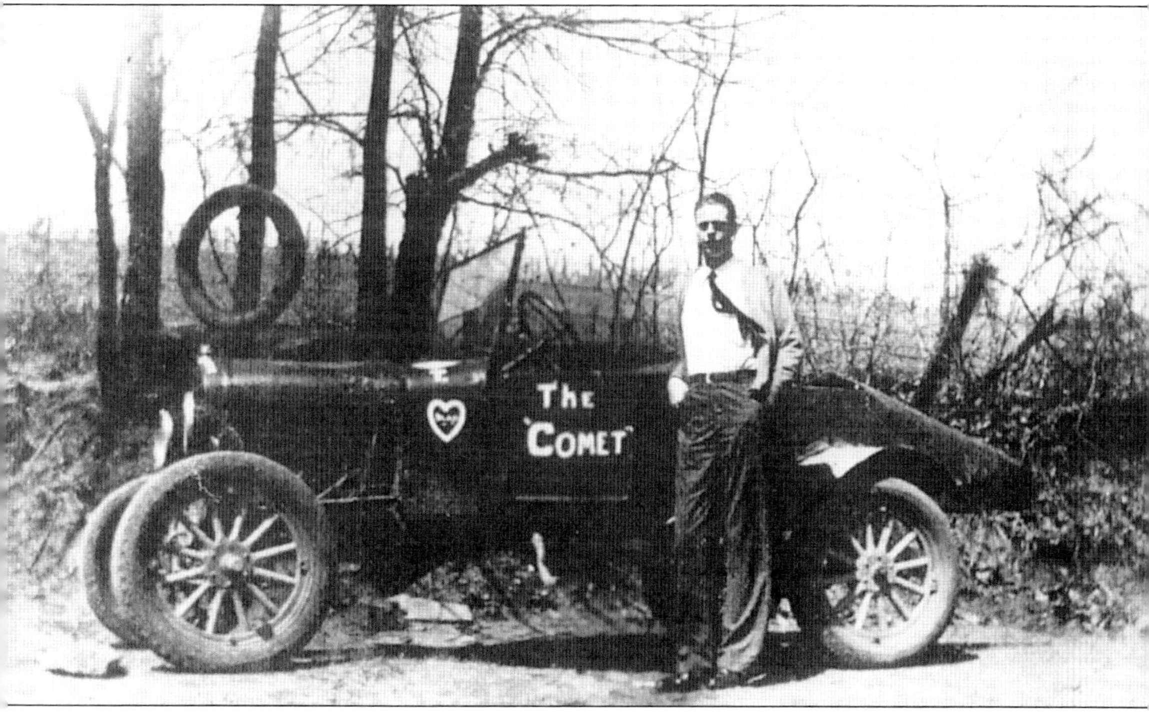

In 1935, Maurice Hudson, at the age of 20 may have been one of the first to "customize" his automobile. It could be said that he owned the first Ford Comet. This car, a 1925 Model-T Ford, was popular with young folks who could afford this kind of transportation. Hudson drove the same vehicle to the wheat harvest in Kansas the year after this photo was taken. Many young men in Arkansas were forced to go out of the area to find employment in those years. Hudson later sold this fine car to his cousin for $25, a handsome sum at the time. Other photos from the era show tourists traveling Arkansas's muddy, rutty roads in Model-T Fords. Tourist travel into the beautiful Ozarks was just beginning, and the automobile as a mode of transportation was still rare. Young people would see just how many of them could pile into a Model-T. A picture taken near Blackburn shows 11 youngsters doing just that. Their vehicle, a 1920 Model-T, had the new-fangled balloon tires, which came into vogue in the 1930s. The tires eased the ride on the rough roads.

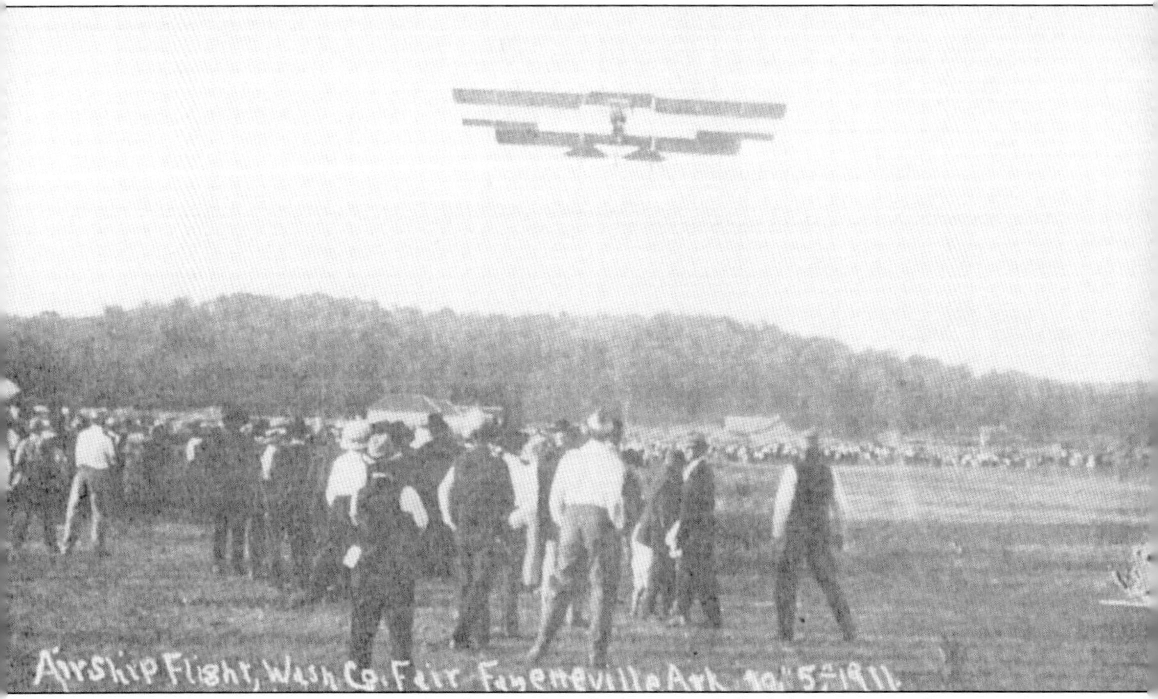

Pictured in this 1911 view is the first airship flight to be billed during a Washington County Fair. Early pilot Glenn Martin later became famous as an aircraft designer and builder. The airship flight was the highlight for visitors to the county fair that year. Within about 15 years, airship flights over the fairgrounds were "old hat," and to draw a large crowd it took a daredevil jumping from a plane to land on the fairgrounds. By World War II, Drake Airfield in Greenland became the headquarters for flight training of pilots going to war.

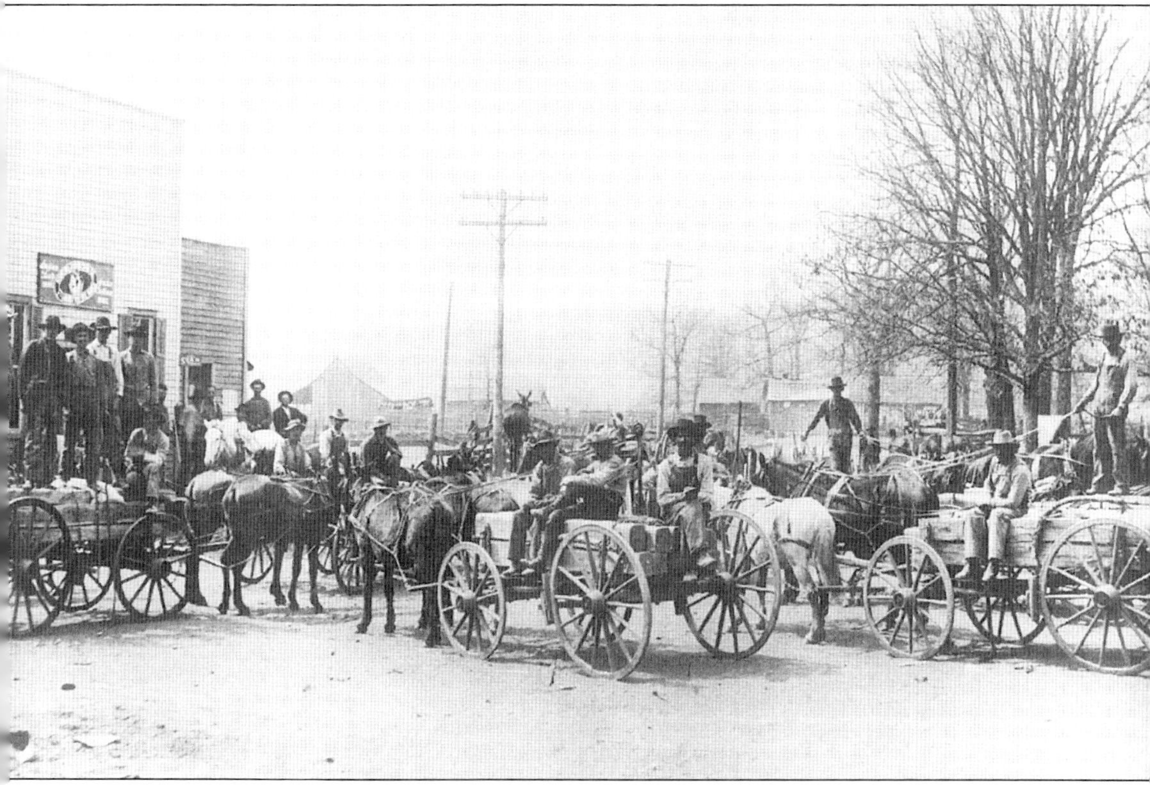

A Saturday morning in any small town in the county brought out residents from miles around to pick up supplies, deliver goods for barter, haul in lumber and ties, or simply visit with neighbors. The family of Daniel Ritter was among the first settlers to homestead in Elkins in 1827. They settled near a fine spring of water and accumulated a lot of land. The town, once known as Hood, became a thriving community when the St. Paul branch of the Frisco railroad brought it and others along the route to life. The logging industry in the White River valley supported several boomtowns. By 1897, the Frisco railroad had extended the line another 12 miles into Madison County, toward the headwaters of the White River. There were more than a dozen lumber and stave mills along the line. Once timber ran out, there was no longer a need for the railroad. In July 1937, a train made a final run and the branch became history. Timber was no longer king. Elkins, however, which is located about 12 miles from Fayetteville, has survived and continues to grow.

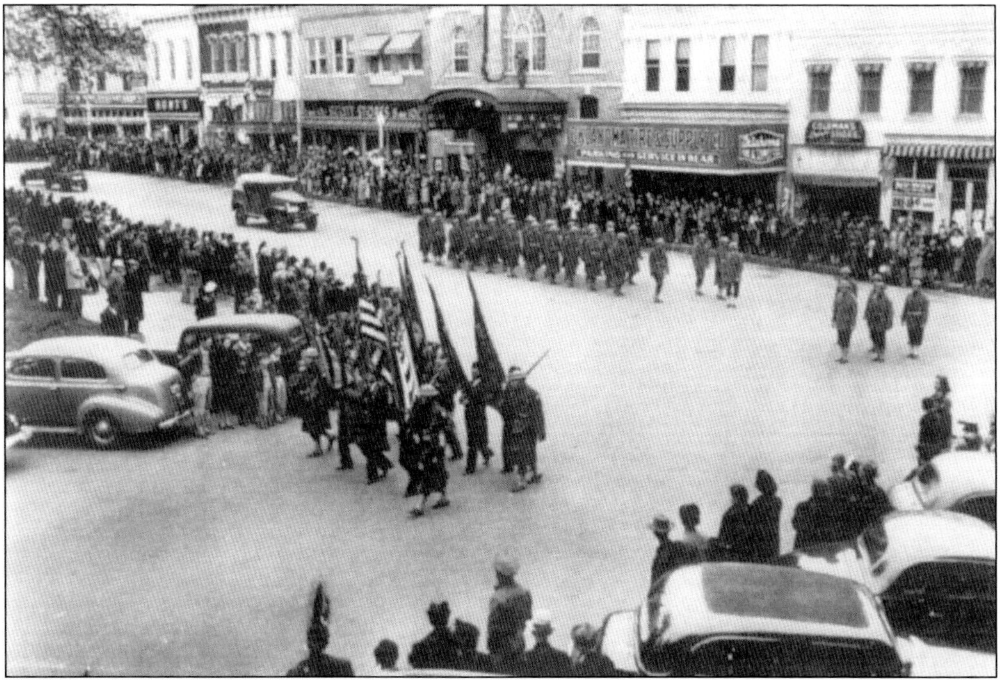

Pictured is the Fayetteville Square in its heyday during World War II. *Goodspeed's History* lists six families as the first families of Fayetteville: two McGarrahs, two Simpsons, one Shannon, and one Alexander. Also on hand to greet following settlers in 1827 were Mark Bean, Lewis Evans, another Alexander, Samuel, and the Latta family. The family of James Leeper, a Revolutionary War soldier, came to Fayetteville in 1830. His son, Matthew, owned most of the land on East Mountain all the way into the valley to the White River near Fayetteville. During the Civil War, Union soldiers occupied the town and before the battles ended, it was burned.

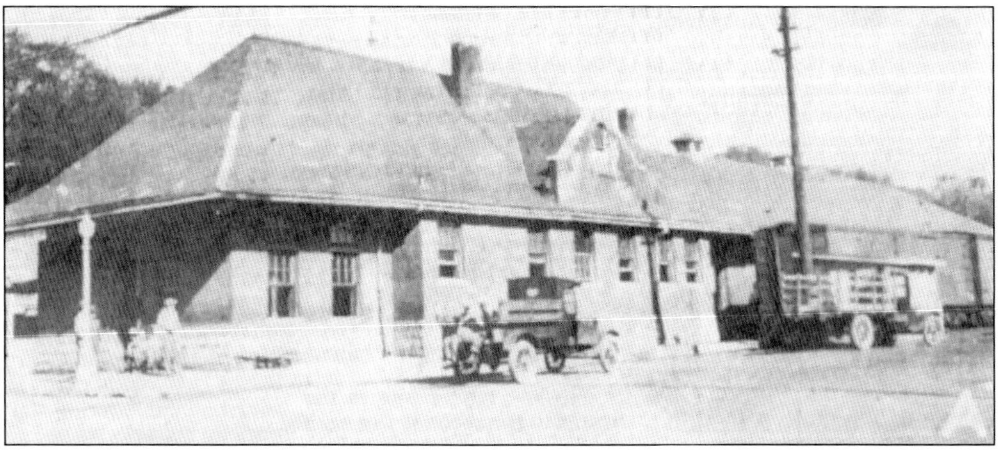

The first courthouse had been built in 1854, but the city wasn't chartered until 1859. J.W. Walker was mayor, and P.P. Van Hoose served as city councilman, along with E.C. Boudinot, C.E. Butterfield, A. Crouch, J.B. Simpson, and J.H. Stirman. In her famous published diaries, author Marian Tebbetts Banes describes Fayetteville as "Often thought of as a cache for thieves, cutthroats and murderers, Fayetteville was actually a charming town, isolated from the outside world, a hundred miles from the railroad and fifty miles across the hills from the Arkansas River."

Three

Makin' a Livin'

Making a living in the Ozarks was tough after the Great Depression. Before that time, however, it was one of the richest areas in the state. Families from Tennessee and Kentucky migrated in hopes of escaping the poverty in which they lived. Following statehood in 1836 and the Indian Removal in 1839, farmers and businessmen prospered. There were apple orchards and strawberry and tomato fields. The logging industry grew by leaps and bounds as men harvested stands of virgin timber hardwoods, and the railroad cut through the rugged Boston Mountains of the Ozarks to bring more prosperity. Homesteaders had little cash money, but the land was rich; a man could work, feed his family, and barter for the goods he couldn't grow. Best of all, the land was open to homesteaders.

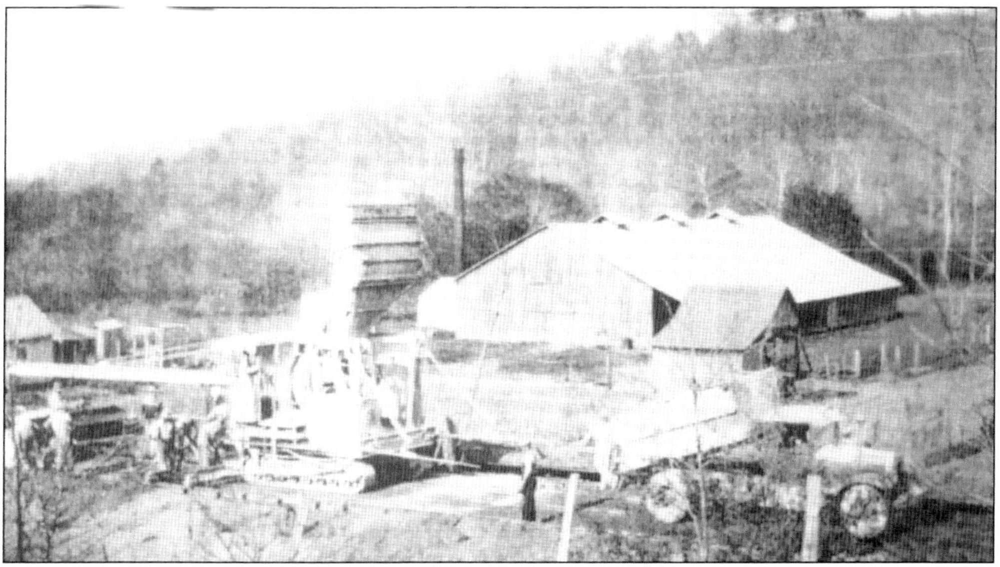

One of the first canning factories near Winslow only canned tomatoes. Shown in the foreground is a road crew paving the first slab of U.S. Highway 71, just north of Winslow at Sunset Road. This factory was soon replaced by a larger one that was closer to the railroad. By 1930, these small canning factories were closing due to the availability of transportation and new roads; produce could now be hauled to larger canning factories.

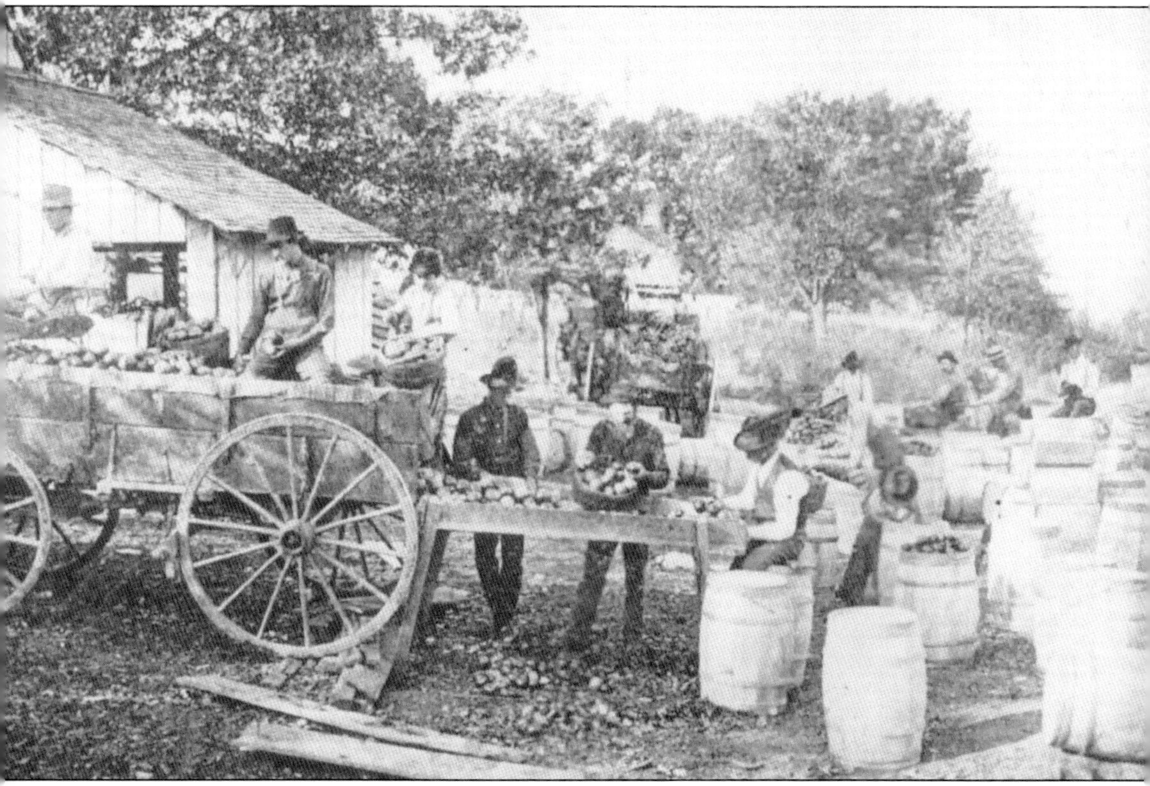

Around the turn of the century, orchards and vineyards dotted the hillsides and valleys. Apples became a principal product of area orchards. The west ridge of mountains, from Blackburn to Fayetteville, contained numerous apple orchards. As seen in this *c.* 1900 view at the M.F. Caldwell orchard near Greenland, fruit was hauled in from the orchards in wagons and graded right off the wagon.The driver is unknown, but seated beside him are Frank Alexander, Everett Alexander, unidentified, unidentified, M.F. Caldwell (at the end of the grading table), Taylor Lee (at the barrel in the foreground), Jim Crider, John Webb, and M.B. Crider. The man on the right is also unknown. Apples that did not grade high enough for shipment were taken to the evaporation building in the left background. There they were sliced for drying, or they were used to make cider. The best apples were packed in barrels and shipped to market by rail. In 1904, apples from the Caldwell orchard took first place in the first World's Fair. Apple picking was the highlight of the season, with apple pies and cobblers to be made and apple butter to be canned for winter.

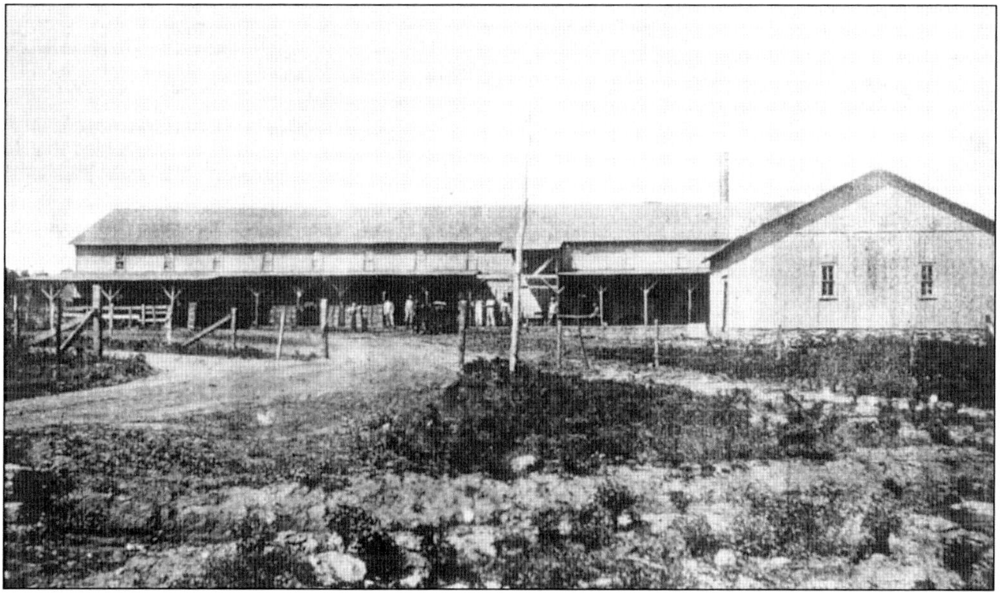

This canning factory was built in 1917, just north of West Fork between the railroad and the road that leads to the gravel pits. It continued to operate through the 1920s. At first, only tomatoes were canned; then blackberries, green beans, turnip greens, and poke were added. The Depression years of the 1930s put an end to the canning operations.

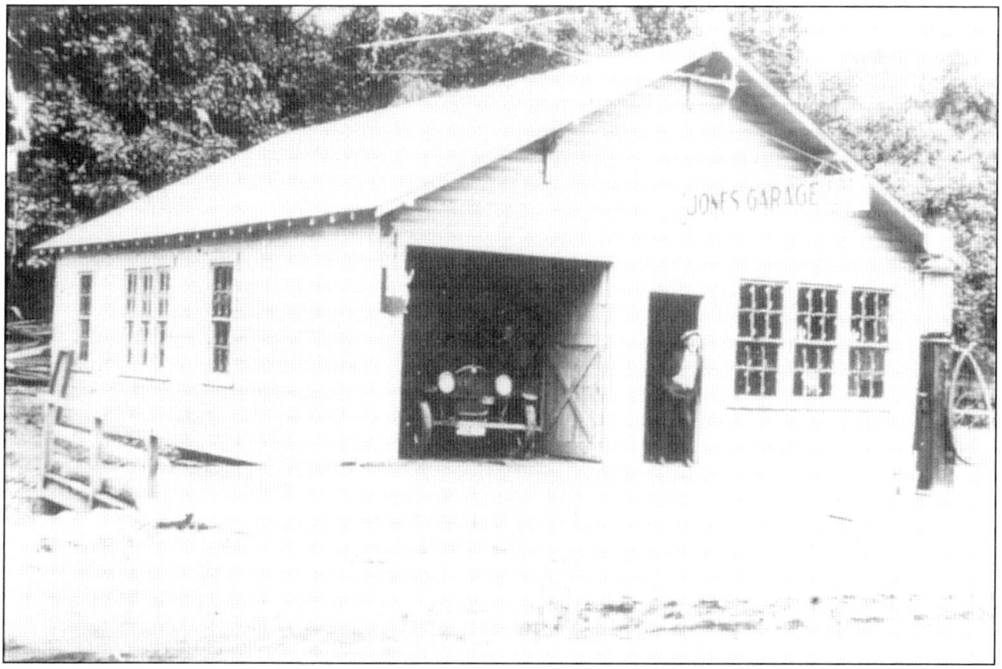

With the advent of the automobile, mechanics were needed, and that became another way to make a living in the county. Jones Garage was located in Winslow. Note the gravity-fed gasoline pump in the right foreground. The canning factory built in Winslow was located to the left of this garage. The railroad can be seen on the hill in the background.

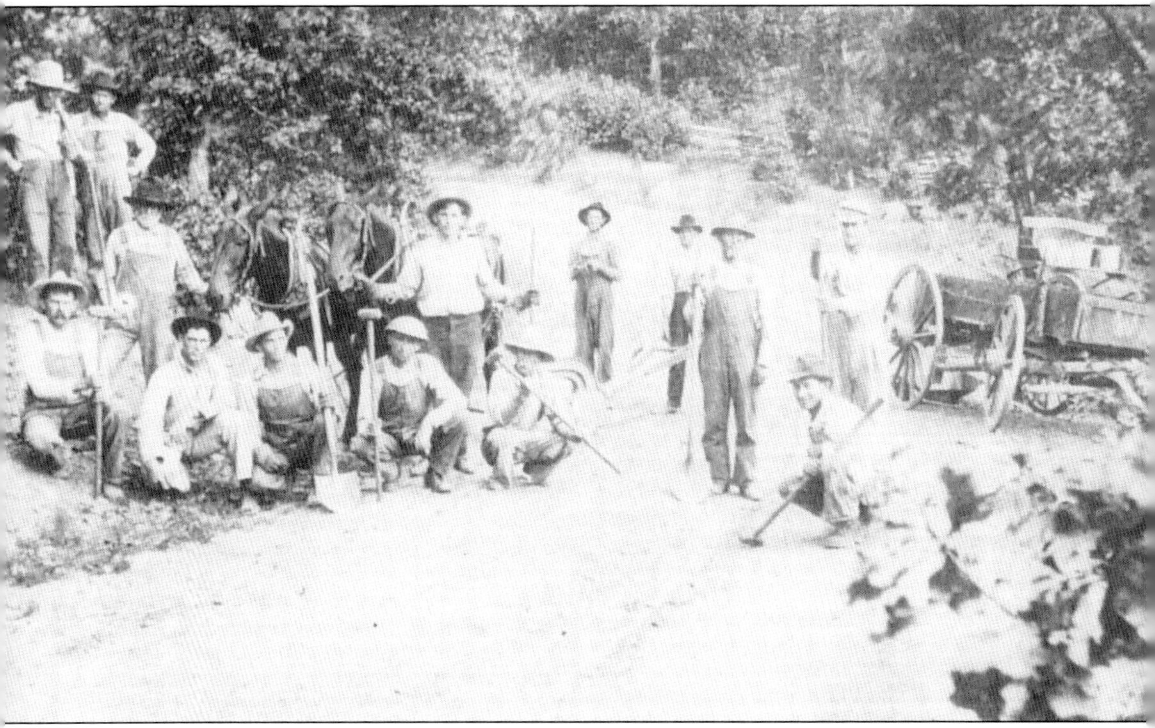

A work crew builds the road to Devil's Den from the West Fork side in this 1915 view. For many years during this time, every able-bodied man between the age of 21 and 45 was required to give four days of road work per year, or two days if he furnished a team of horses or mules. A road overseer was elected from each township. Jim Jones is the overseer in this photo. He was the only one of the crew that drew a salary. Some men who had available cash would pay someone to take their place on the road crew. Other than the equipment pulled by the mules, shovels were the mainstay of the road crew. This photo was taken by George Frederick, a Spanish-American War veteran who lived nearby. He often took photos of weddings and school and church groups; the family kitchen doubled as his darkroom.

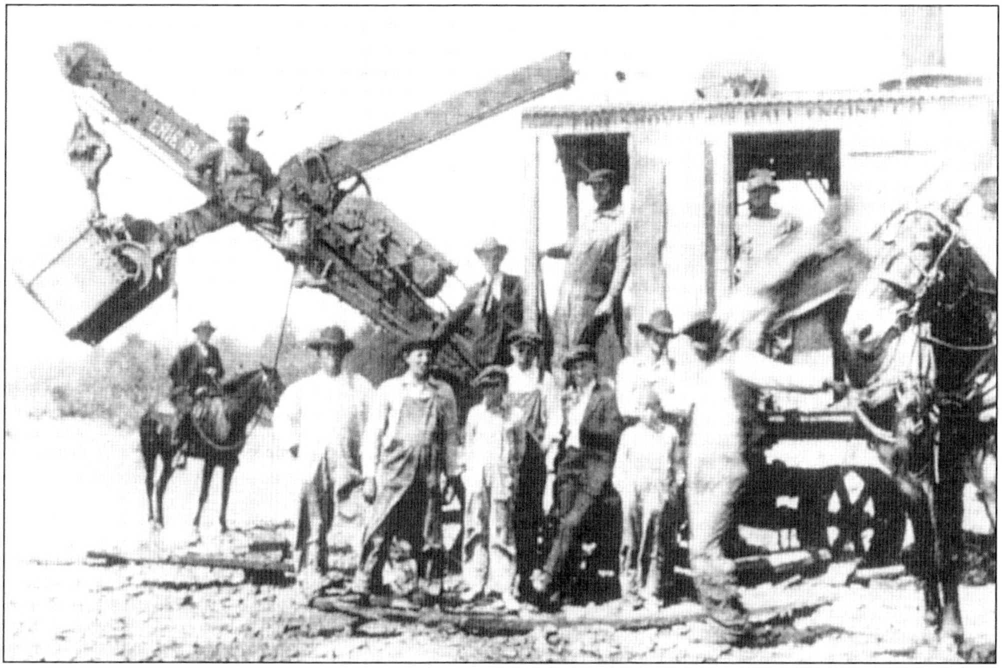

The Civilian Conservation Corps constructed state parks all over the United States in the late 1930s, until the outbreak of World War II. In this view, construction on the park at Devil's Den is enhanced by the heavy equipment of the day, such as the steam shovel, which took much of the back-breaking work out of this type of construction. The only person identified, Uncle George Latham, is standing in the door of the steam shovel.

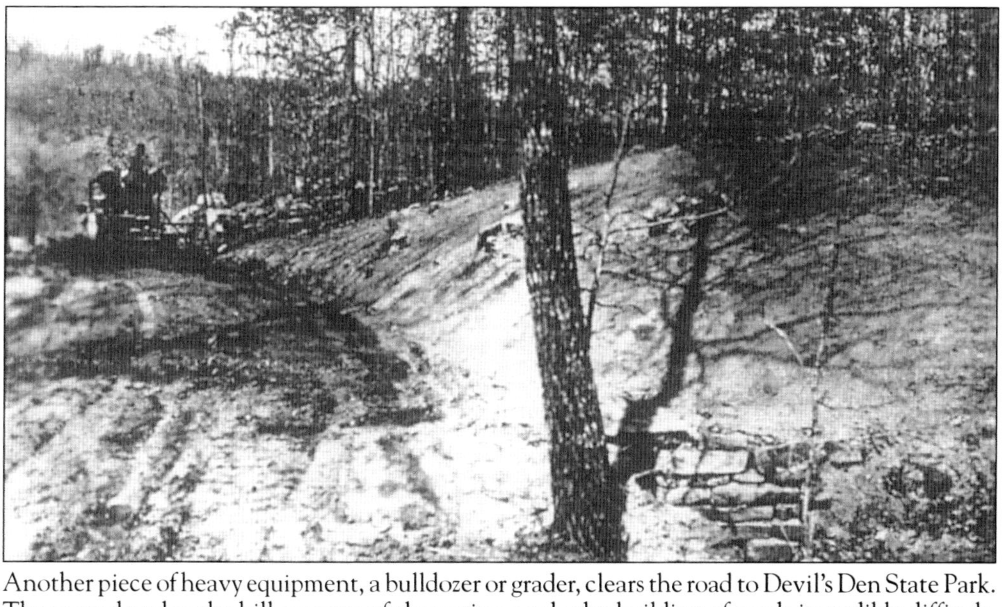

Another piece of heavy equipment, a bulldozer or grader, clears the road to Devil's Den State Park. The rugged and rocky hill country of the region made the building of roads incredibly difficult. Prior to the development of steam equipment, horses and mules pulled slips and graders.

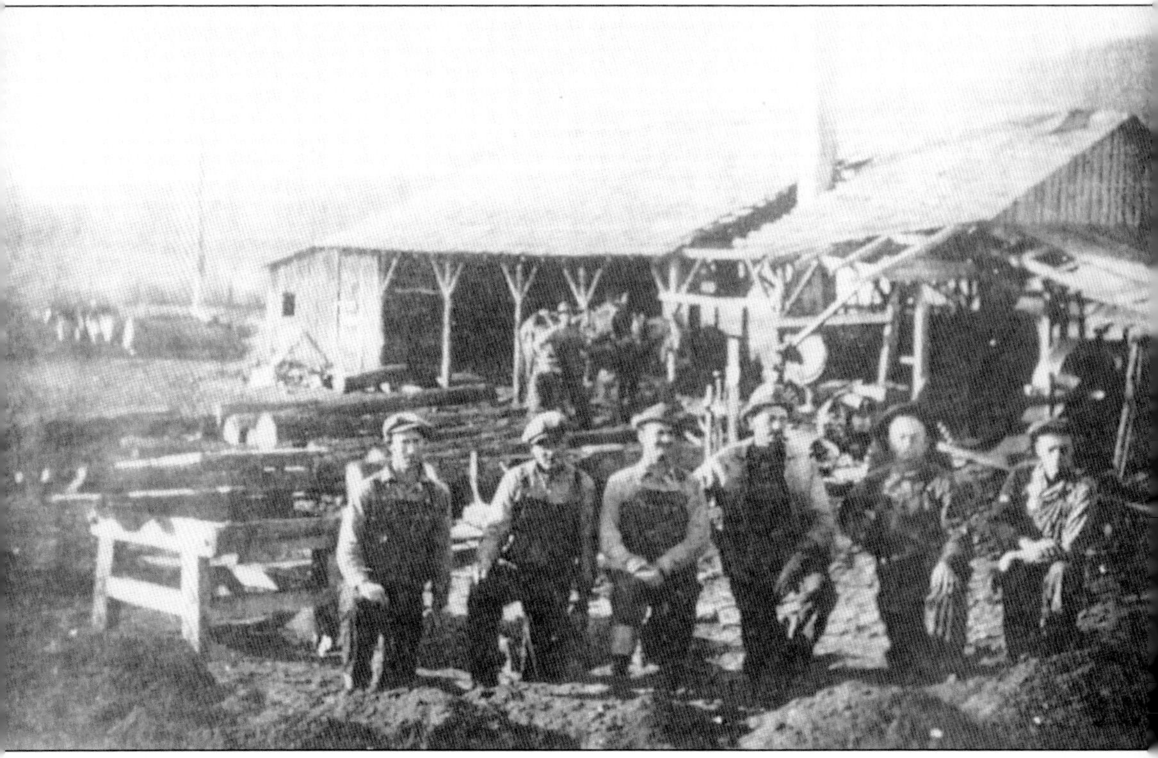

Because of the virgin timber in the area, many men owned and/or worked at sawmills. This one operated at Brentwood between 1915 and 1920. The timber boom was beginning to fade in the county. John Chandler lived nearby and may have owned this mill at Brentwood. From left to right are as follows: Aubrie McKenzie, Hobson Hughes, Clyde McKenzie, Claude Prater, unidentified, and Everett Parrish. The area was sparsely settled until after the Homestead Act of 1862, when the fertile valleys and river bottoms and the timbered hills and free range for livestock offered a good living to homesteaders. Several small communities developed into larger trade centers, but most faded away with the advent of motorized transportation. During the timber boom, one could look in almost any direction at daybreak and see smoke rising from a sawmill that was powered by an old steam boiler. In the crisp morning air, the creak of log wagons could be heard as they rolled out of the timber, headed for the sawmill. Some days, wagonloads of timber would line up for miles on either side of the rail yard sidings.

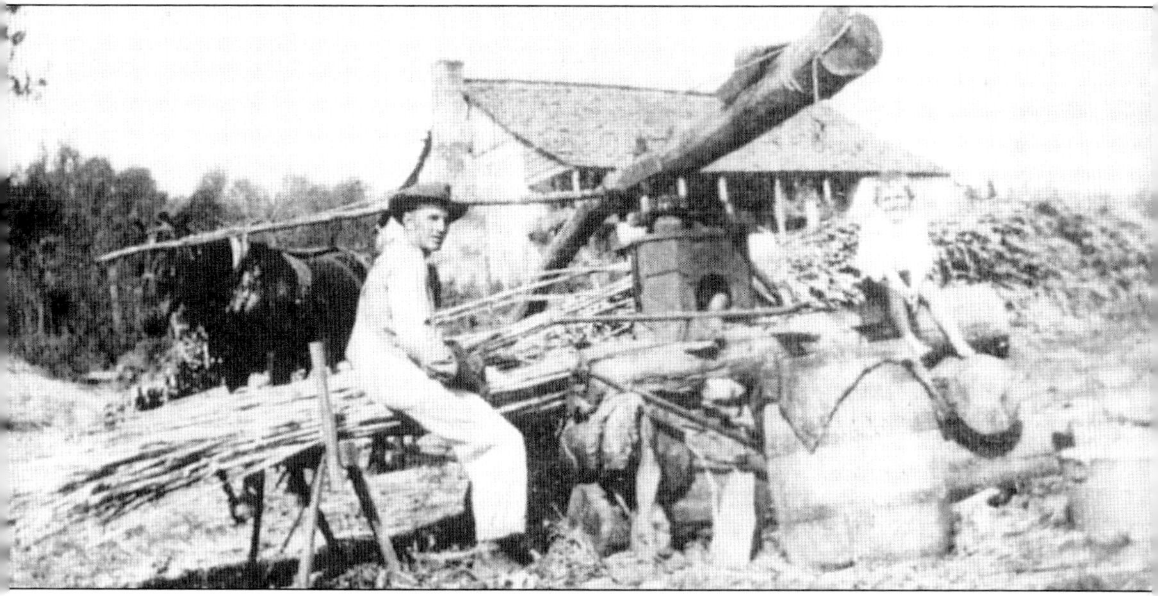

Sorghum-making time in the Ozarks was a special time for the children, who would hurry home from school and race out to the mill to peel a few joints of cane and chew out the sweet juice. Yellow jackets were also attracted to the juice and could give a good sting to the unsuspecting child sliding down the pummy pile (cane that has gone through the mill and discarded). Sorghum was used by most families as "sweetnin'" because sugar wasn't affordable or available. The cane was stripped and headed in the field, cut with a large cane knife, and hauled to the mill. The fodder stripped from the cane was fed to livestock. Many people would haul cane to the mill; it was made into sorghum on the shares. Once the juice was squeezed out, it was carried to the cooking vat. This photo is a view of the Hutcheson mill on Winn's Creek. A mule was hitched up and walked around and around, powering the press.

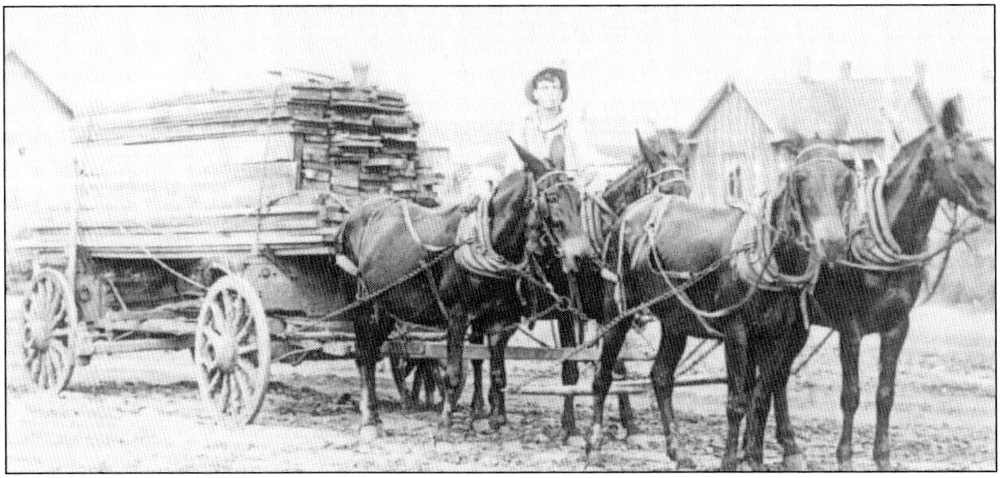

This is a typical load of lumber arriving at the railroad tie yard, which was usually done on Saturdays. By dawn, wagons would be lined up and drivers would visit with neighbors who, like them, had labored in the timber and at the sawmills all week. This young man, who is not identified, has a fine team of mules. They probably spent the week skidding logs out of the woods to haul to the mill for sawing.

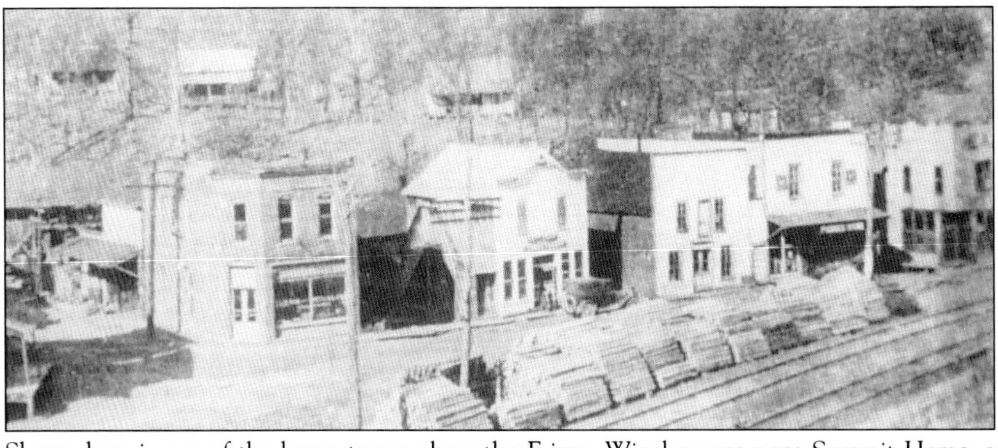

Shown here is one of the boom towns along the Frisco. Winslow was once Summit Home, a stage stop along a branch of the Butterfield Stage Line south to Van Buren and Fort Smith. The railroad turned the small one-hotel stop into a large community that became a resort area in the early 1900s. The resort attracted many summer visitors who sought relief from the hot Arkansas River Valley.

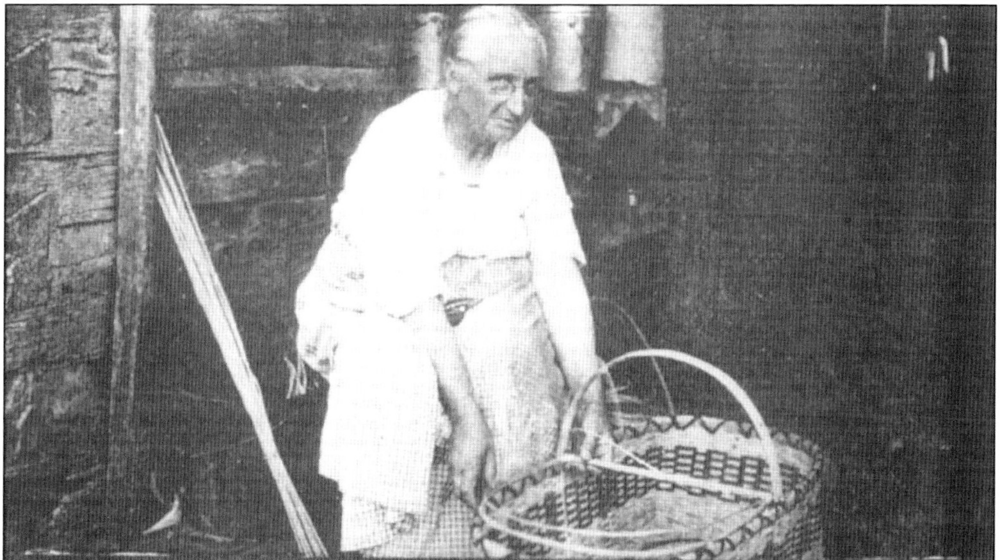

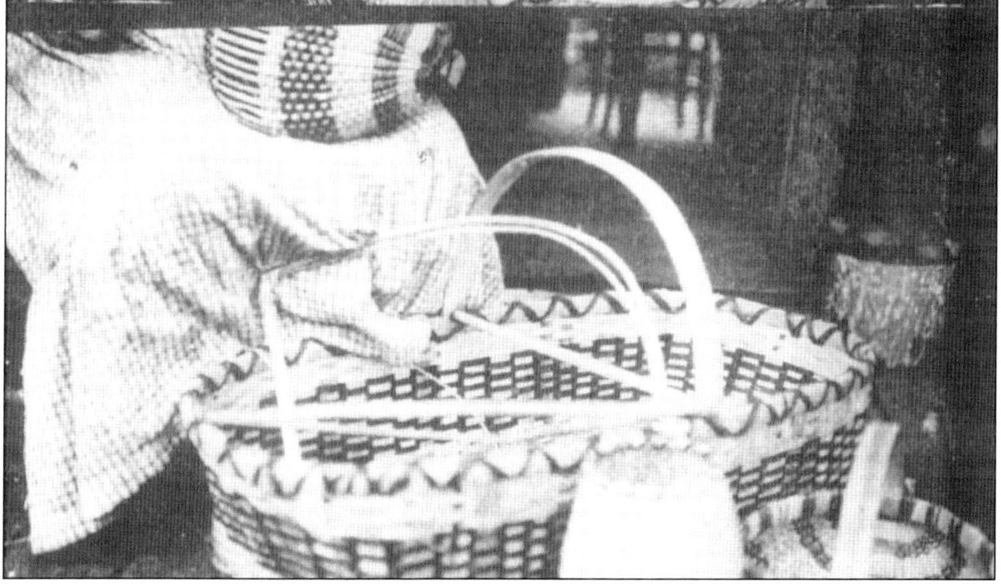

When the Depression hit the area in the 1920s and 1930s, it made earlier deprivations seem like a picnic in comparison. Many residents searched for and found ways to make the elusive dollar and help feed their families. From this need emerged the art of white oak basket-making, which remains to this day one of the most popular native crafts in the area. Grandma Ida Southern was considered one of the best basket makers in the mountains. The basket-making began when Grandpa Will took to the woods around the log house where the couple had raised 11 children. He selected straight, untwisted saplings four to six inches in diameter and mostly free of knots and limbs. A froe and mallet, or drawing knife, was used to make splits for baskets and chair bottoms. The white oak was put down in the creek to keep it from drying out if grandpa couldn't get to it right away. Grandma started the basket by making two hoops. The splits were then woven into a basket, but this is a simplification of the intricate and difficult work that took place. Grandpa took the baskets in by the wagonload for the tourist trade and to sell to retail stores. In those days, hard work far into the dark of evening was the order of the day for those who wanted to eat.

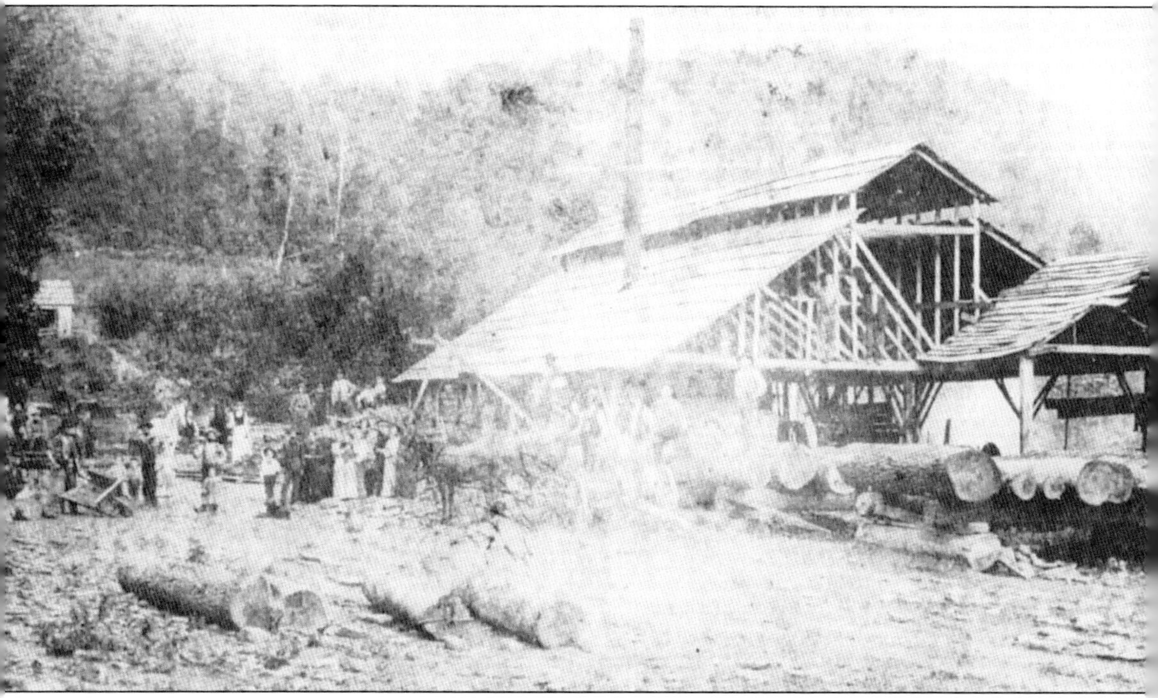

This photo of the J.C. Myers sawmill was taken September 5, 1889. The mill was located in Hazel Valley, on the Middle Fork of the White River. The triangular frame in the center appears to hold a block and tackle, which was used to lift logs from wagons into the mill. Compare the size of the logs on the right to those in the background for an idea of the enormity of the virgin timber that was cut at the time. One log would be a full load for a wagon, and it was all a team could do to pull it up the steep mountainsides. The age of the picture and its damage made it impossible to identify anyone shown. Hazel Valley remains today one of the most historically rich areas in Washington County. It was considered as a listing by the Arkansas Historic Preservation Association but residents there declined, wishing to continue their own efforts of preservation without government help or intervention.

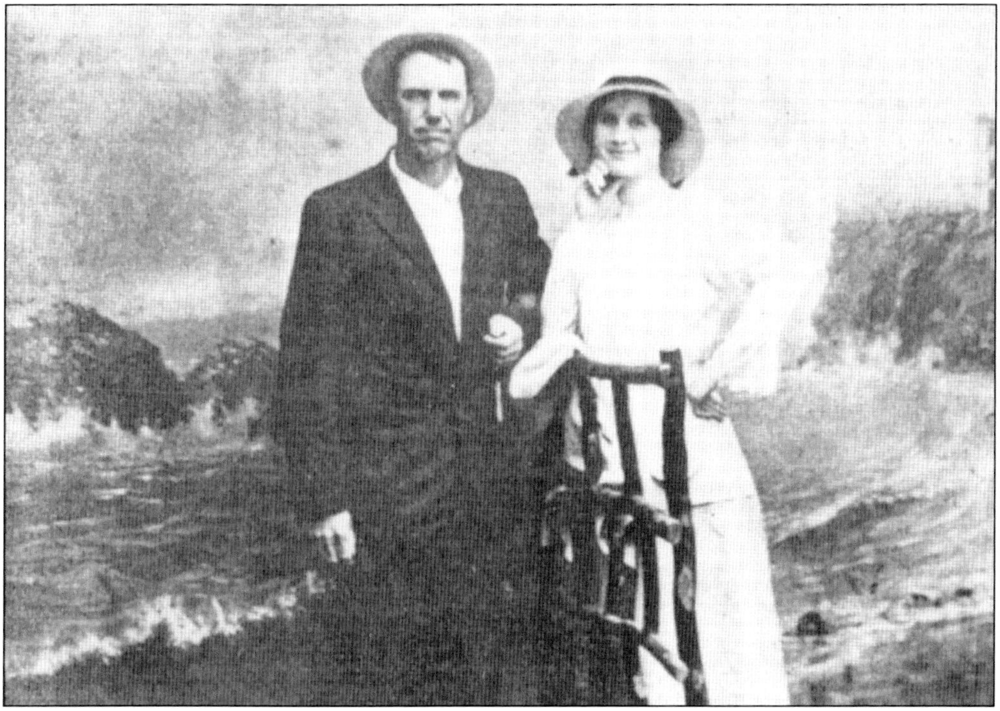

Makin' a Livin' history would not be complete without inclusion of E.A. Budd and his young wife, Rose Shackelford Budd. Budd was the owner of the Budd Post Company and became known as the Man who Fenced the West. A phenomenal entrepreneur, Budd built business establishments in nearly every railroad town along the Frisco, from Fayetteville to Van Buren. He also owned almost all of the south side of the Fayetteville Square. One of his largest establishments was located in Winslow during its boom days. Here Budd and his adored wife made what was then a daring and unusual automobile trip from their home in Winslow to attend the World's Fair in San Francisco. Tragically, on October 28 of that year, Rose died in childbirth at the couple's home. She and the newborn baby were buried in Brentwood Cemetery. Budd left Winslow and moved the headquarters of his business to Fayetteville after their deaths, and most say he never recovered from the loss.

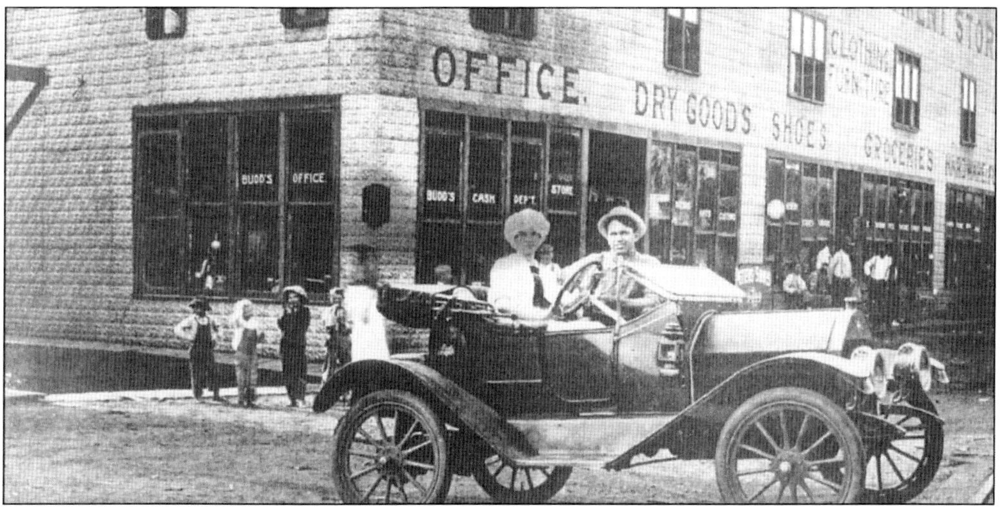

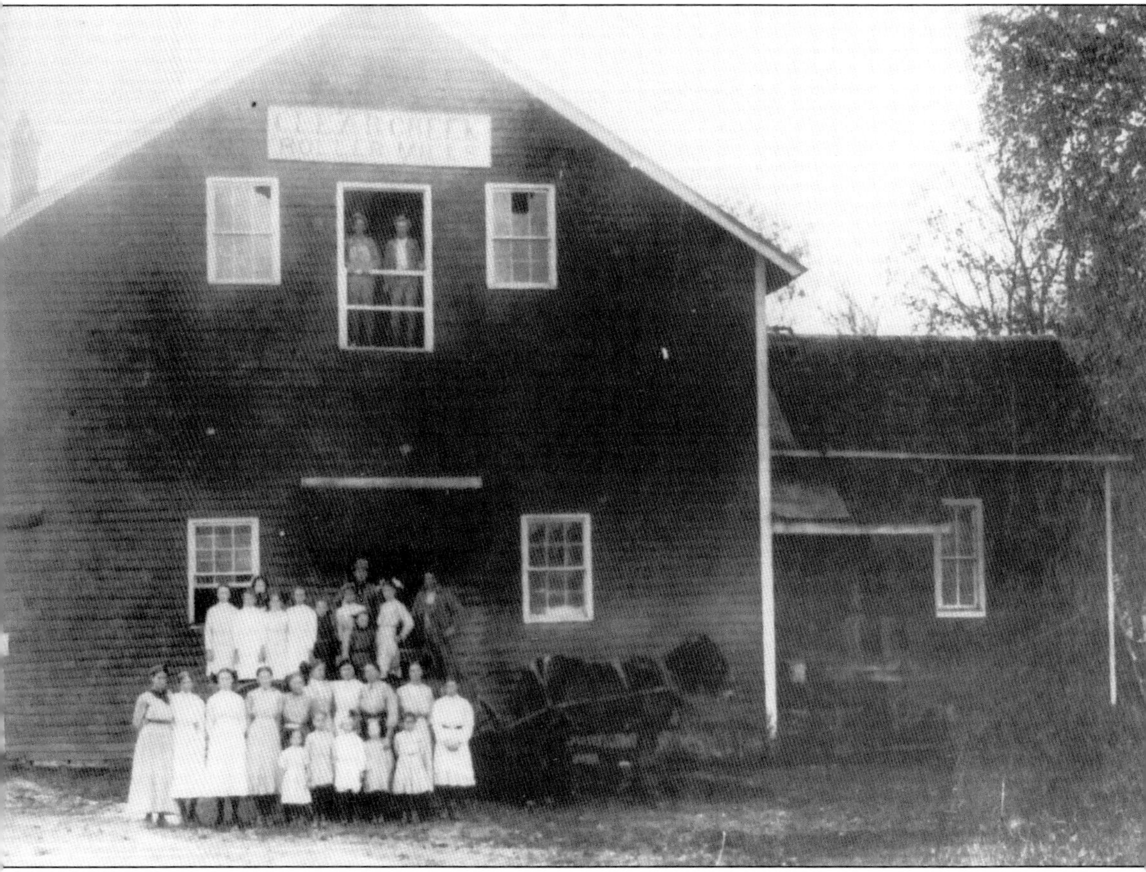

Savoy Mill was located on Clear Creek near Farmington. This photo was taken in 1911. Built in the early 1800s, the mill stood on this spot until it burned in 1960. In 1911, J.K. Cowan began the American Milling Company there. At one time, the picturesque village of Savoy, located east of Lake Wedington, had a post office, three grocery stores, two blacksmith shops, and the Cowan Mill with its gigantic water wheel. Today, there is little left but a community building, several homes, and a beautiful lake behind the dam on Clear Creek. The Cowan family built the dam in 1920. They allowed the public to stroll the lush green banks and to picnic and swim, but due to changing times it is now closed.

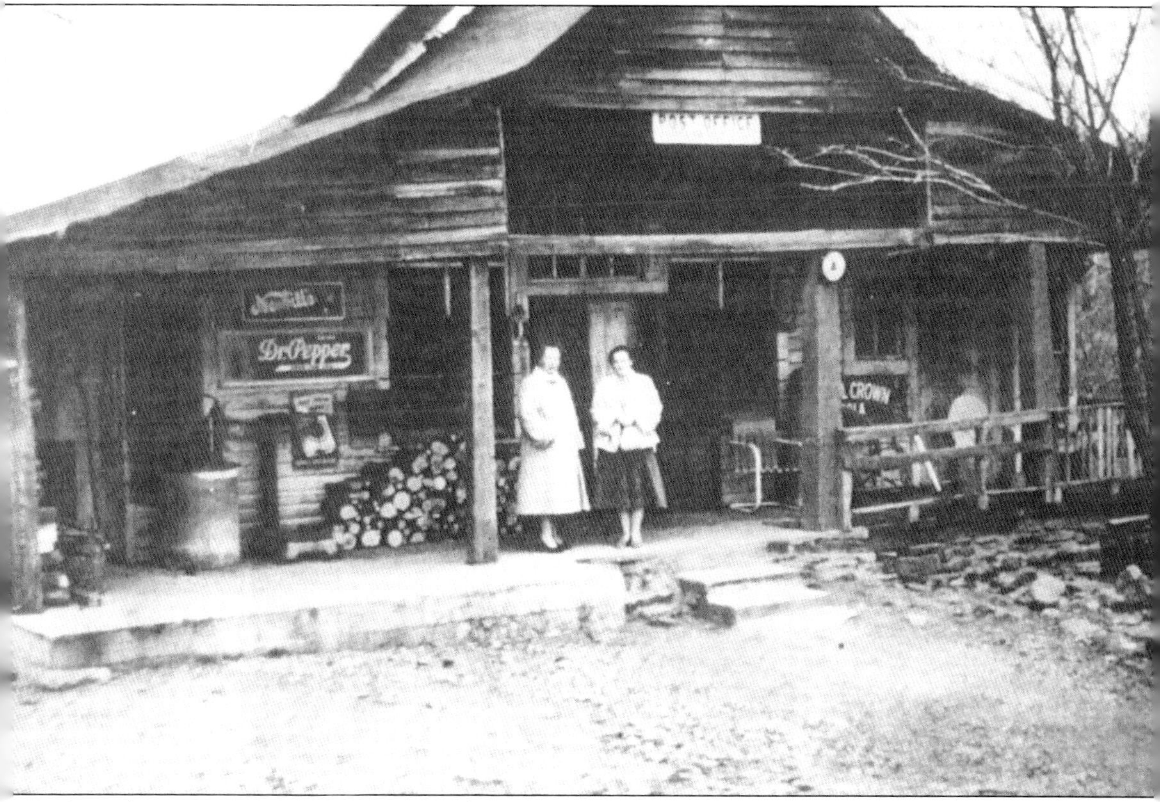

Over the past 100 years, 50 to 100 of Washington County's post offices have closed. Better transportation has shortened the distance in time between communities, and one by one, the small stores that once housed post offices have closed their doors. This photo, taken in the 1950s, shows how little those stores changed from their inception up to that time. The Brentwood Post Office was established January 19, 1880. For the first three years, the town was known as Gunter. It was named for its first postmaster, Thomas Gunter. The last postmaster to serve Brentwood was Frank J. Waggoner in 1960. Located on the banks of the West Fork of the White River and along the Frisco Railroad line, Brentwood was a busy community center for years. Nelle Jett Duncan and Ione Miles Duncan are shown standing on their porch.

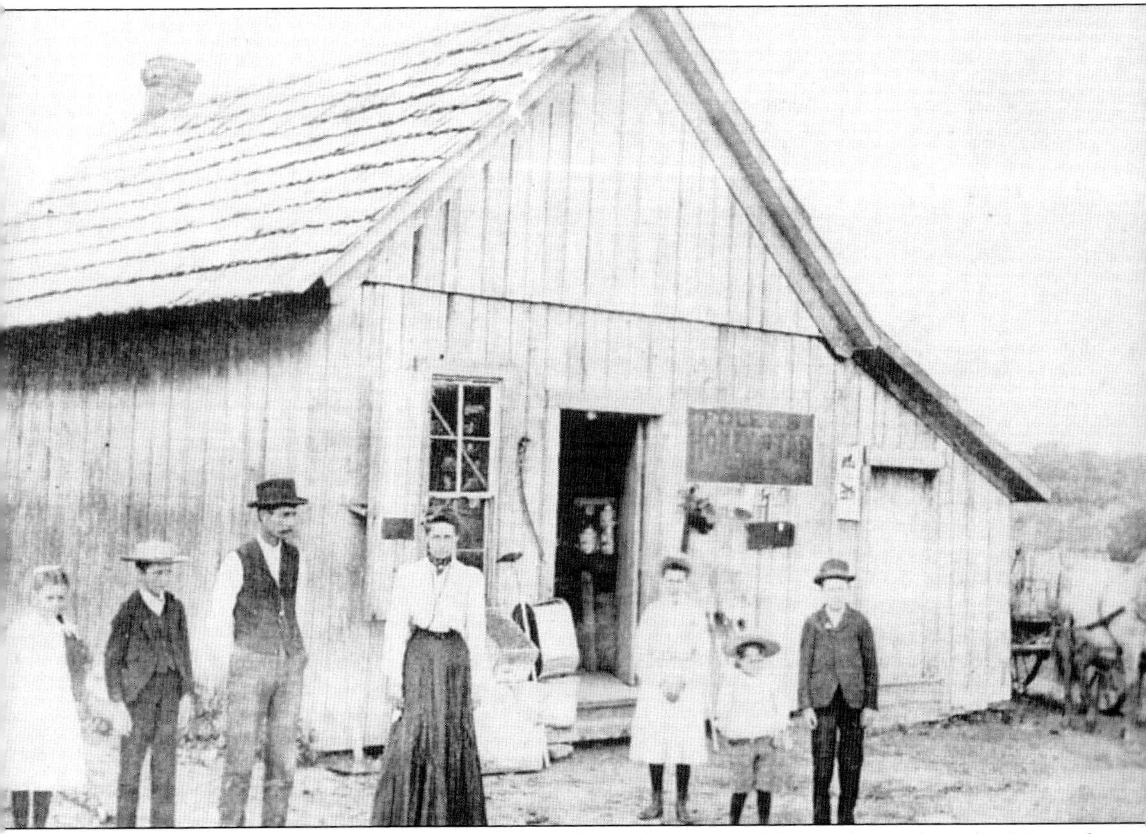

The Ridge Post Office and General Store, shown here in 1905, was located in the Mineral Springs community. It was owned and operated by W.S. Payton. Each day, Walker Woods would bring the mail by horseback from the West Fork Post Office. Residents picked up their own mail because there were no rural route deliveries. The post office became a daily gathering and gossiping place for residents as they waited for mail time. The year after this photo was taken, the building and all its contents were destroyed by fire. Mr. Payton rebuilt the store, this time larger and better, and opened it the following year. From left to right are as follows: Mamie Payton Winfred, E.A. Payton, W.S. Payton, Mrs. Lavina Payton, Alice Payton Malone, Edgar L. Payton, and Ivan Payton.

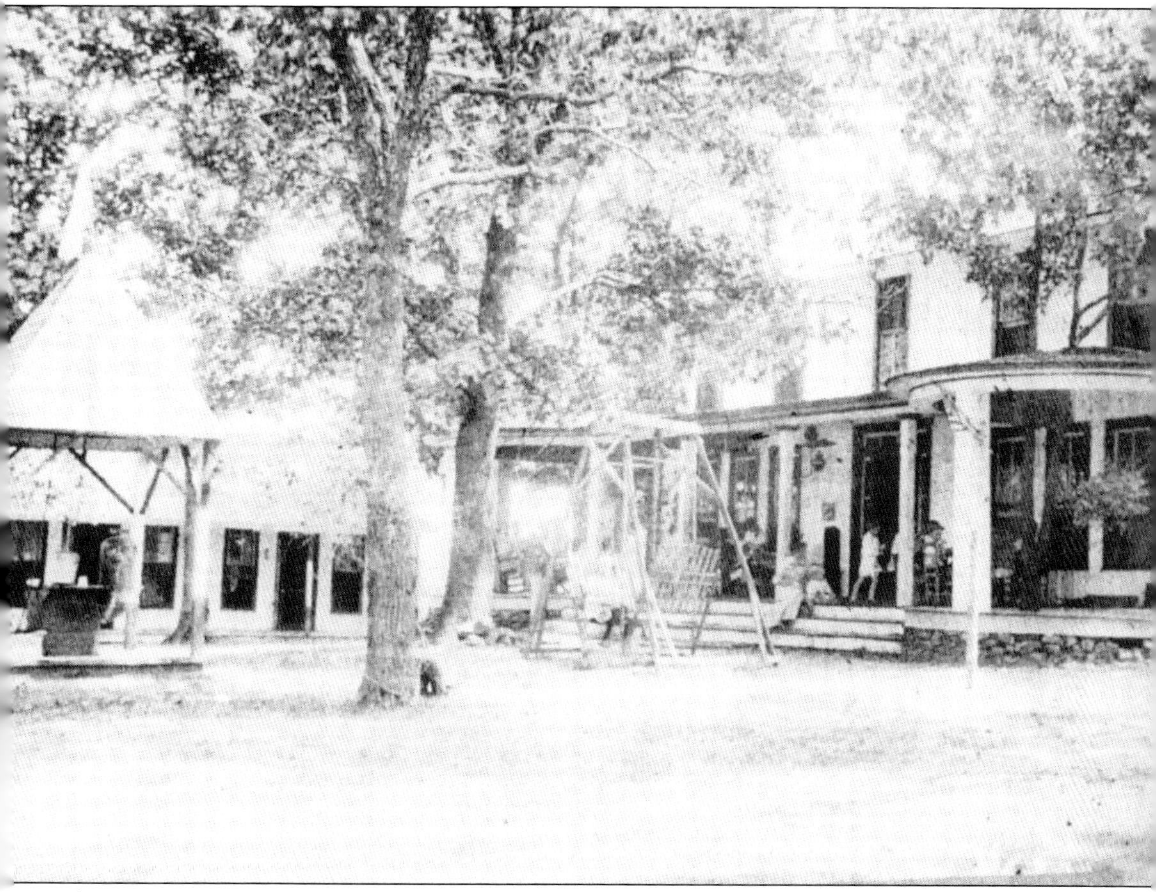

The Summit Hotel in Winslow was built as a stage stop by Mr. E.J. Woolum (or Woolem) in 1872. It was the first and largest privately owned resort hotel in Winslow. The branch of the Butterfield Stage Line was known as the Woolum Branch by some, but history holds several disputes over the exact route of the line through the area. In the 1880s, after the railroad replaced the stage, the place was purchased by Mr. and Mrs. R.G. Williams of Springfield. They operated the hotel until the main building was destroyed by fire in January 1930. The site is now part of the Winslow Public School property. In addition to the main building, there were cottages on each side; together they could accommodate up to 80 guests at one time. At the height of Winslow's boom, some 10,000 summer visitors stayed in area hotels, cottages, and summer homes.

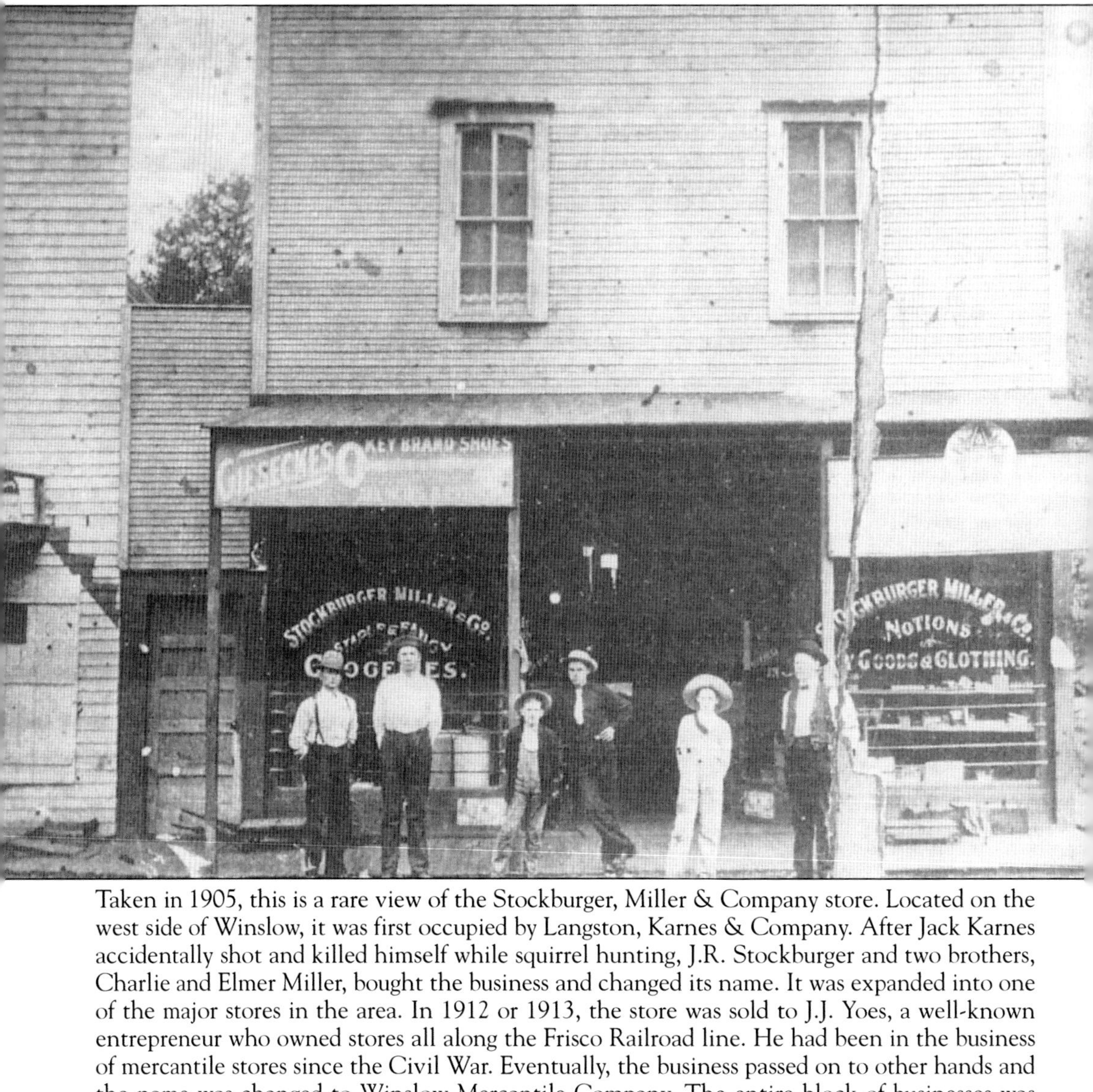

Taken in 1905, this is a rare view of the Stockburger, Miller & Company store. Located on the west side of Winslow, it was first occupied by Langston, Karnes & Company. After Jack Karnes accidentally shot and killed himself while squirrel hunting, J.R. Stockburger and two brothers, Charlie and Elmer Miller, bought the business and changed its name. It was expanded into one of the major stores in the area. In 1912 or 1913, the store was sold to J.J. Yoes, a well-known entrepreneur who owned stores all along the Frisco Railroad line. He had been in the business of mercantile stores since the Civil War. Eventually, the business passed on to other hands and the name was changed to Winslow Mercantile Company. The entire block of businesses was destroyed by fire in the 1950s and was never rebuilt. Once, the store was burglarized after a large shipment of clothing had been received for the summer season. The merchandise was recovered at the hideaway of Pearl Starr, daughter of Belle, who owned a home less than a mile outside of town, off Bunyard Road.

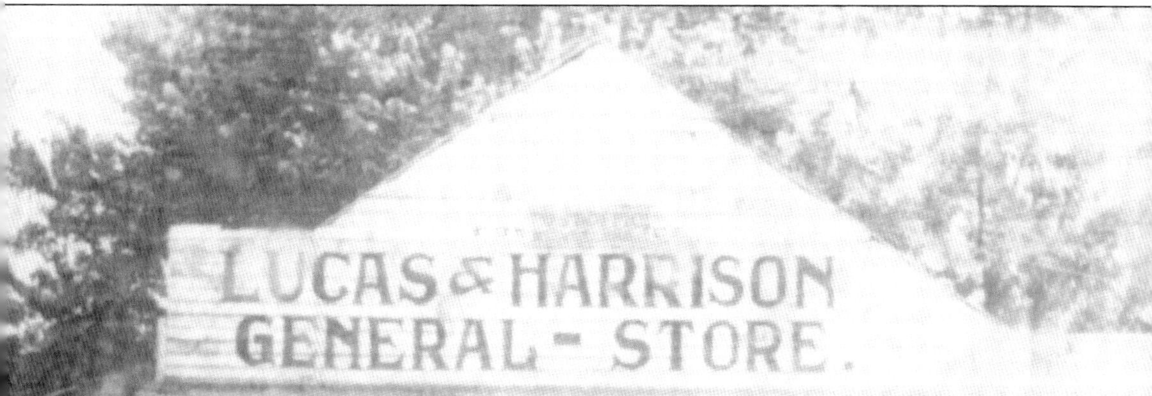

This old photo of the Lucas & Harrison General Store in Durham was taken c. 1914. Durham, located east of Elkins in the White River Valley, was also once a thriving community. A cannery located there was one of the largest in the county. It was later moved deeper into Hazel Valley, where there was an endless supply of water from Tatum Springs. The spring was used by travelers from the time of the Cherokee and Osage. A large catch-bowl was built of rock to capture the heavy flow of water. People who live in the area continue to haul water from the spring during dry seasons when their wells dry up. It adequately furnished the Durham Cannery with plenty of water, and it has never been known to go dry. The community of Arnett, which was located nearby, did not survive. Only a huge, old barn marks the spot where the cannery once stood. Durham was recently the seat of a large dispute over landfills; a small, grass-roots organization known as the White River Environmental Protection Agency managed to bring a huge company to its knees in a 10-year battle to prevent a landfill from being placed on Hobbs Mountain near Durham. All waters from that point flow into the water supply of Northwest Arkansas.

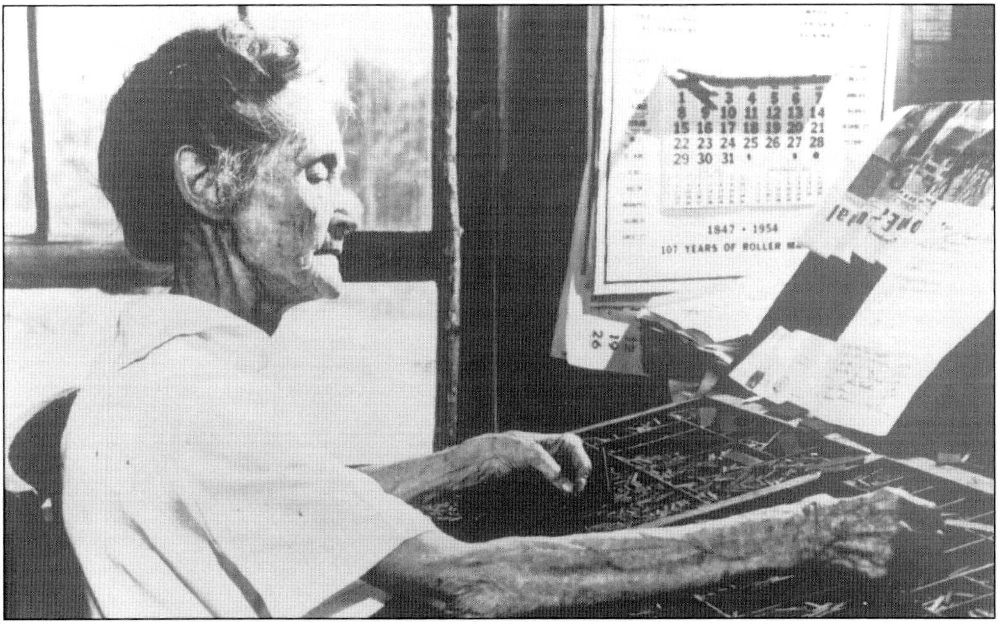

Maud Dunlap Duncan sets type on an old printing press for the *Winslow American* newspaper that she and her husband, Gilbert Nelson Duncan, owned. They put out the weekly paper from 1908 through the 1950s, but it was at its peak during World War I. Duncan died on Armistice Day, November 11, 1918. Maud died in January 1958 at the age of 84.

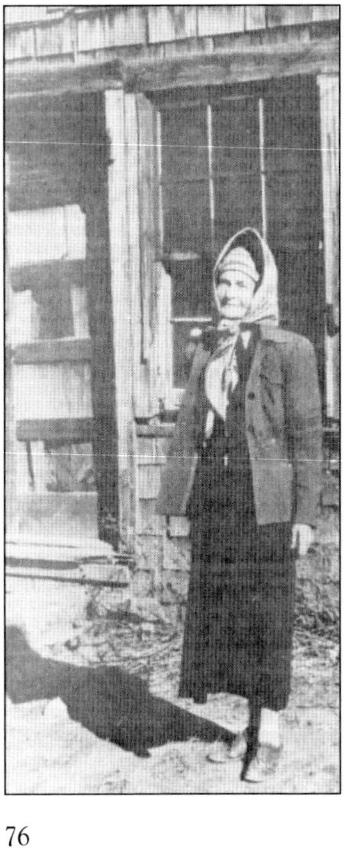

Pictured is Maud Duncan in later years, when she still published weekly issues of the paper. It was usually printed on a single 8x10 sheet on which she sold ads to finance her meager existence. During an illustrious but often sad life, she accomplished much and was truly a woman ahead of her time. She was never able to manage her own money, however, and in her waning years, relied on the kindness of her many friends.

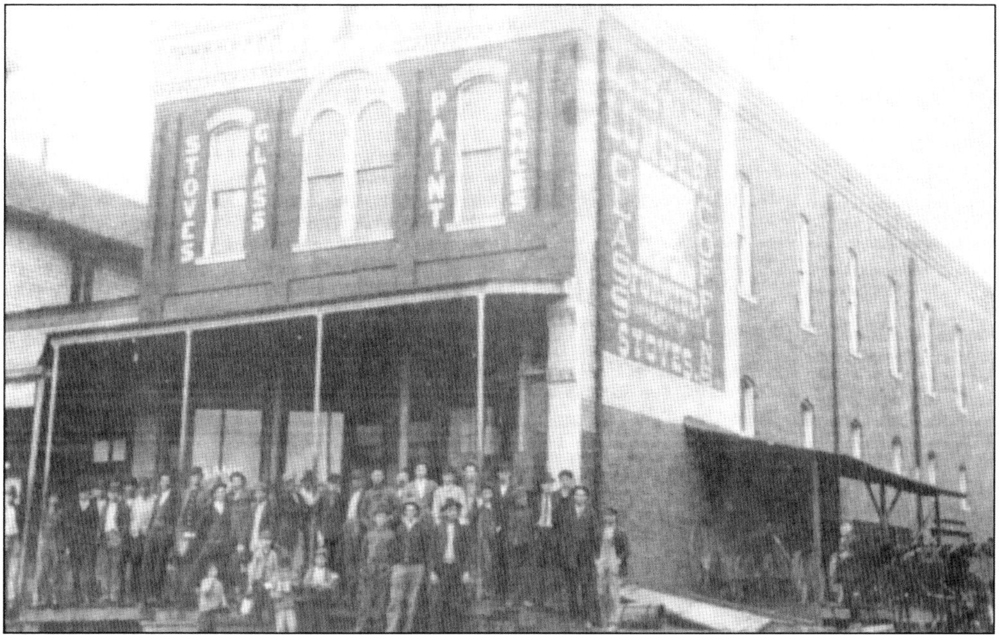

This later photo, taken just before WW I, shows the hardware store from the West Fork street scene on the following page. Later known as the Northwest Arkansas Lumber Company, the building also housed the Bank of West Fork. The reason for the large gathering is not known; however, when a photographer came to town the word spread like wildfire, and everyone wanted in on the photos he would take. The building was originally built by Jacob (Jake) Yoes in the 1880s.

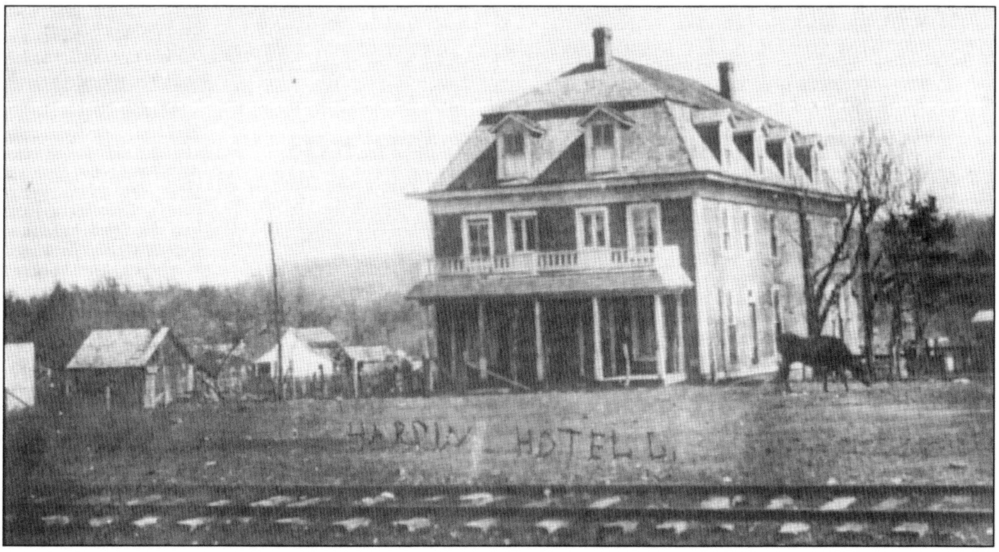

The Hardin Hotel at West Fork stood on the east side of the railroad in the southern part of town. Excellent food was served in the establishment that catered to traveling salesmen, known as drummers, and sometimes, to the local farmers who came to town for more than one day. It was also a favorite social gathering place for young people. Note the cow grazing in the yard. No date is available for the photo.

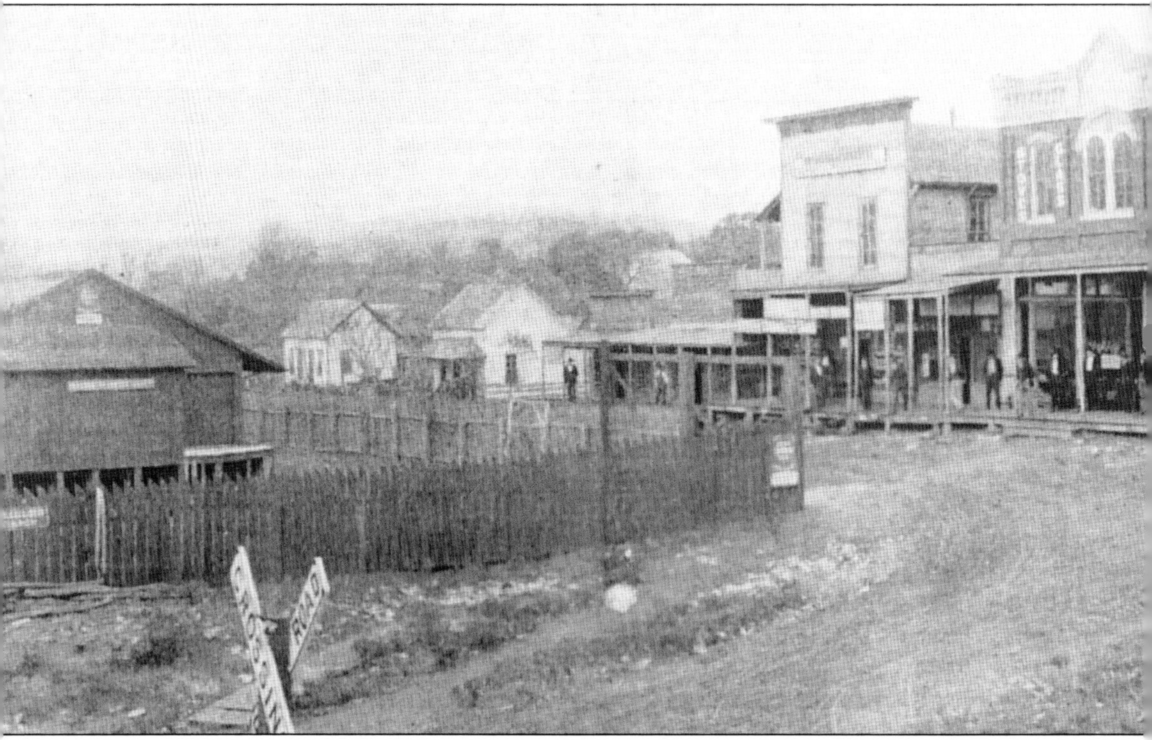

This photo of the city of West Fork was taken *c.* 1906. Inside the fence is the lumber yard, and to the far right is the hardware store featured on the preceding page. The bank was earlier located in a corner of the old hardware store until it was moved across the street. It remained in that location until 1929, when the owner paid off all the depositors and closed on the national "bank holiday" that was declared after the stock market crash. Next to the hardware store is Karnes Drug Store, a later version of which is shown on the following page. The two-story building beside the drug store is West Fork Mercantile. Upstairs, the local doctor had an office beside a land office. Two barber shops were operated in this area of the block, and there was also a restaurant there in the early 1930s. Today, West Fork struggles for its own identity amidst a booming business economy, but it operates one of the most progressive schools in the county.

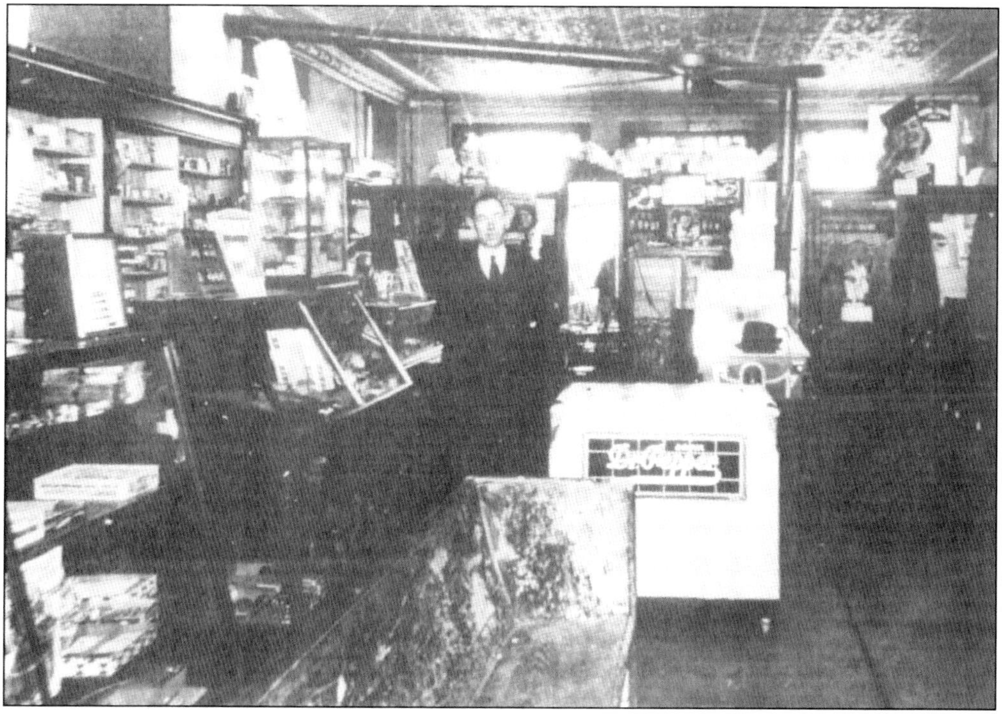

Karnes Drug Store and owner Roy Karnes are shown here, probably in the early 1930s, after the store was moved across the street from its earlier location. In the foreground is a scratched and well-worn bench where anyone was welcome to "sit a spell," whether they had the money to buy anything or not. There were booths where a frosty mug of root beer could be shared by the young men and women who dropped by.

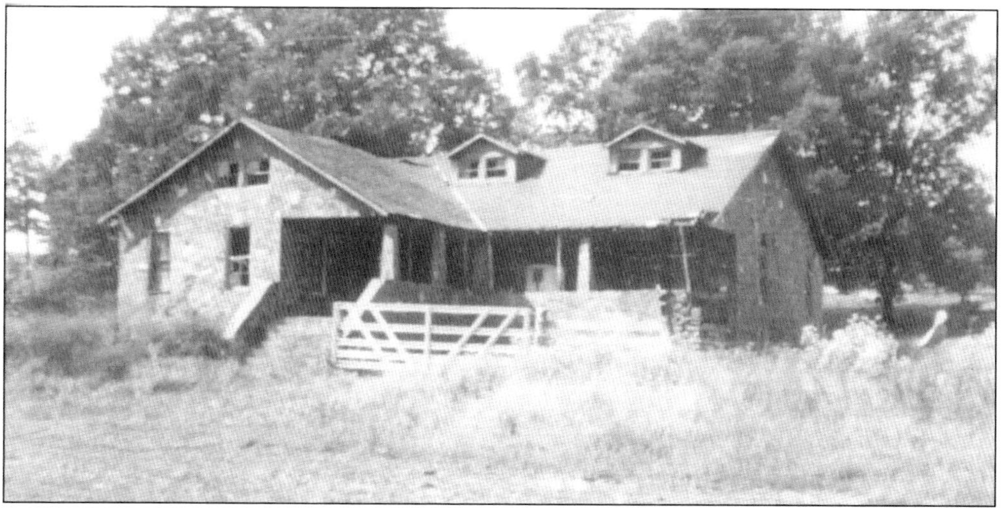

Pictured are the remains of the Sunset store and post office in the early 1970s. The post office was established here in 1888 and closed in 1951. This is probably not the original location of the first post office—and it is certainly not the original building—but the native rock stonework is a work of art and a fine example of the many stone structures throughout the county. Most of the stone schools were built by workers with the WPA; the builders for this structure are unknown.

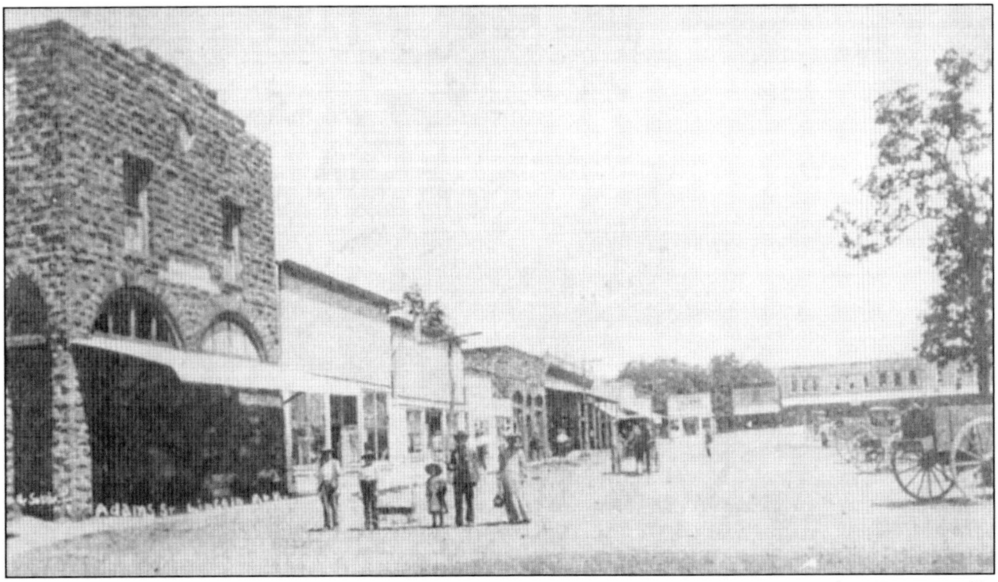

This photo, taken from a postcard, shows the town of Lincoln in 1911. It appears that Fayetteville and Lincoln were the only two towns in the county that were planned in advance and built around a square with some important structure or park in the center. Most towns grew along a main street as businesses were established. The two-story building on the left was the IOOF lodge hall upstairs and the J.M. Smith Hardware and Furniture shop was on the ground floor.

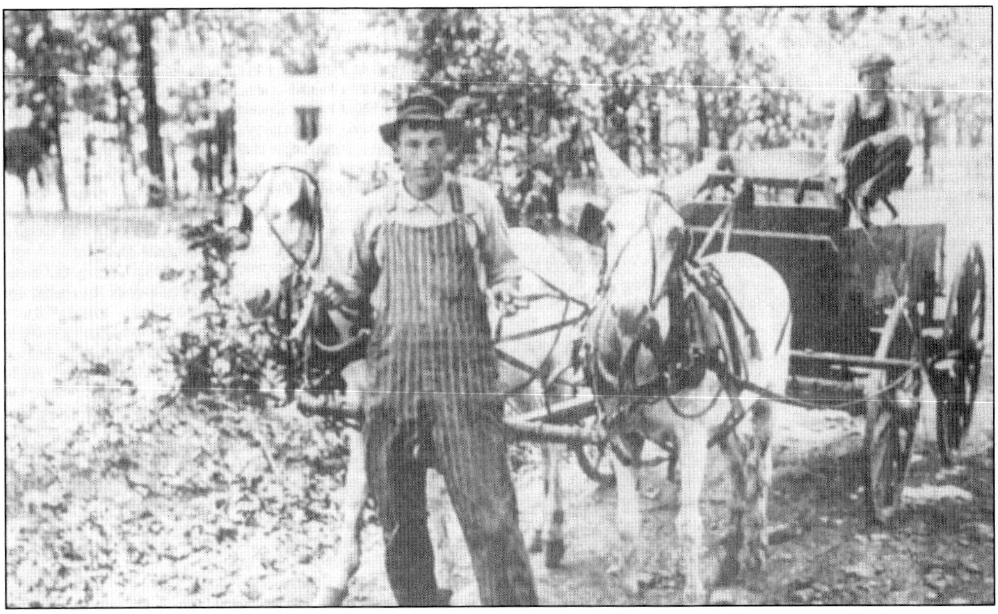

Taken from an undated post card, this picture shows Roy Kelton and his span of white mules. Roy delivered ice for J.F. Black when Black's was the only ice house in Winslow (prior to WW I). He also used his rig for general dray work and to take groups of young folks on outings, picnics, and evening affairs.

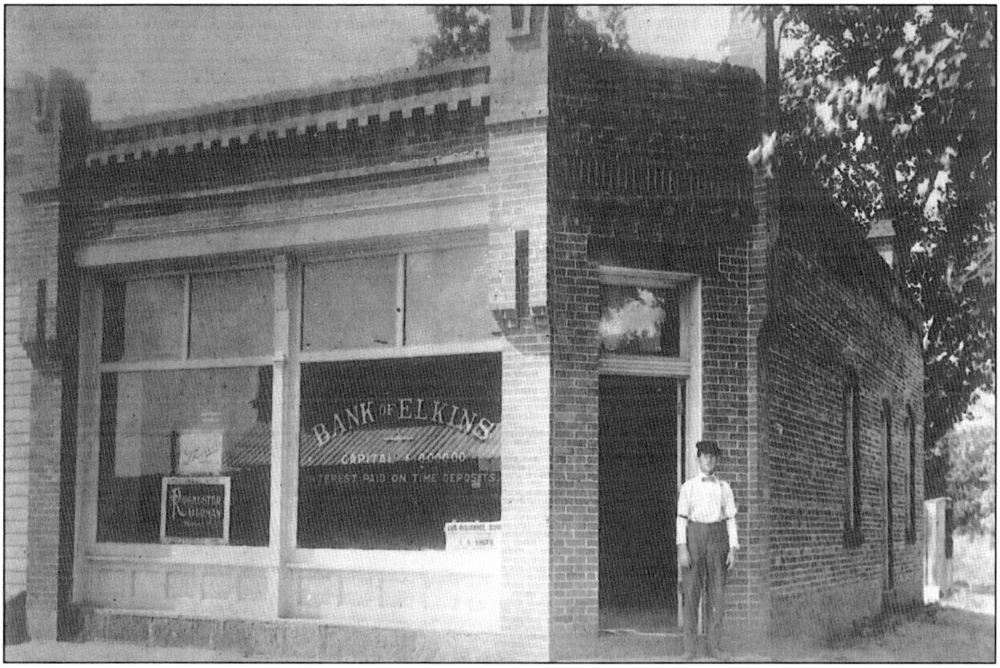

The *Titanic* sank a scant month before a group of folks met in Elkins on May 14, 1912, at 10:30 in the morning, to establish a new bank. It was 12 clay-mud miles to Fayetteville, and many wondered if such a venture could succeed. Surrounding settlements were booming from the cattle, lumber, and grain business, and businessmen and customers needed a convenient bank. At the time, Elkins's population was 100. Members of the Bunch family have been involved in banking in the area since that day. (Photo courtesy of Joel Bunch.)

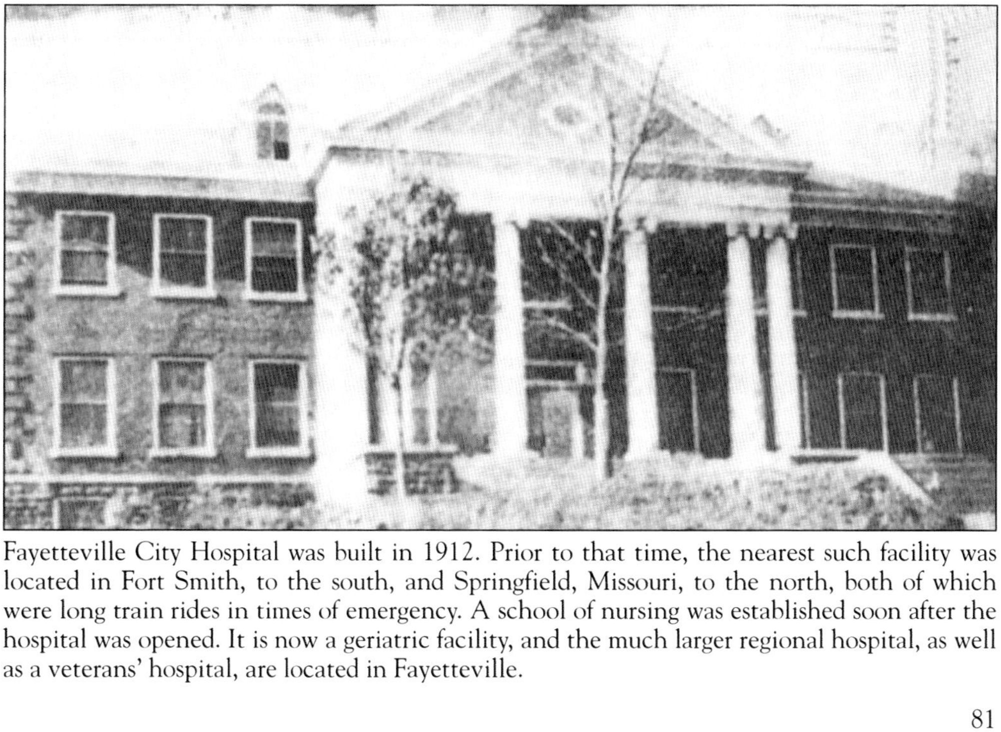

Fayetteville City Hospital was built in 1912. Prior to that time, the nearest such facility was located in Fort Smith, to the south, and Springfield, Missouri, to the north, both of which were long train rides in times of emergency. A school of nursing was established soon after the hospital was opened. It is now a geriatric facility, and the much larger regional hospital, as well as a veterans' hospital, are located in Fayetteville.

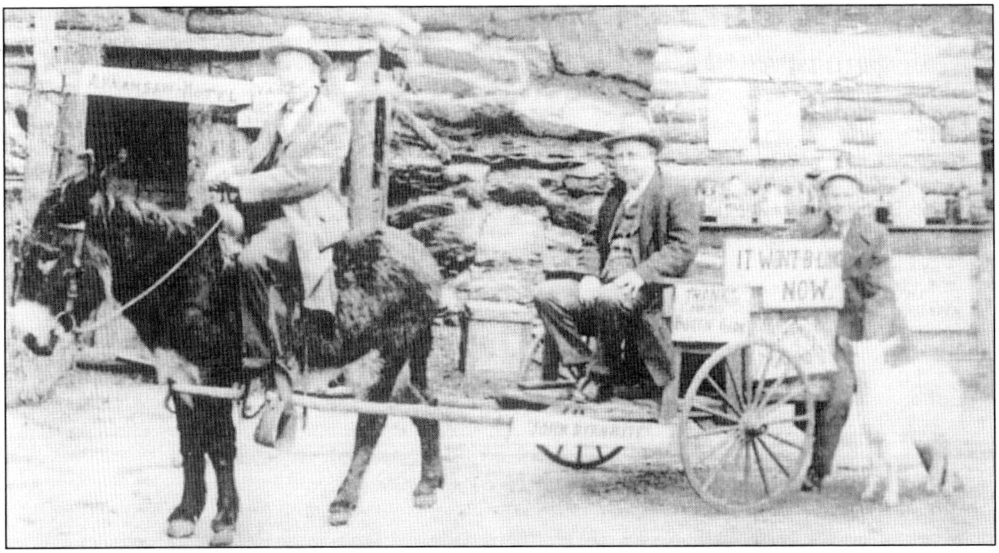

"Lobbying in the 1930s" was the title of this photo when it ran in *The Observer*. It shows three Winslow gentlemen in Little Rock: Clint Shook on the donkey, A.N. Cole riding in the cart, and J.A. Winn holding the goat. They had appeared before the legislature to present their case to prevent Winslow School from closing due to lack of funds. They must have been successful; the school remains in operation to this day.

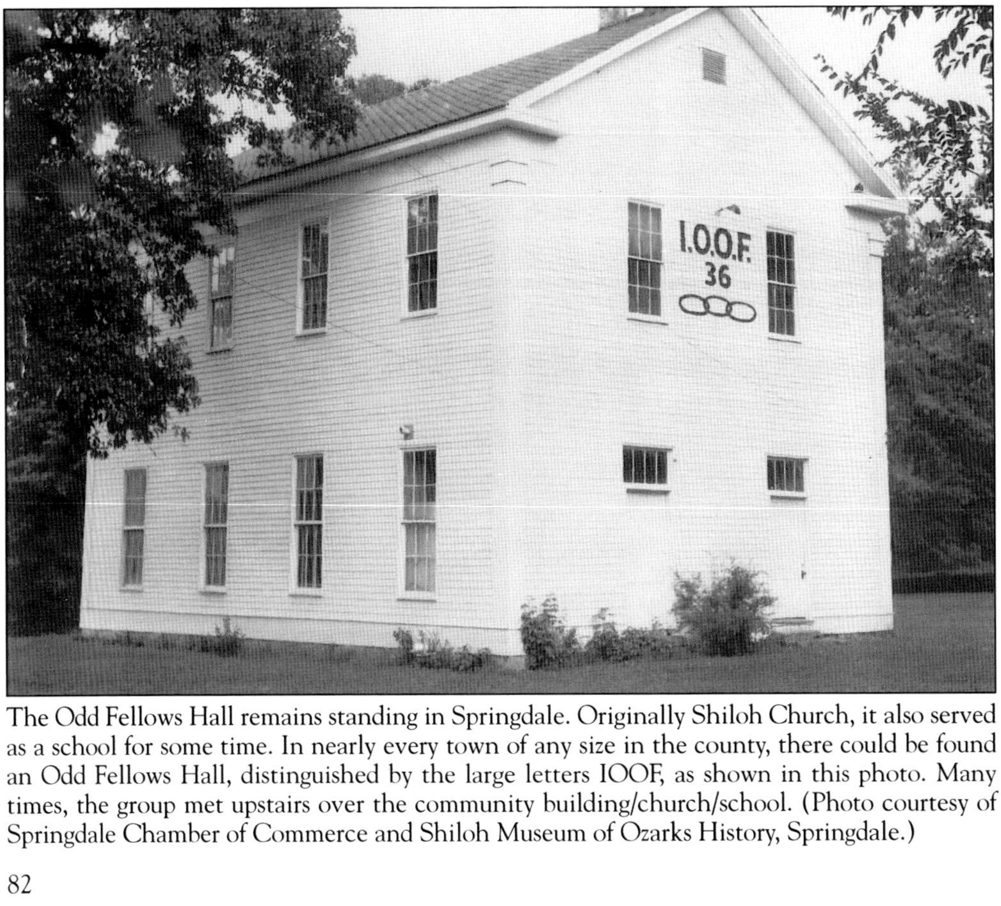

The Odd Fellows Hall remains standing in Springdale. Originally Shiloh Church, it also served as a school for some time. In nearly every town of any size in the county, there could be found an Odd Fellows Hall, distinguished by the large letters IOOF, as shown in this photo. Many times, the group met upstairs over the community building/church/school. (Photo courtesy of Springdale Chamber of Commerce and Shiloh Museum of Ozarks History, Springdale.)

Four

Hearth, Home and Kin

Many descendants of homesteading families in the county still live in the area, and some of the earliest homes have survived as well. Others have crumbled into dust. Scattered throughout the hills, however, are remnants of the old, simpler way of life. In Hazel Valley stands one of the oldest surviving cabins in the state. It was restored and is lived in by a descendant of those who built it in the early 1800s. South of West Fork, on the east side of U.S. Highway 71, stands another old log cabin that was once part of a small resort. Here and there, barns sag away from the prevailing winds, most of them ready to collapse. Progress destroyed many of the early structures.

Home and family was very important to early settlers, because they often went for weeks without seeing another living soul. Their lives were bound by hearth and kin. Often, the children attending a one-room school in the wilderness were related to one another. Family reunions, decorations, picnics, birthday parties, and the like revolved around several generations of the same few families. How they celebrated life together is the focus of this chapter.

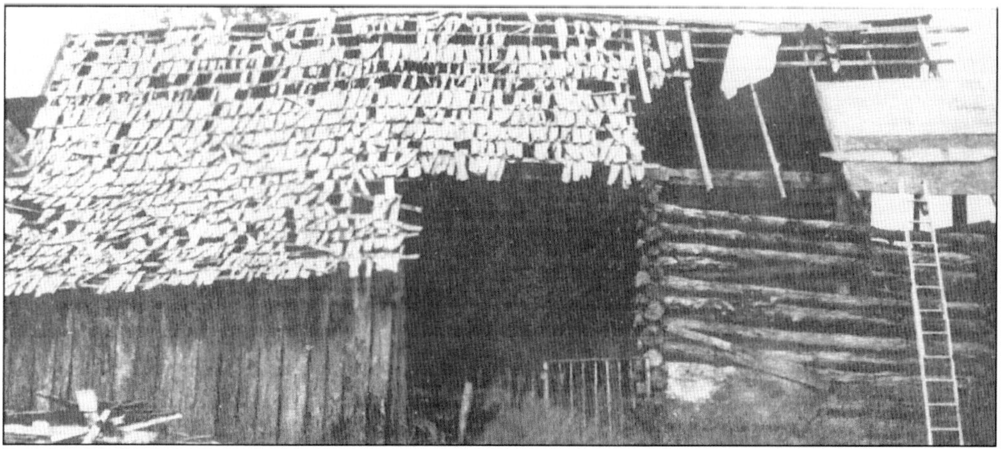

A ladder leans against this relic Ozarks barn in the Black Oak community southeast of Fayetteville. In the 1970s, the owner gave some thought to restoring the old log structure. Shakes on the roof were hewn, the logs were probably cut by hand; patches have been nailed up here and there in later years. This historical monument stands in mute testimony to the past and faces a very uncertain future.

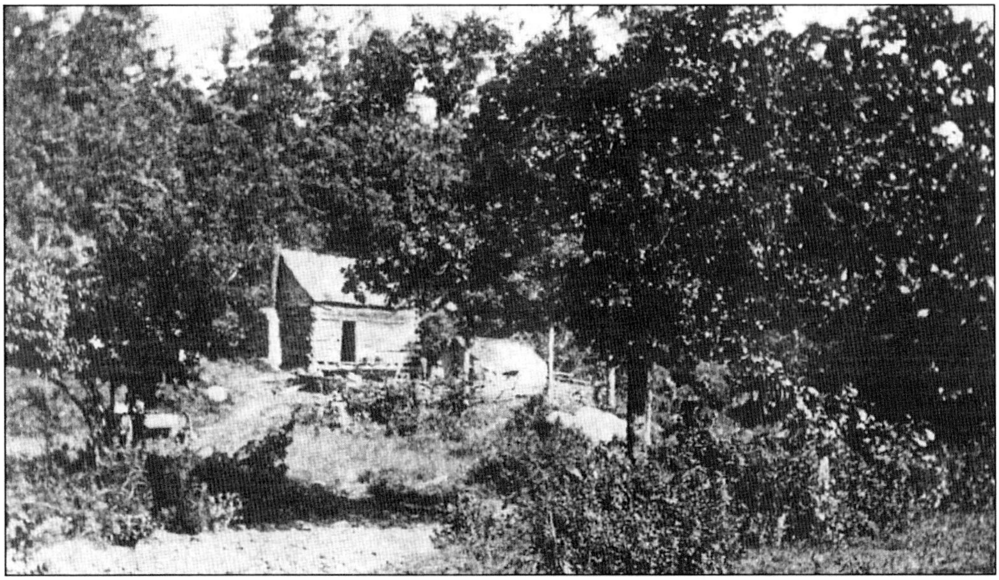

Ben Hysell's log cabin has long disappeared, a victim of a highway roadbed. It is said to have stood right in the center of what is now U.S. Highway 71, in front of the Winslow Ball Park. This photo is not dated, but the cabin still stood in 1919. The highway has been drastically elevated at this spot so that the surrounding area no longer resembles this photo.

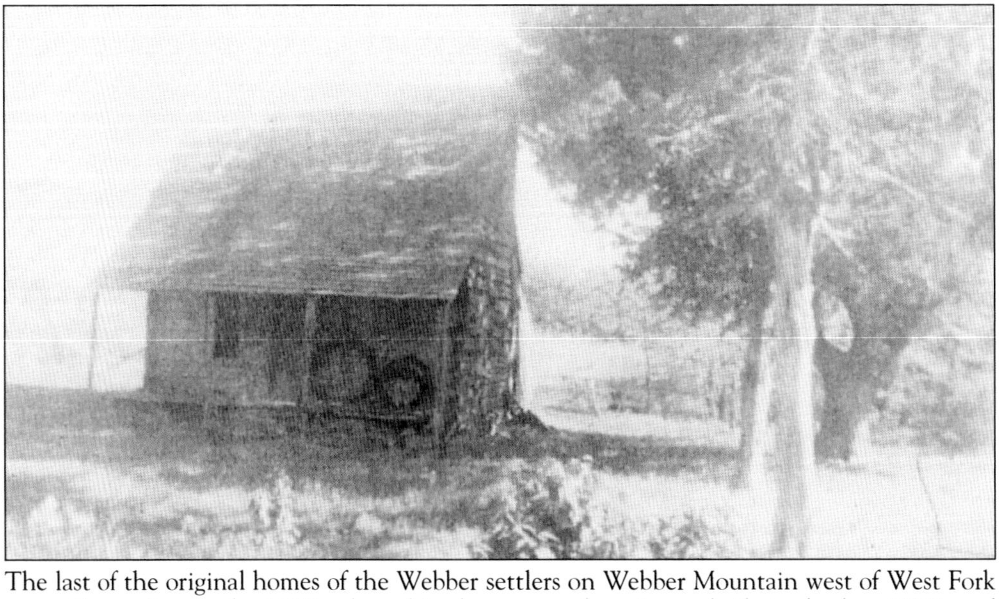

The last of the original homes of the Webber settlers on Webber Mountain west of West Fork was still standing in the 1960s when this photo was taken. It was built in the late 1800s and was home for a family of six children: Bertha Webber, Adolph Webber, Celia Webber Skelton, Anna Webber Hudson, Otto Webber, and Walter Webber.

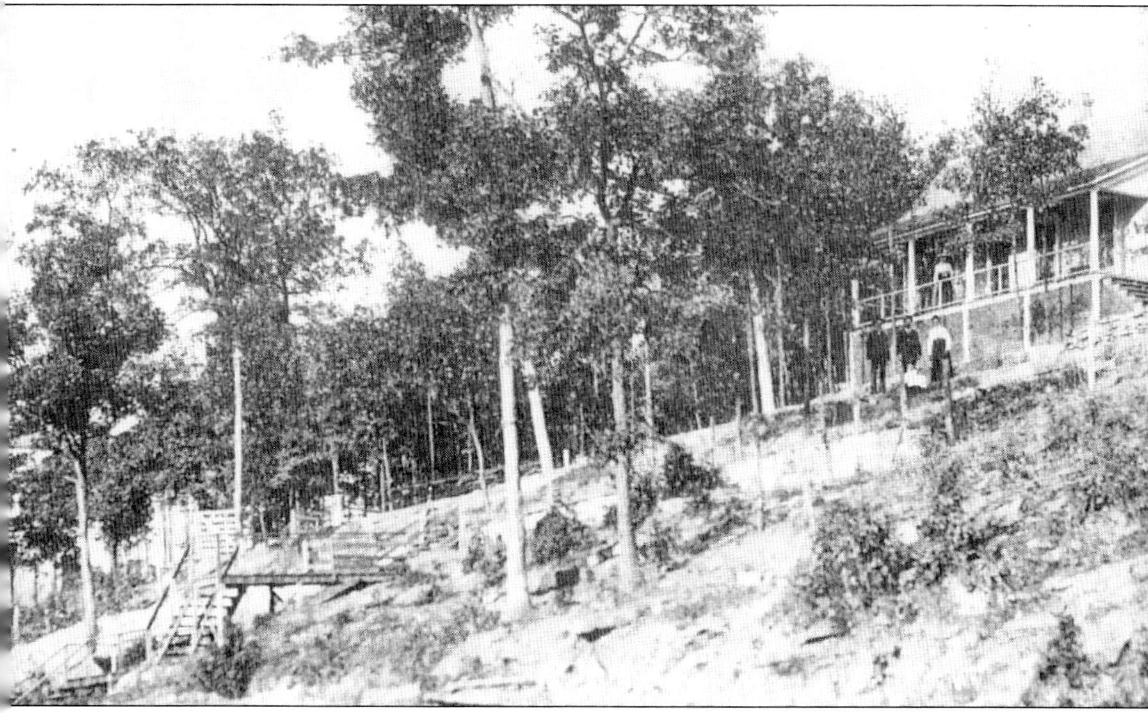

The J.A. Winn home in Winslow was photographed in 1905, soon after the house was built on the hill, directly east of the train depot. The wooden steps with four or five landings extended all the way from the depot to the house, which was typical of homes in the mountain hamlet. Standing in the front yard are J.A., his wife Laura Karnes Winn, and their two small children, Burl and Ruby. The other people are not identified.

Winslow is situated in a deep hollow that was filled in to lay the railroad tracks so that homes and the various resort hotels would be perched on hillsides. At one time, most homes and buildings had steps leading up from the main thoroughfare because people were used to walking, and such an arrangement was more convenient. Winn was a stockholder in the Winslow bank when it was organized in 1907, and eventually, he became president. It was his duty during the Great Depression, in November 1931, to make the following announcement in the *Winslow American*: "Bank of Winslow asks depositors to call for their money, the bank sold to First National Bank of Fayetteville." It was the only bank in Arkansas forced to close during that harsh time that paid its depositors 100¢ on the dollar.

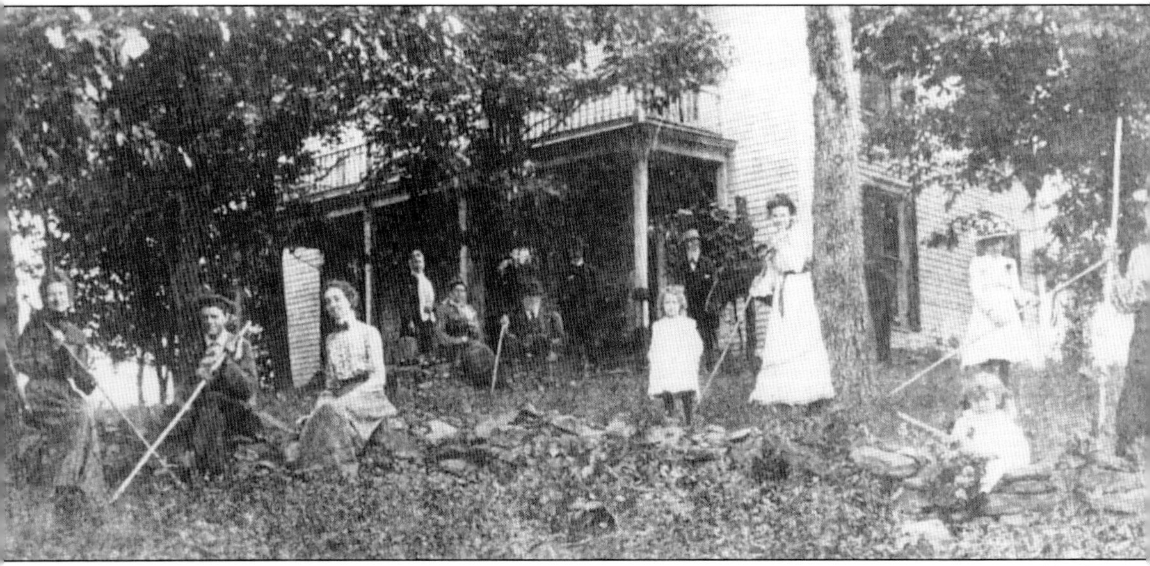

Visitors to the glamorous home of Dr. Albert Duncan and his wife, Virginia, no doubt walked there, though some lived as far as two and three miles away. The gathering in this photo also included some summer visitors. No explanation of the sticks is available. Note how the lawn is grown up; in those days, no one cut the grass around their home. The small child sitting on the rock wall (right) is Celester Perkins Shipley, who was known to her friends as Johnny. She recently celebrated her 100th birthday and is the only survivor of those pictured. Boston Heights, as the home was known, became a school for girls not too long after the death of Helen (Pierce) Dunlap, the other young child in the foreground. She was the granddaughter of the Dunlaps and the daughter of Maud Duncan. The Helen Dunlap Memorial School operated for several years and took in young ladies who could not otherwise afford an education. As long as Albert Dunlap was alive, he continued his philanthropy toward his adopted hometown. The family was instrumental in forming the first church, St. Stephens Episcopal, and they donated the land where the public school was built.

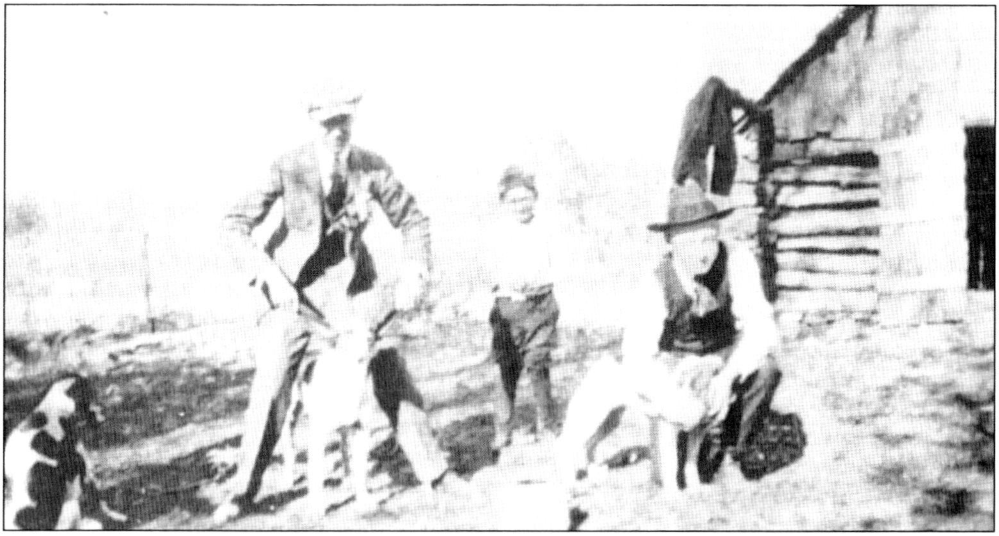

Fox hunting was a popular sport in the Ozarks at the turn of the century. This picture, taken in the early spring of 1920, shows Earl Land astride a foxhound; the other man is Clyde Jones. The young lad in the background is Jack Stockburger, son of Noah Stockburger, owner of the place and the hounds. This photo was probably taken on a Sunday since these fellows are just "horsing around" and not getting ready for the hunt.

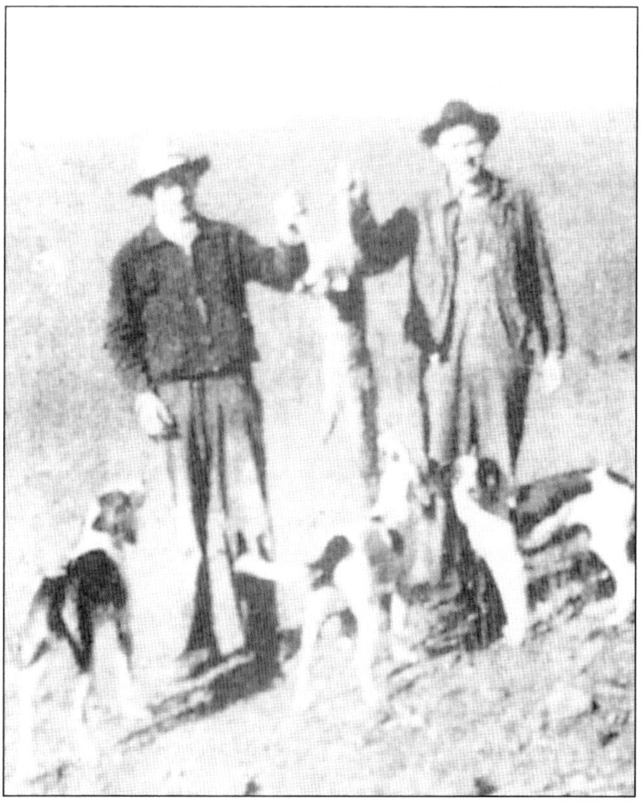

Down to more serious fox hunting business are these two, Hugh Smith (left) and Noble Breeden. The hunts would start before daybreak, and throughout the misty hills could be heard the "song" of the hounds on track as they pursued the wily red fox over hill and dale, through creeks and bramble bushes until the animal "went to ground."

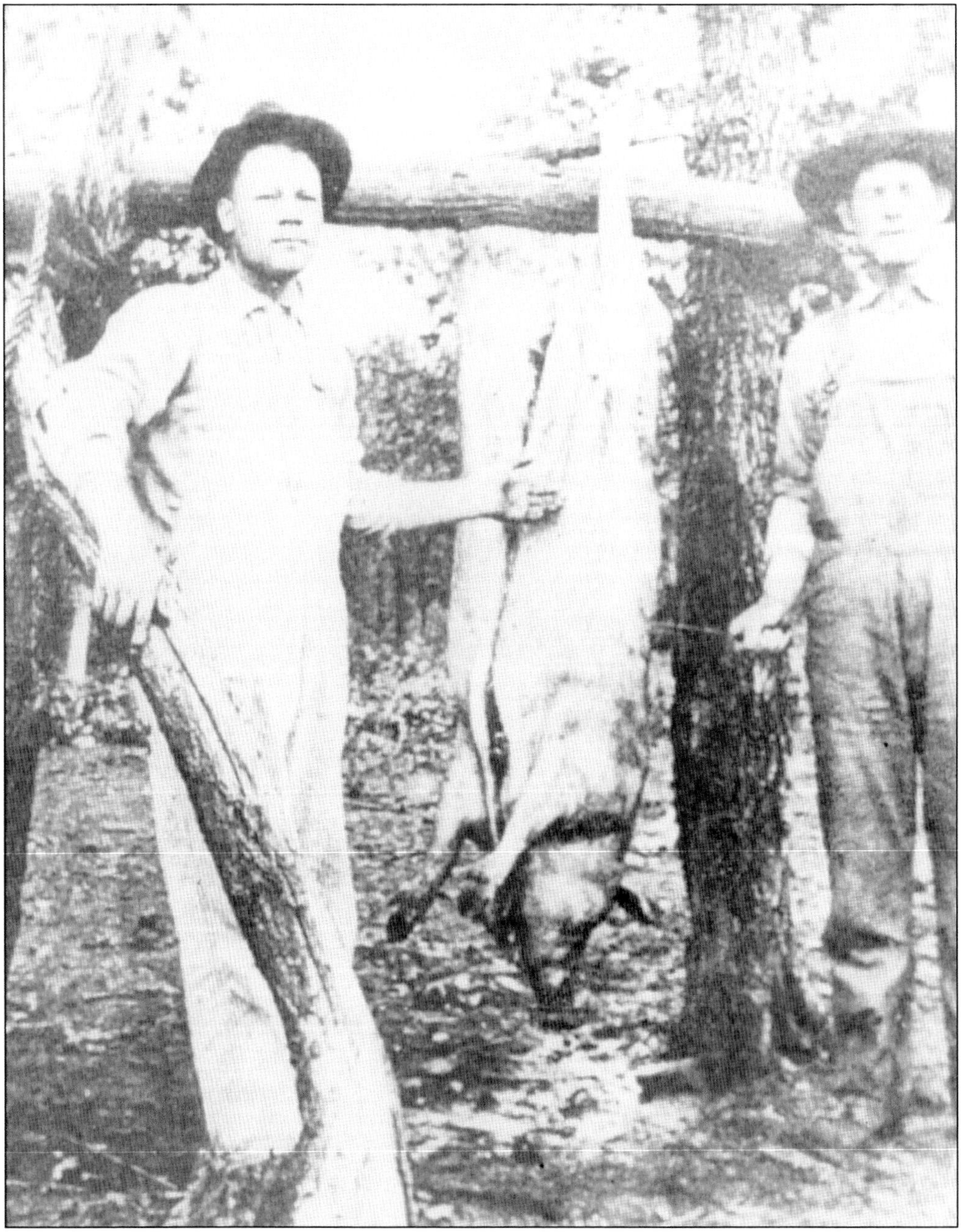

After the first few cold mornings in November, farmers began to think of butchering and laying in a supply of meat for the winter. In 1919, E.E. Osburn (left) has just returned from serving in France during the war. He arrived at his mother Casana Osburn Bruton's home just in time to help with the hog butchering. On the right is his stepfather, only identified as Mr. Bruton. E.E. had previously won the platoon sharp-shooting award in the AEF and probably had little trouble placing a bullet in the head of the hog. Once the animal was put down in that way, its throat would be cut and it would be hung up for butchering and scraping. In those days, not a morsel of the animal was wasted; even its ears, feet, and tail were used for food. Head cheese was a favorite treat; the brains, tongue, and heart also were well liked.

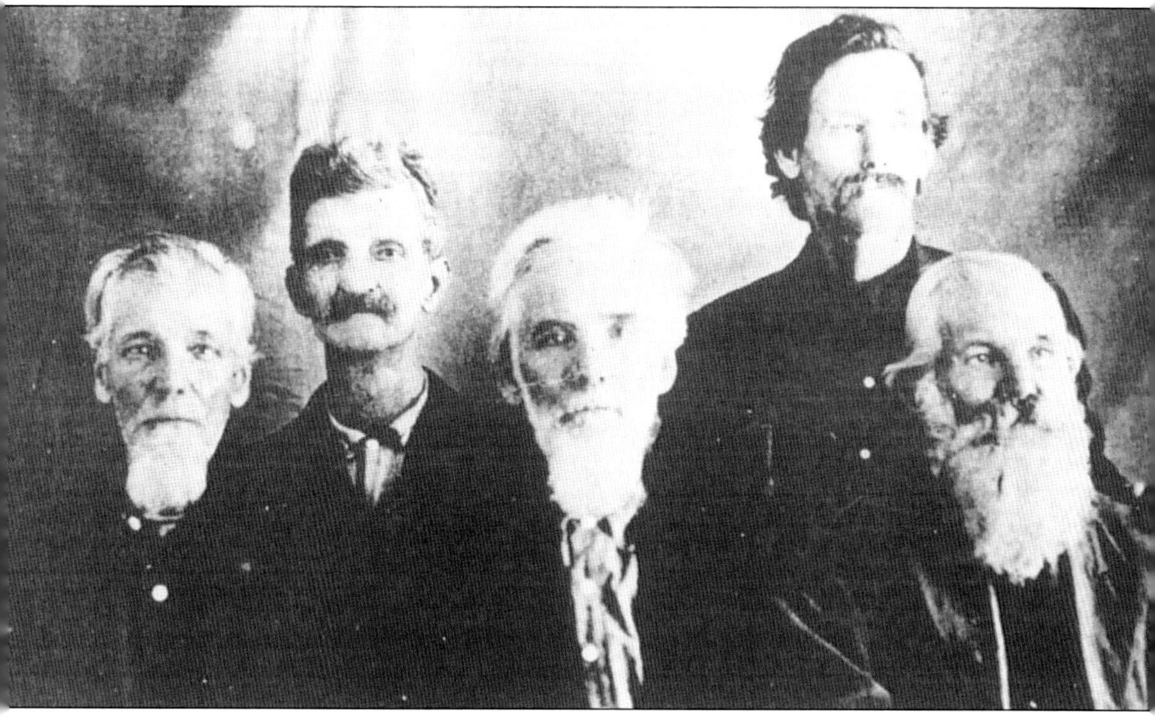

Though families in Arkansas were divided in sympathies during the Civil War, many of the area men and boys wore the blue of the U.S. Army. The two men on the right in this photo, John and Mark Center, were too young to serve in the army. The first three men on the left, Riley Center, Nathan Caughman, and Nick Center, were veterans of that conflict. Many stories were told of the tragedy of the division within families. Brother literally fought against brother, son against father. Neighbors would lay in wait for return visits from boys fighting on the "wrong side." More than one unwary soldier was strung up and nearly every community had a "hanging tree." Funerals were held at night for fear of being caught by someone on the other side. Bushwhackers ran wild, using the war as an excuse to murder and pillage homes where a lone woman stood guard over her pitiful food supplies or starving animals. In addition to the Battles of Prairie Grove and Pea Ridge, hundreds of small skirmishes were fought throughout the county. Those who fell were buried where they lay. A field on Winn Creek Road is known to contain several bodies of fallen soldiers. Nearby is Union Bluff, where U.S. troops would lie in wait for the Confederates known to pass through the area.

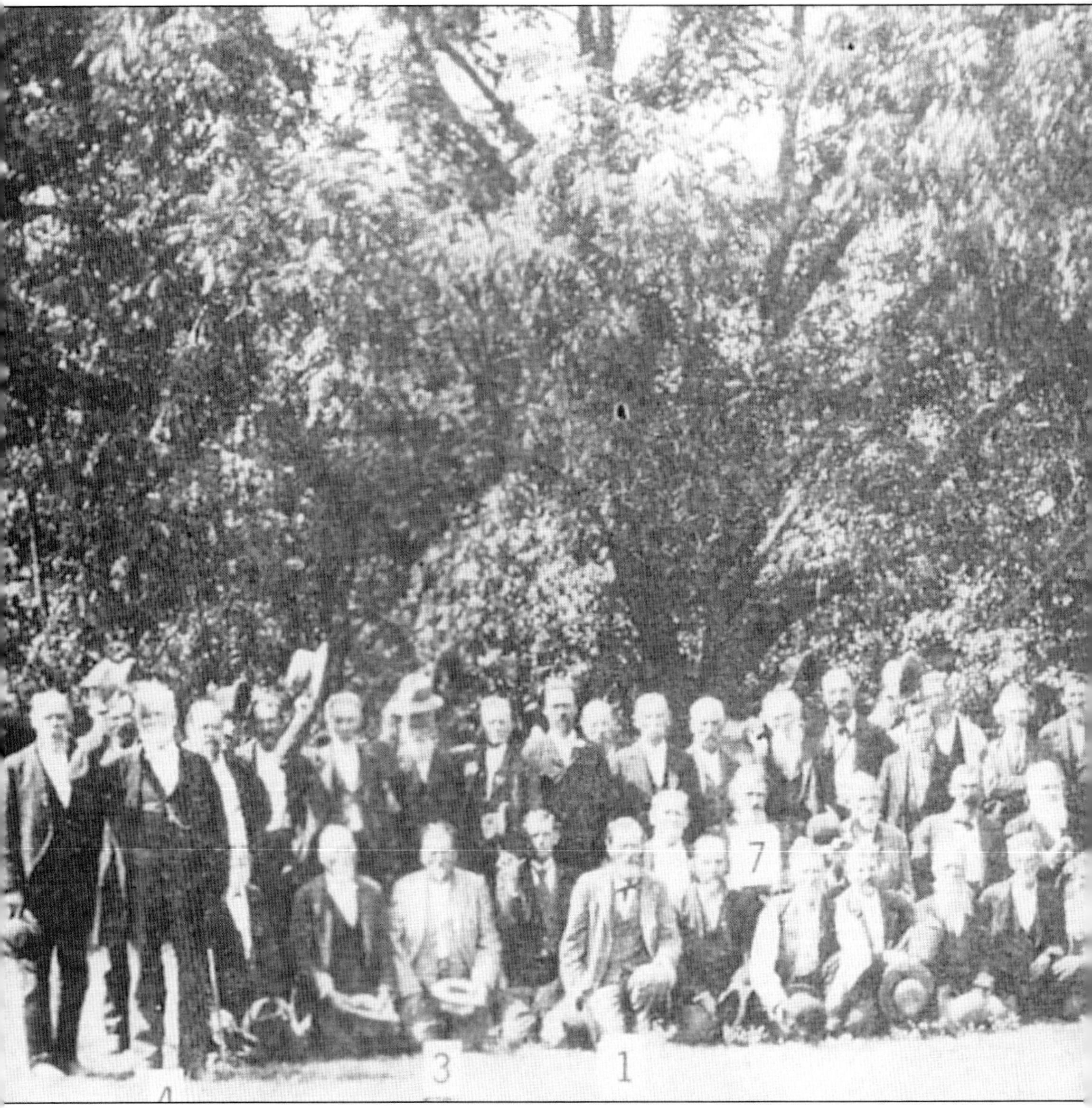

After the end of the Civil War, veterans of both sides held annual reunions in Washington County. The Federals gathered at Fayetteville and the Confederates at Prairie Grove Battlefield. This picture was taken at the Confederate reunion. Though some numbers were placed, identification did not then match properly with the file at the County Historical Society. Only #4 was correctly identified as Major Earle. Other names listed, but not matched, include Judge James Middleton, J. Marlar, Kibbe Cummings, Senator Berry, W.E. Pittman, Bart Carl, and J.C. Bain. The battle at Prairie Grove was fought on Dec. 7, 1862. One Confederate soldier wrote in his memoirs, "At this time all Northwest Arkansas and Southwestern Missouri were

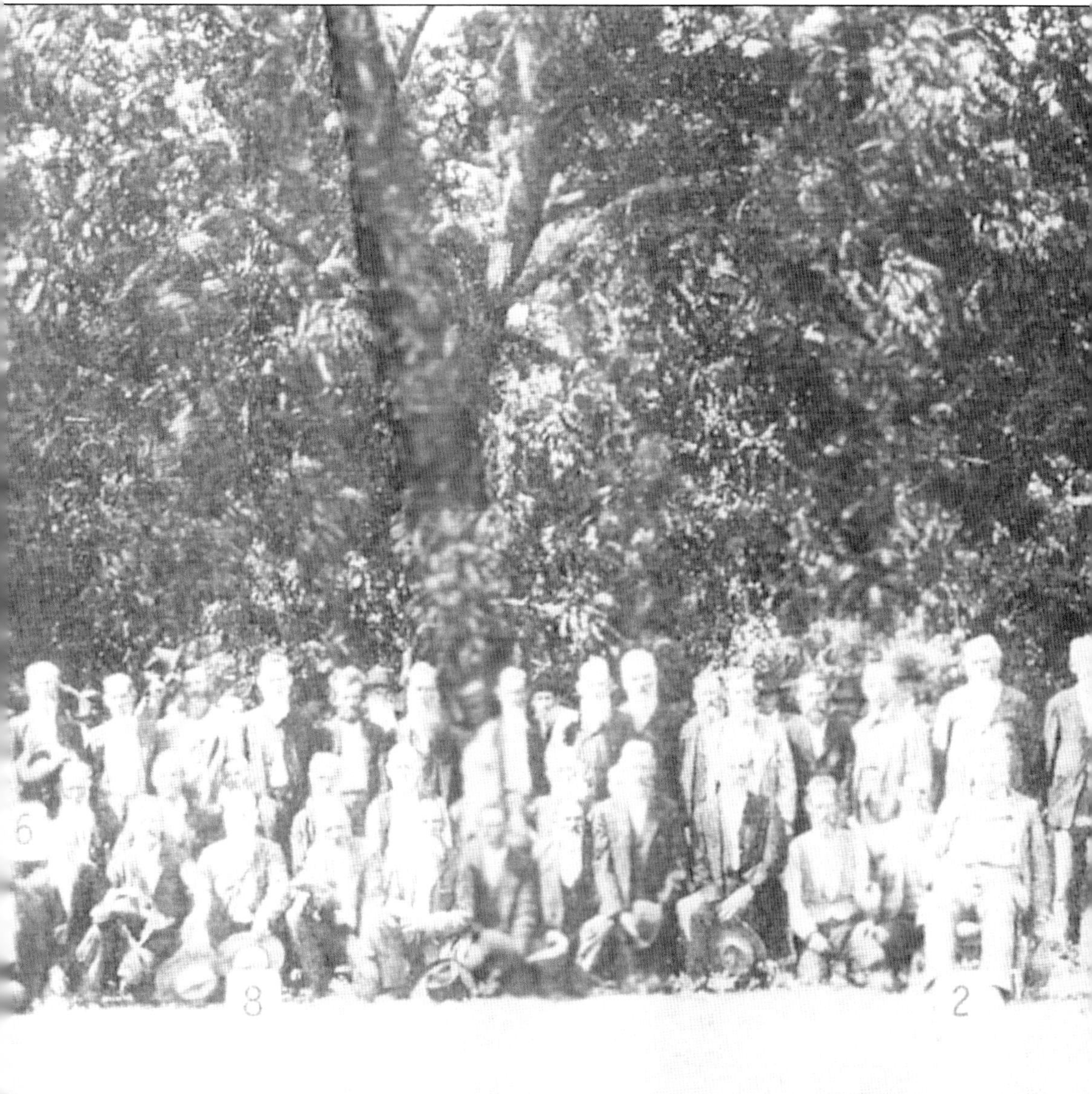

involved in a desperate guerrilla warfare. Fayetteville, Ark., was in the hands of the Federals, but the country was in the hands of the Confederates." U.S. troops had taken Fayetteville in February of that year. In the months after the battle at Prairie Grove, U.S. troops, incensed by those "boys from Cane Hill," marched through the area, burning at least 11 homes. Confederate Captain Buchanan received a commission to raise a cavalry company and, in May, attached his men with Capt. Buck Brown of Benton County. Constantly on the move, they engaged in many skirmishes with the Federals.

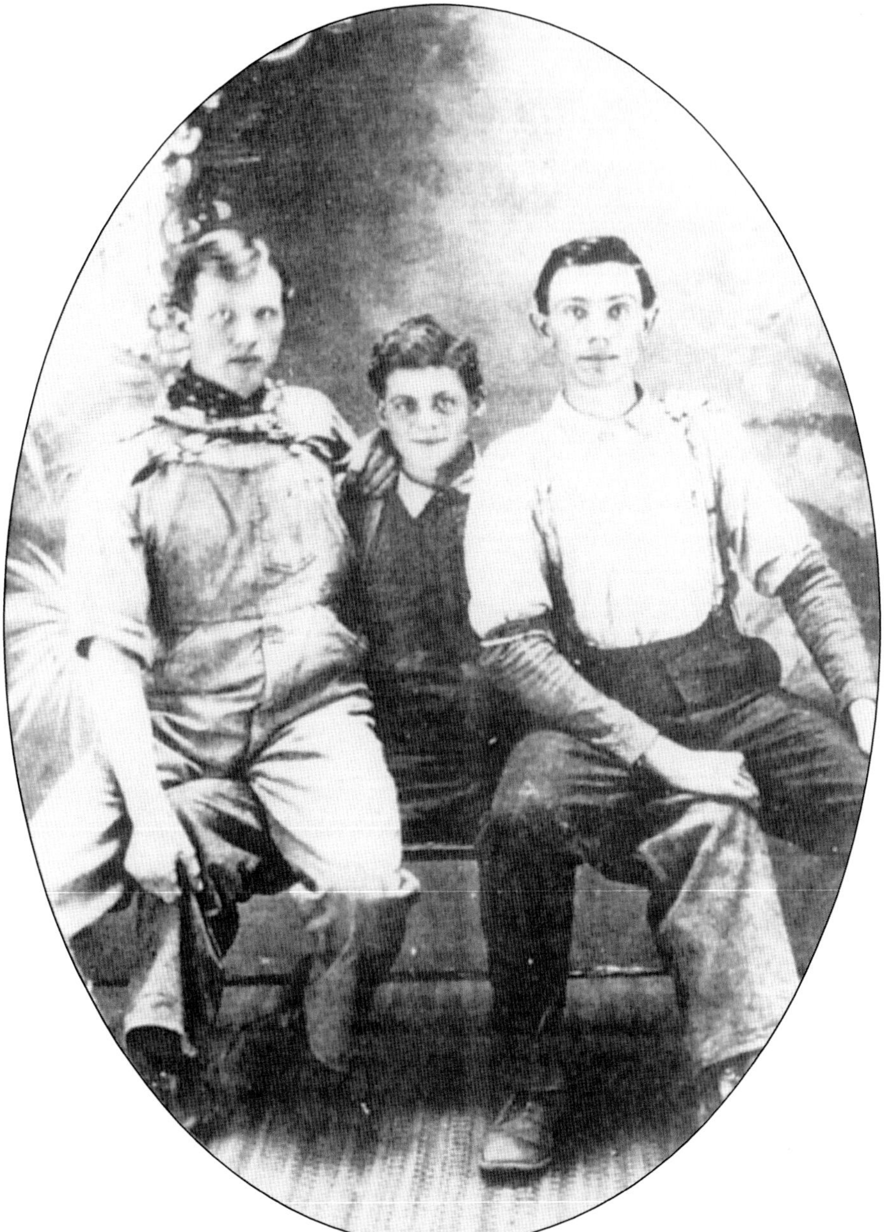

In all probability, these boys worked at the apple drier in Winslow, a business that employed practically all the available work force during each autumn's apple season. Myron Barnhill (left) and Oda Miller (right) are sitting on John Guinn's knees. Myron is wearing a bandanna around his neck, a popular fashion fad with young men in 1905. Oda may have had a clerical job; he is carrying a pen or pencil in his shirt pocket and is wearing long-sleeve protectors to prevent getting his white shirt dirty. The garter-like bands above his elbows were to keep the protectors from slipping down over his hands. Like many towns in the county, Winslow was surrounded by apple orchards. Working at the apple drier would have been far less labor intensive than logging.

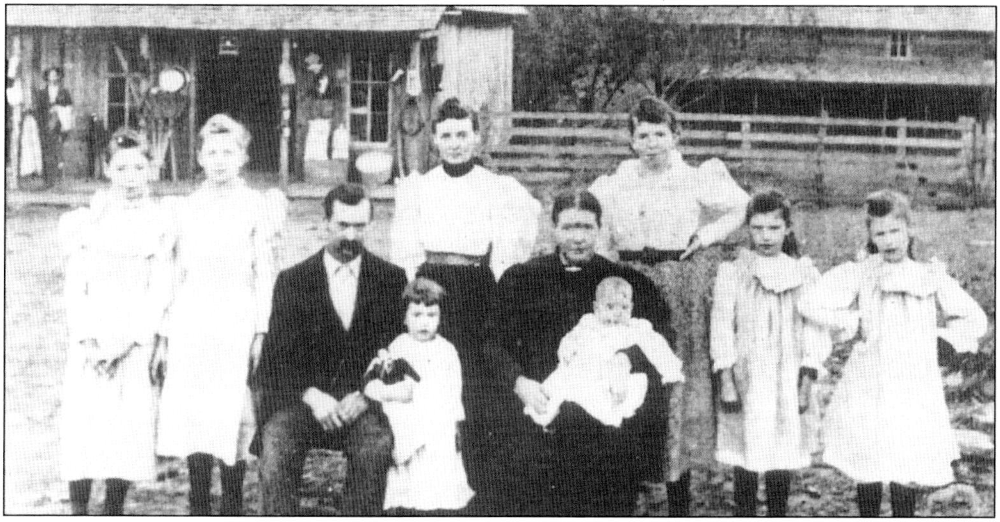

This photo of the family of J.H. and Alice Bailey Mannon was taken in 1898 in front of their home and store at Blackburn. The Mannons were some of the earliest settlers to the Blackburn area and created homesteads on much of the land there. From left to right are as follows: (standing) Jennie, Carrie, Ella Beele, Sidney, and Fronia; (seated) Mr. Mannon (with Laura standing at his knee) and Mrs. Mannon (holding Clifton). Charlie Price is standing on the porch of the store in the background.

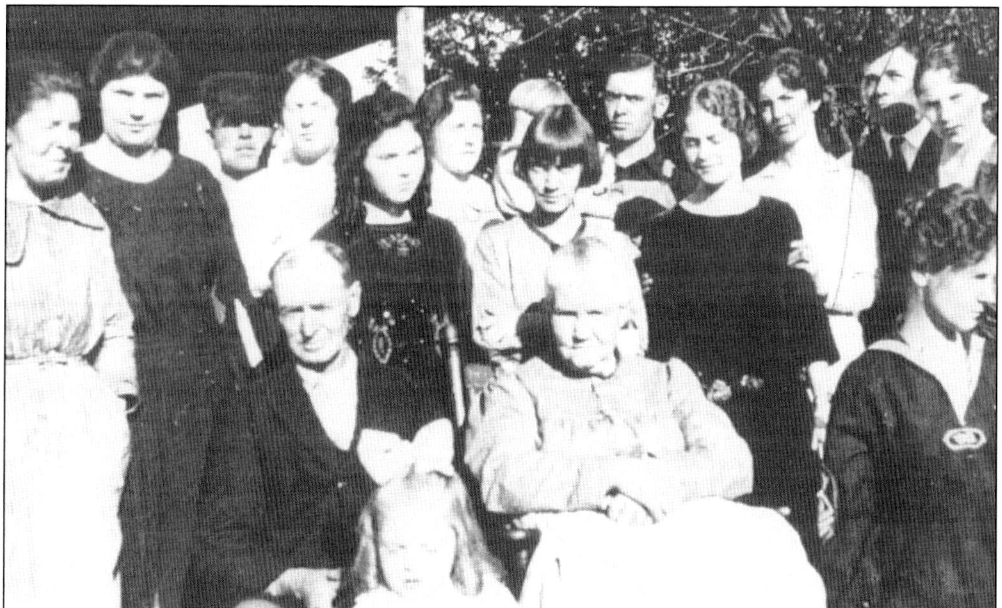

This photo of the Mannon family was taken c. 1923. They are, from left to right, as follows: (front row) John Hiram Mannon, Alice Bailey Mannon, and Fronia Mannon Poor; (middle row) Wanita Taylor Reed, Lucretia Mannon Rosacker, and Ophelia Reid; (back row) Belle Mannon, Sidney Mannon Taylor, Paul Reid, Carrie Mannon Reid, Pearl Davis Mannon, Clifton Mannon holding Gracie, Laura Mannon Houston, Luther Lee Houston, and Leighton Taylor Faulk. The small child in front is Mabel Mannon. Another daughter, Jennie Mannon, was not home at the time of this photograph.

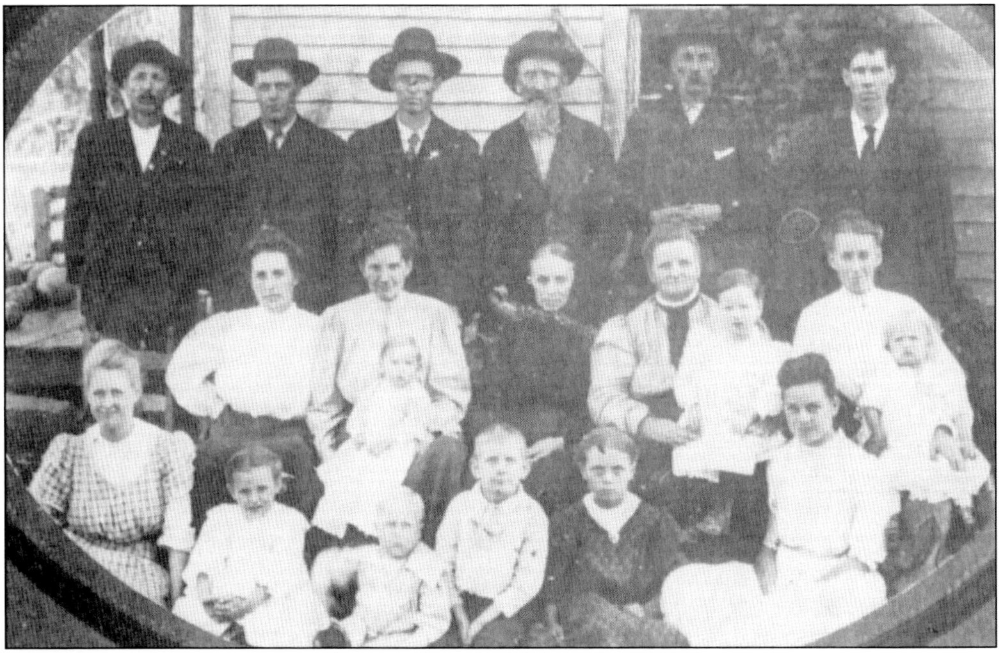

This 1907 photo was taken at the home of Shrilda and S.H. Guinn near Winslow. From left to right are as follows: (front row) Ollie and Florence Nickell, Earl Land, Tom and Mollie Nickell, and Rachel Guinn; (second row) Ida Nail Guinn, Sarah Elizabeth Ann McClendon Nickell, R.C. Nickell (holding son Robert), Rosa Grubs, Shrilda Guinn (holding grandson Roy), and Ollie Land (holding daughter Violet); (back row) Mr. Osburn, Lem Guinn, R.C. Nickell, Grandpa Grubbs, S.H. Guinn, and W.V. Land.

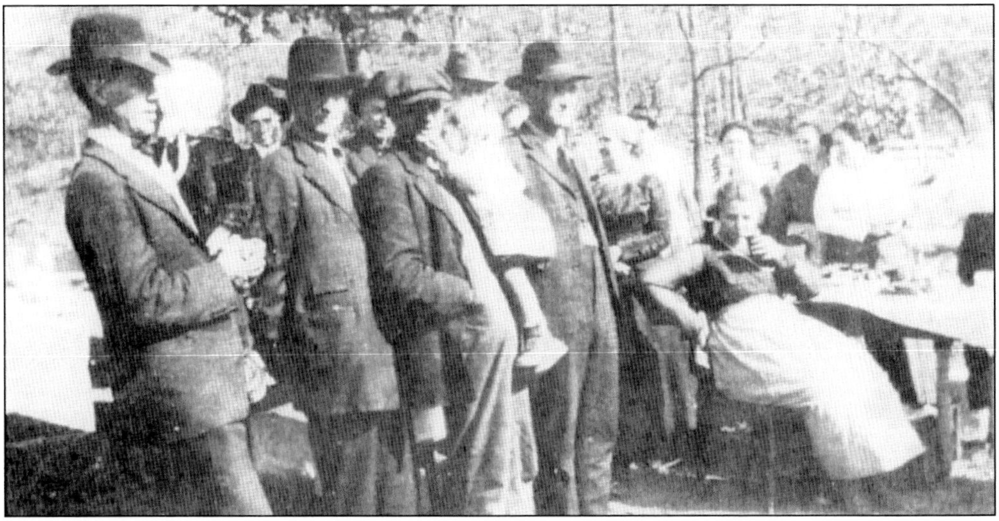

The Guinn family gathers for potluck in 1920 to celebrate a visit by relatives Ped Nickell and his wife. From left to right are as follows: W.V. Land (holding daughter Geneva) Ped Nickell, R.C. Nickell, Sam Guinn (holding daughter Helen), Will Dockery (wearing hat), Cleve Bogan, Mrs. Sam Guinn (her head barely showing), Mrs. Ped Nickell (white-haired woman), Mrs. R.C. Nickell; Mrs. Clara Bogan, Mrs. John Guinn, Mrs. Will Dockery, Mrs. W.V. Land, and Bertha Guinn Jones (seated).

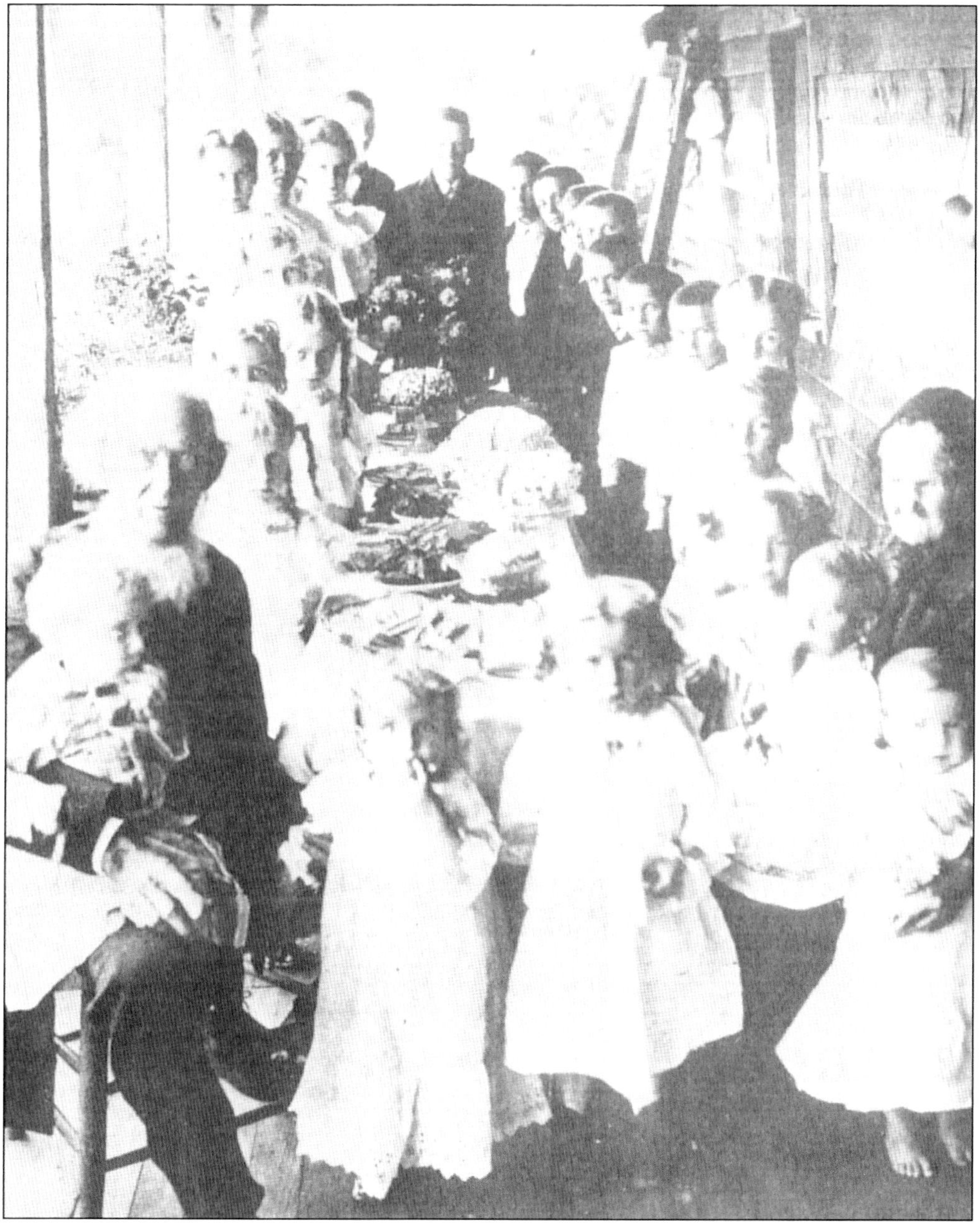

This 1905 reunion of Stockburger relatives shows Grandpa John Calvin and Grandma Martha Reed Stockburger with only a few of their grandchildren and great-grandchildren. More mature grandchildren considered themselves too big to have their picture taken with the youngsters. Pictured clockwise, from left to right, are as follows: Grandpa John Calvin (holding Robert Winn), Jewell Curtis, Gladys Curtis, Prella Stockburger, Winona Stockburger, Mamie Stockburger, Irma Karnes, Iva Stockburger, Martha Winn, Edgar Karnes, Omer Winn; at the foot of the table are Howard Karnes, Oscar Curtis, George Stockburger, Jim Wyatt (a neighbor), Bryan Curtis, Olin Karnes, Robert Stockburger, Lyda Winn, Troy Stockburger, Verna Stockburger, and Grandma Calvin (holding two neighbor children of Bill White). Bethel Stockburger and Hazel Stockburger are in front of the table.

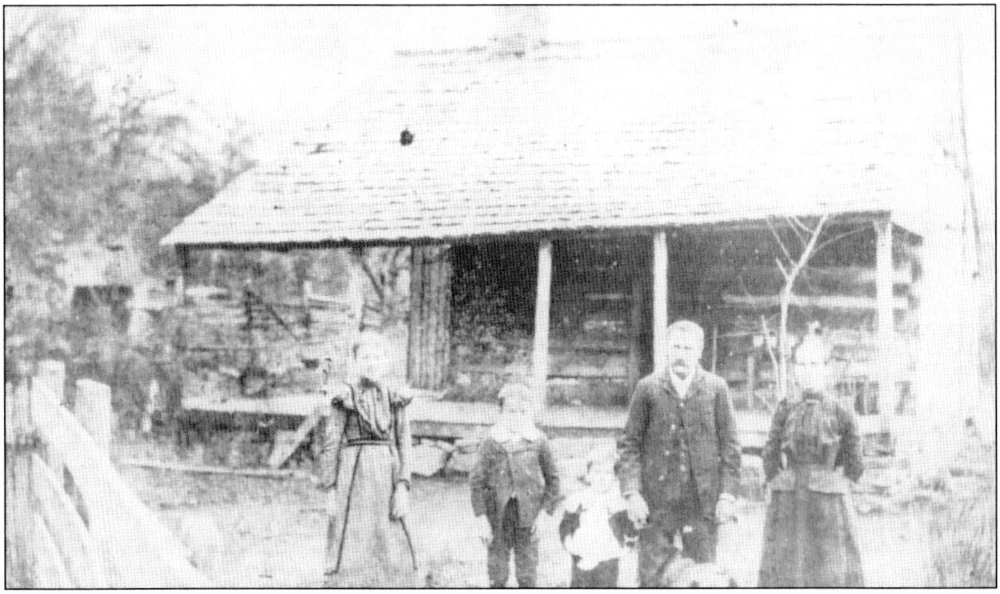

Within a stone's throw of West Fork school is Clark's Bluff, where many students once attended school picnics for their annual outing. The John Clark family lived in this log house on Woolsey Road before the turn of the century. They later moved to the bluff site. From left to right are as follows: Maude Caudle, Bert, Newell, John Clark, and his wife, Ellen Karnes Clark.

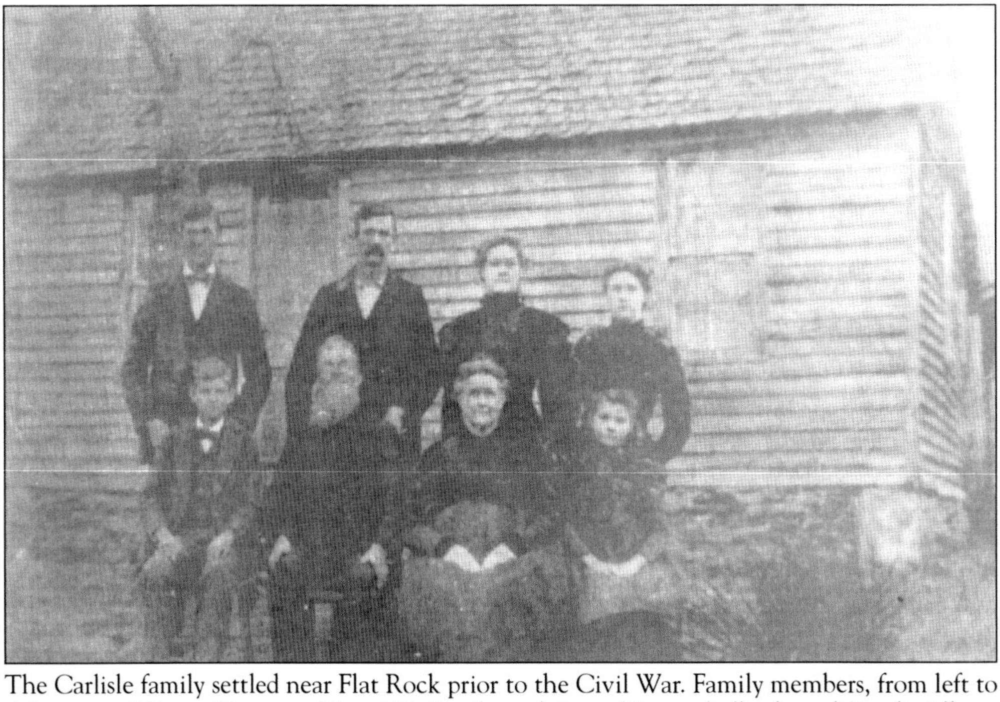

The Carlisle family settled near Flat Rock prior to the Civil War. Family members, from left to right, are as follows: (front row) Joe, J.D., Sarah, and Anna (Parsons); (back row) Frank, Albert, Lena, and Myrtle (Gibbs). Flat Rock community was located east of Baptist Ford. The Carlisle children attended school there, and although records show Flat Rock School as coming into existence in 1877, there was probably a subscription school prior to that date.

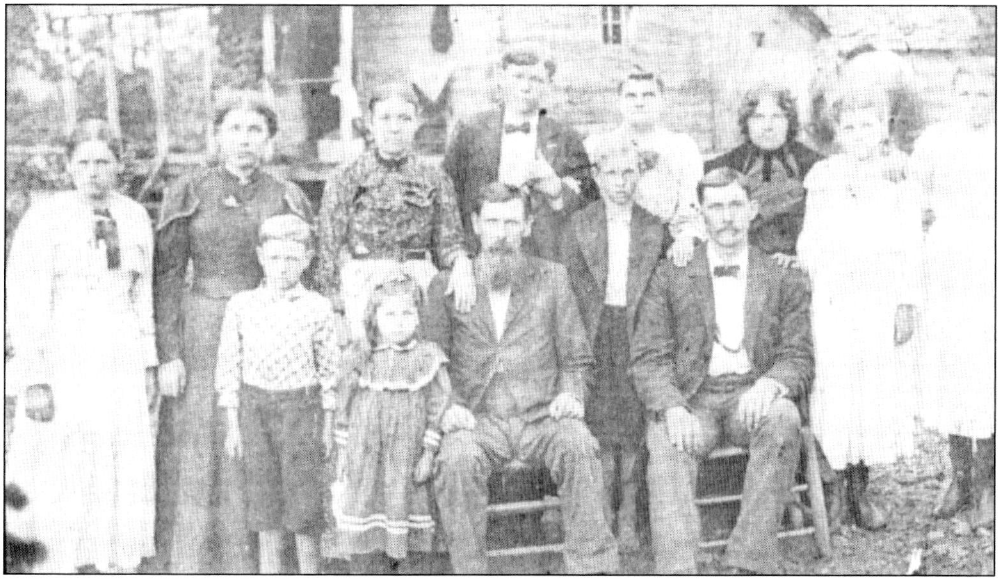

The Malen Spyres family was one of the most influential in the southern part of the county at the turn of the century. Known as Uncle Grab, Malen was a circuit-riding missionary Baptist preacher. All members of the family had beautiful singing voices. The family, seen here in 1898, are from left to right as follows: (sitting) Albert Spyres, Tennie Spyres (Tanner), Malen, Sylvester "Ves" Wells (a grandson), and Logan; (standing) Nettie Spyres, Daisy Spyres, Hannah Jane (mother), Lenora (Logan's wife), Alice Spyres Wells (a widow who later married G.L. Smith), Myrtle, and Lillie.

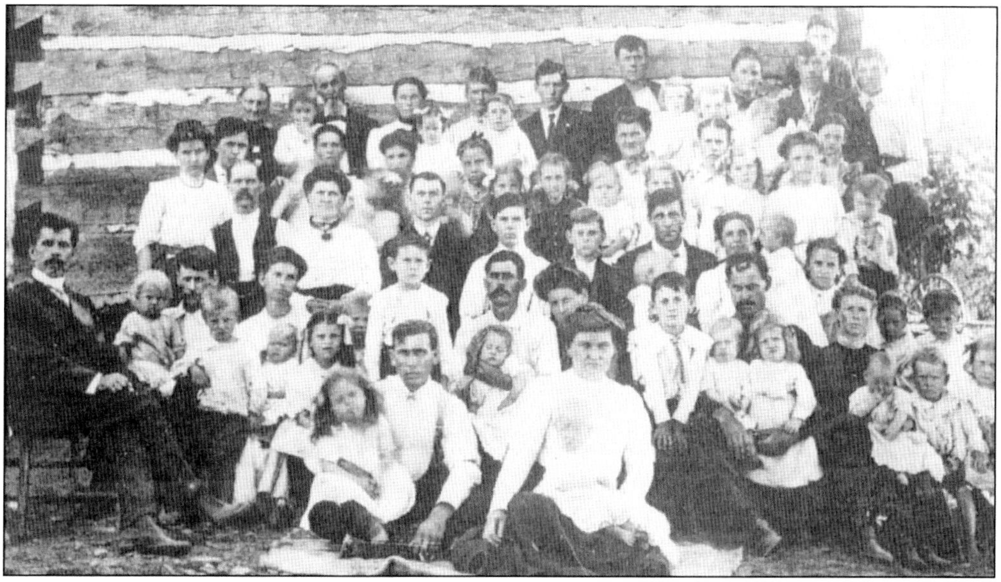

Pictured is the G.L. Smith family reunion in 1906. Family members shown are either descendants or related by marriage to G.L. and his wife. G.L. was also a circuit-riding preacher and a prosperous farmer in the Oak Grove community northwest of Winslow. After his wife died, he married Alice Spyres Wells. Note the chinking in the logs and the dovetail notches in this house; it was constructed without nails. Space does not allow for identification of all family members.

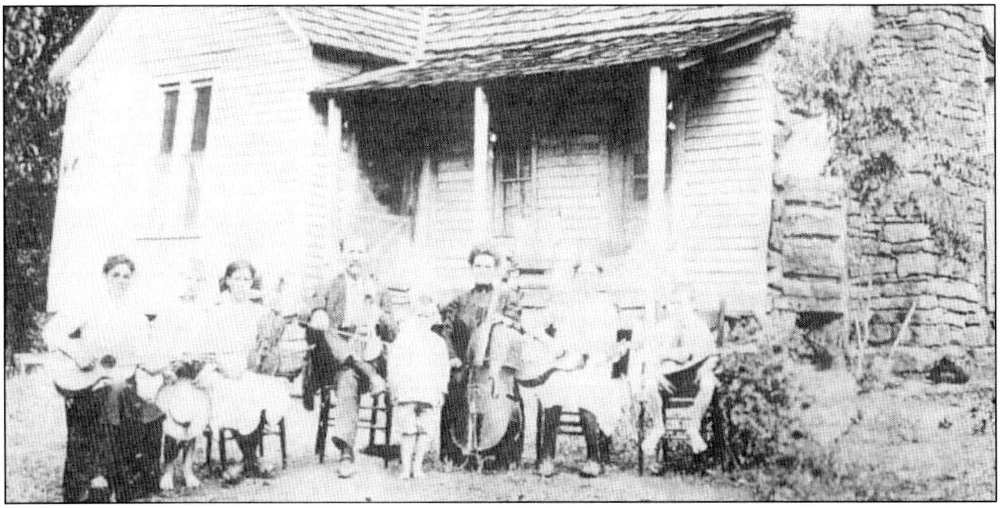

C.E. Jones, known for his wit and love of life, is the best remembered medical practitioner in the small town of Winslow. He preferred to be called Doc and everyone obliged. In this 1912 photo, family members are pictured from left to right as follows: Georgia, Pat, Flora, Dr. Jones, Ray, Mary Alice Hendrixson Jones (mother), Carl, and Dick. Another daughter, Anna, had already married.

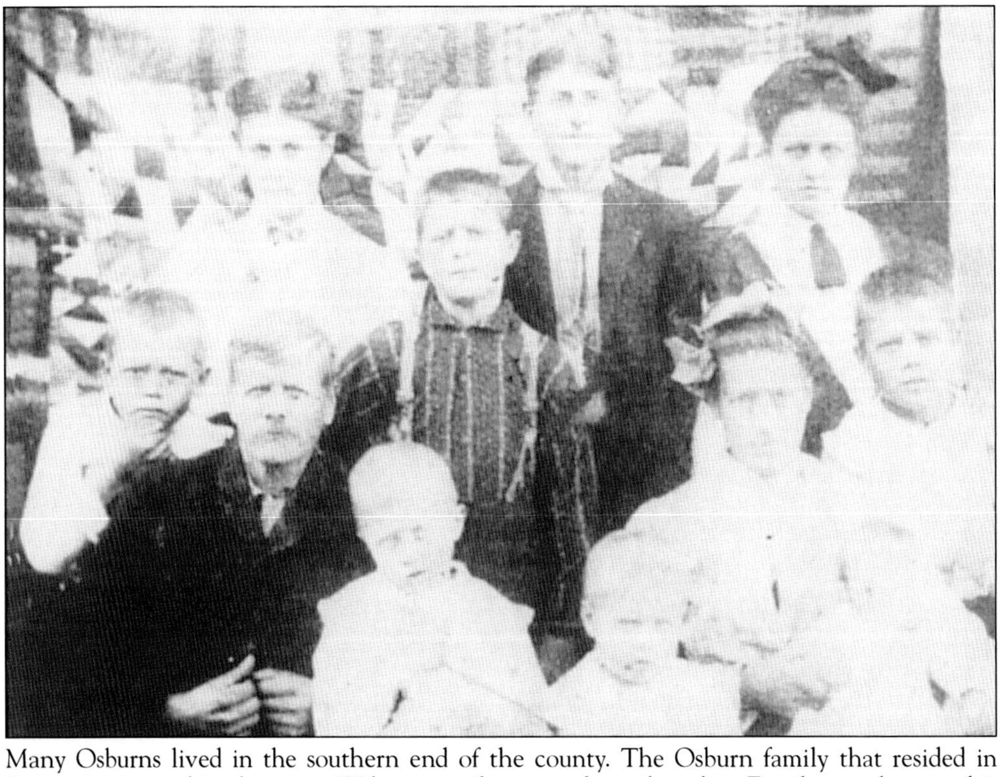

Many Osburns lived in the southern end of the county. The Osburn family that resided in Sunset is pictured in this view. Wiley was a farmer and watch tinker. Family members in this photo include Clyde Osburn (Mills), Henry A., Myrtle Osburn (Bradley), Floyd, Wiley, Luther, Ora, Roy (Dutch), and Alice (holding Jesse). Daughter Violet is not pictured.

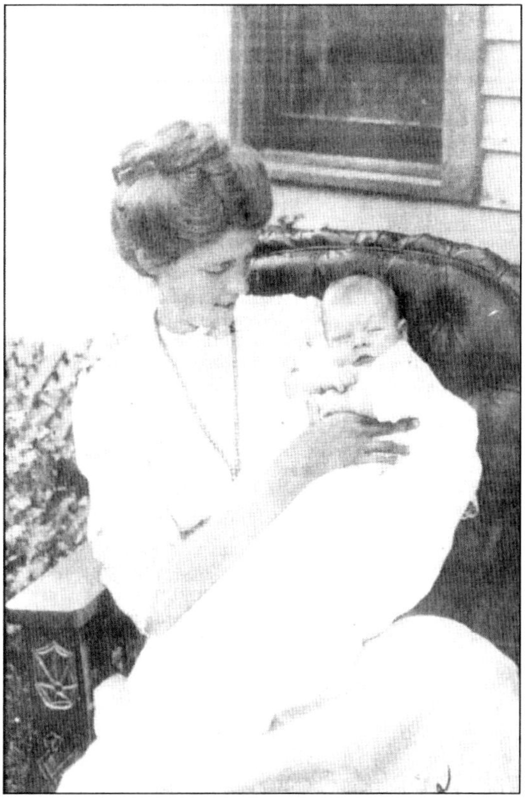

Vienna Gregg Smith is holding her first-born daughter, Georgia, in this early 1900s photo. The hair style and dress are typical of the day. Underneath her clothing, she wore a tightly laced corset and several layers of undergarments. Fred V., Vienna, and their children, Georgia, Mildred, Bonnie, and Max moved to Arkansas around 1920. Fred began working for the Frisco Railroad at the age of 13; he swept floors in a depot. He then worked as a telegrapher in Van Buren and as a school bus driver; after coming to Arkansas, he worked as a mail carrier.

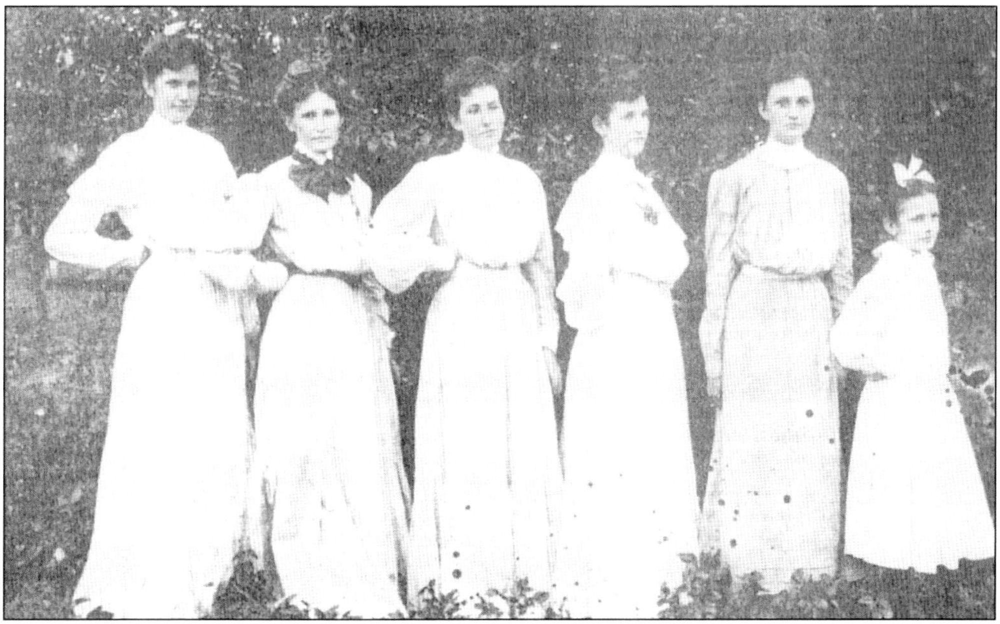

Another prominent pioneer family was that of Preston E. and Mary Ann Texas Lee McClendon. From left to right are their six daughters: Sarah Elizabeth Ann, Frances Emaline, Martha Ella Catherine, Mary Alice, Hattie Jewell, and Jessie Rosabel. The McClendons had one son; he is not pictured.

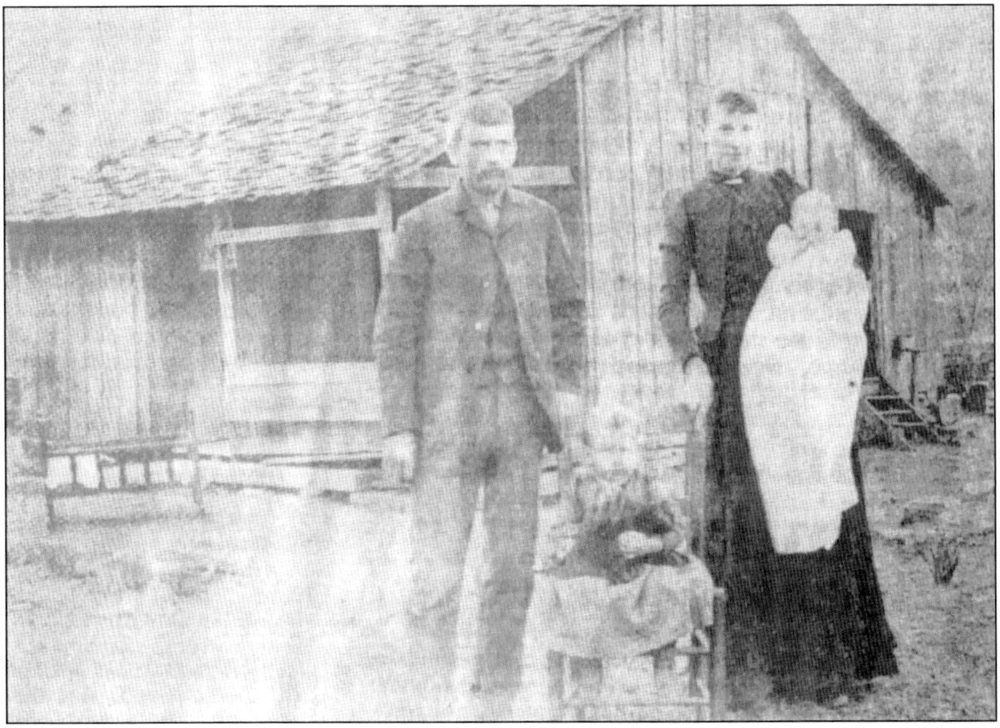

Probably one of the oldest photos in the collection is this one of Walker R. Winn, his wife Margaret Chapman Winn, and their children, Ethel (sitting in the chair) and baby Stella, who was born in 1893. Their home was located on a level bench west of Woolsey Road, halfway between West Fork and Woolsey. It was known as the Combs farm. Combs was the previous owner and, probably, the builder of the house.

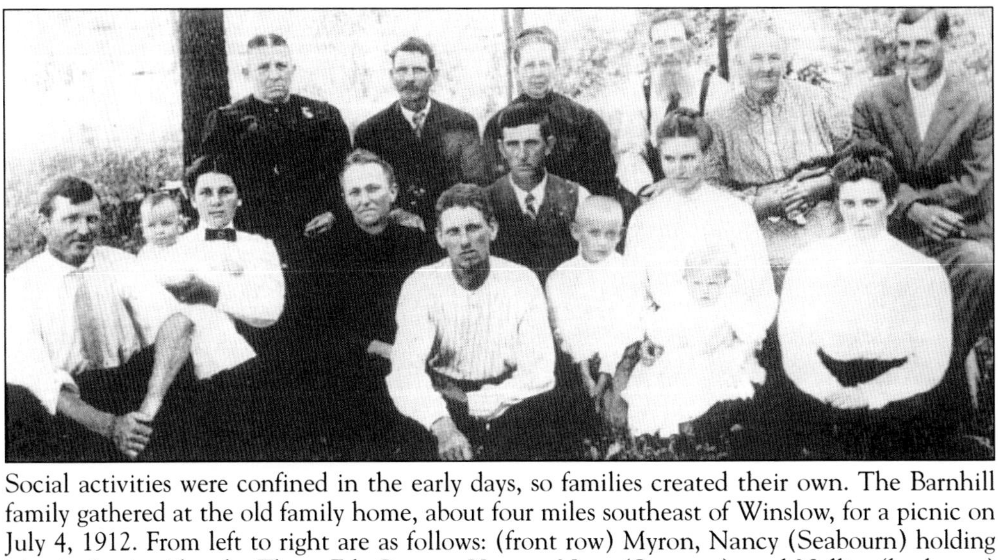

Social activities were confined in the early days, so families created their own. The Barnhill family gathered at the old family home, about four miles southeast of Winslow, for a picnic on July 4, 1912. From left to right are as follows: (front row) Myron, Nancy (Seabourn) holding Martin Louis, Almeda, Than, Ed, George, Harvey, Nora (Stratton), and Nellie; (back row) Letha, Oliver Martin, Ann (Moudy), Will, Jane, and Will Stratton.

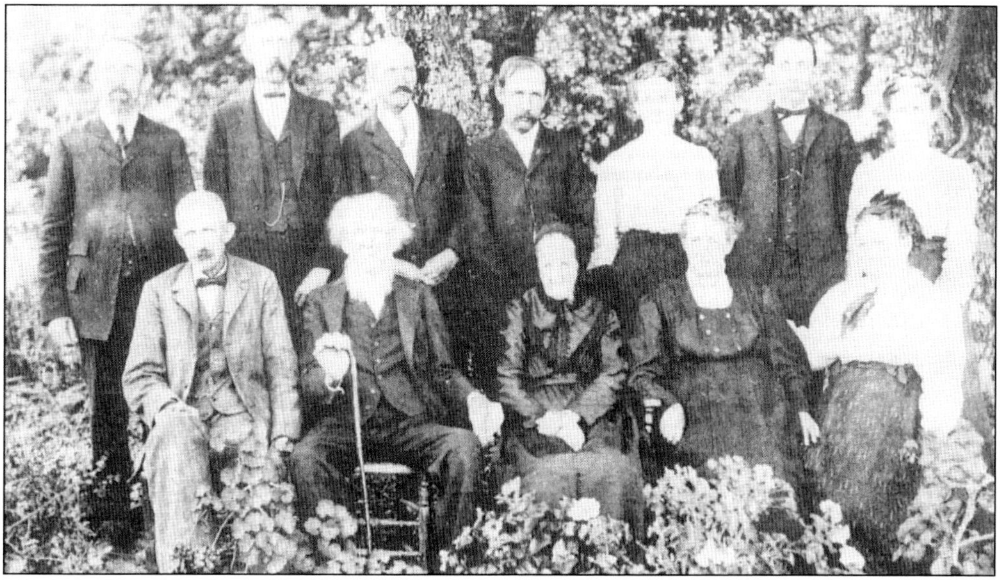

This 1905 photo shows a reunion of the John Calvin Stockburger family of ten children. From left to right are as follows: (standing) Jacob Wilson, John Robert, Joseph Adam, Elisha Edward, Mary Dorinda (Winn), Calvin Columbus (Tum), and Lydia Emma; (seated) Marcus Alexander, John Calvin (father), Martha Ann Reed (mother), Nancy Elizabeth, and Martha Annie (Bishop).

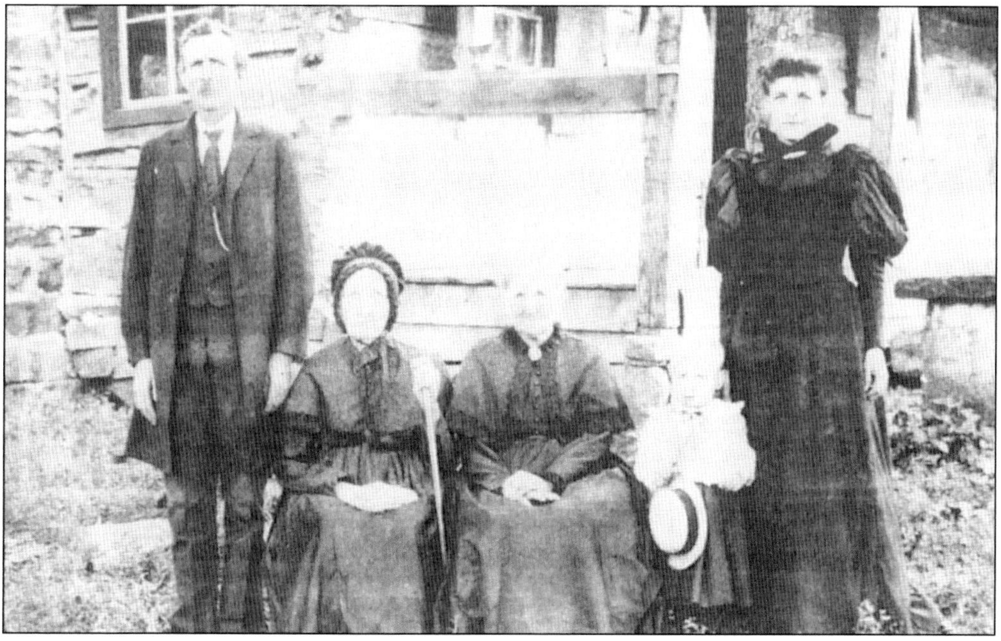

In the summer of 1852, a covered-wagon caravan from the state of Georgia arrived in southern Washington County. The group included Robert Reed, his wife Elizabeth Fagla, their daughter Martha Reed Stockburger, and her husband John Calvin, with their two-year-old son Marcus Alexander. Shown are five generations of Reeds, from left to right: Alex Stockburger, Elizabeth Fagla, Martha Reed Stockburger, Oscar Curtis, and Effie Stockburger Curtis. This photo was taken on the original Reed homesite *c.* 1896.

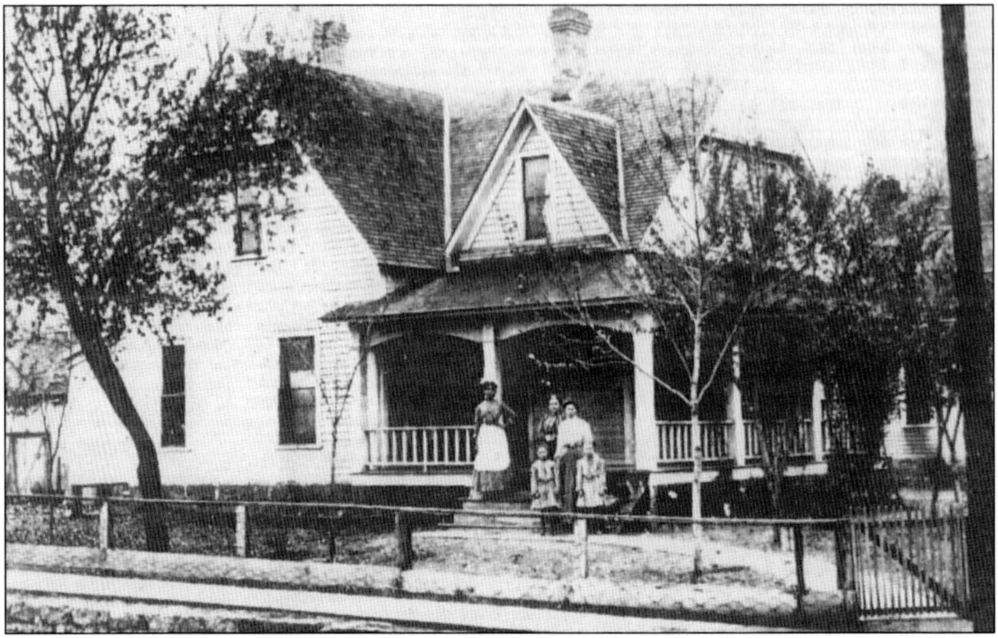

When this photo was taken in 1906, it was the home of Mr. and Mrs. A.N. Cole. The house is typical of the more luxurious homes in Fayetteville at the time. The Coles lived in several homes along Dickson Street before Mrs. Cole was murdered in 1920. On the steps are Addie Lee Land Cole and their two small daughters, Fay and May. At the left is the family maid. The other woman is not identified.

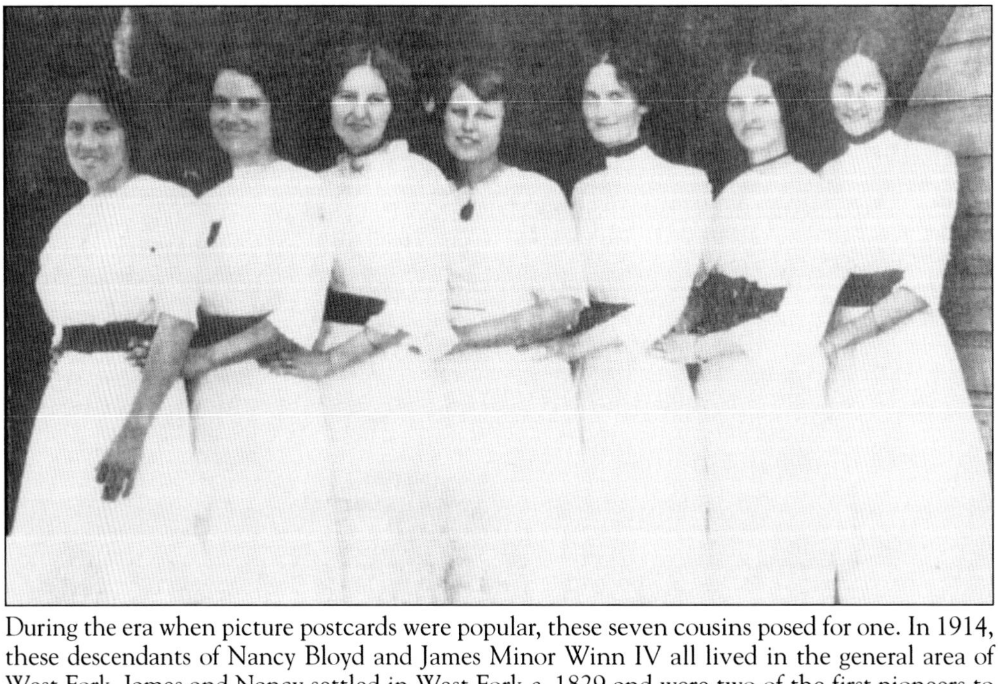

During the era when picture postcards were popular, these seven cousins posed for one. In 1914, these descendants of Nancy Bloyd and James Minor Winn IV all lived in the general area of West Fork. James and Nancy settled in West Fork c. 1829 and were two of the first pioneers to homestead in the area. From left to right are sisters Osa and Elsie Dearing, sisters Drada and Elizabeth Reed, Carrie Alexander, Pearl Reed, and Mary Alexander.

Five

SOCIALIZIN'

Communities revolved around religion and education before modern modes of transportation allowed families to travel more than a few miles away from home. Huge crowds were attracted to baptizings, revivals (sometimes called rallies), decorations, school literary functions, annual Christmas celebrations, pie suppers, and musicals. Some spent a full day traveling one way. Fortunately, many photographers took advantage of these gatherings, and the foresight of families who saved these treasured pictures allows us to look back on the daily lives of our ancestors. Where space will not permit, individuals in the photos have not been identified.

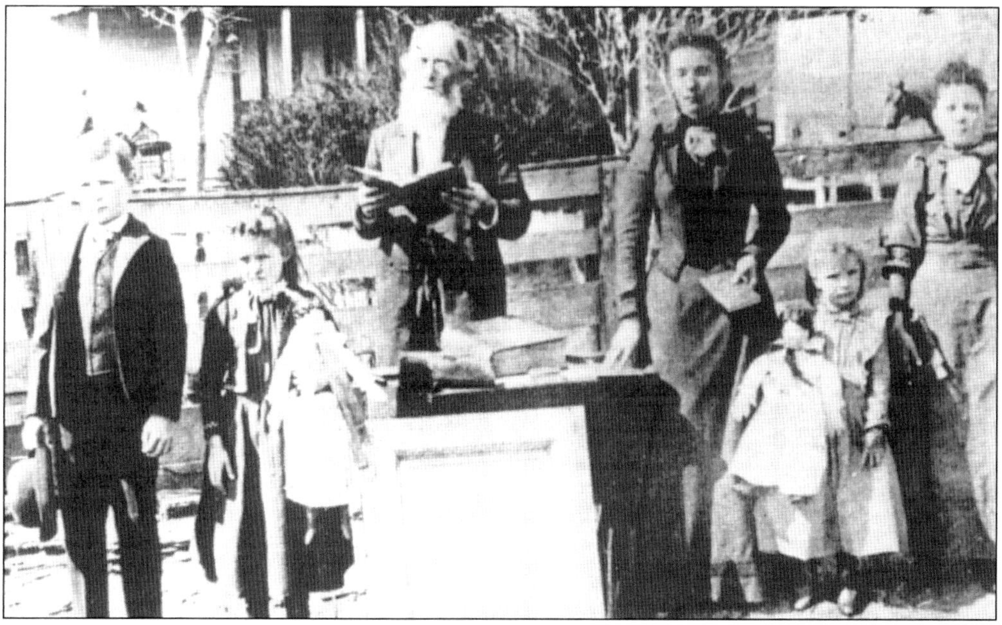

The circuit-riding preacher was once a familiar and welcome sight. Many communities had no preacher and looked forward to the circuit rider's appearance. Thomas Walker was a circuit-riding Methodist preacher. He is shown here with his grandchildren, Earl and Mert Dye. On the right are his daughters, Elizabeth Walker Dye, Icy Dye, and Florence Dye. Thomas also had two sons, John and Dan (not pictured).

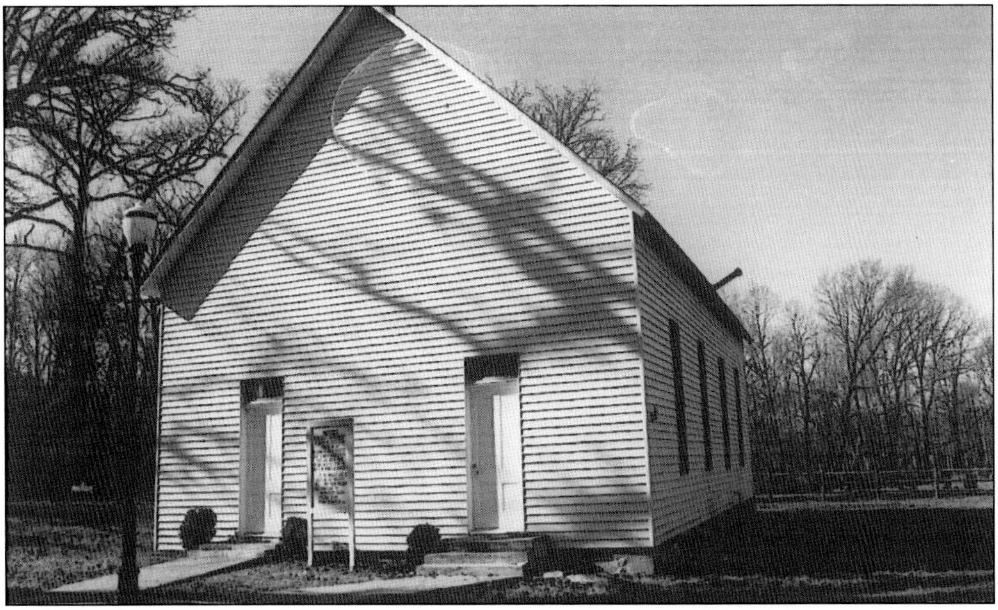

Thornsberry Church, located on the banks of the Little Osage, near the Benton County line, was a campground as early as 1835. In the 1850s, it was donated to the Methodist Church, and every fall they held a six-to-eight-week revival after crops were harvested. Families camped there to attend. Prominent war heroes buried in its cemetery include Revolutionary War soldier John Robinson and Col. Buck Brown of the Confederate Army; Colonel Brown fought the bitter war with McCulloch at Wilson Creek and Prairie Grove. He is thought to have also fought at Pea Ridge. (Photo courtesy of Arkansas Historic Preservation Program; Washington County Historical Society; and Shiloh Museum of Ozark History, Springdale.)

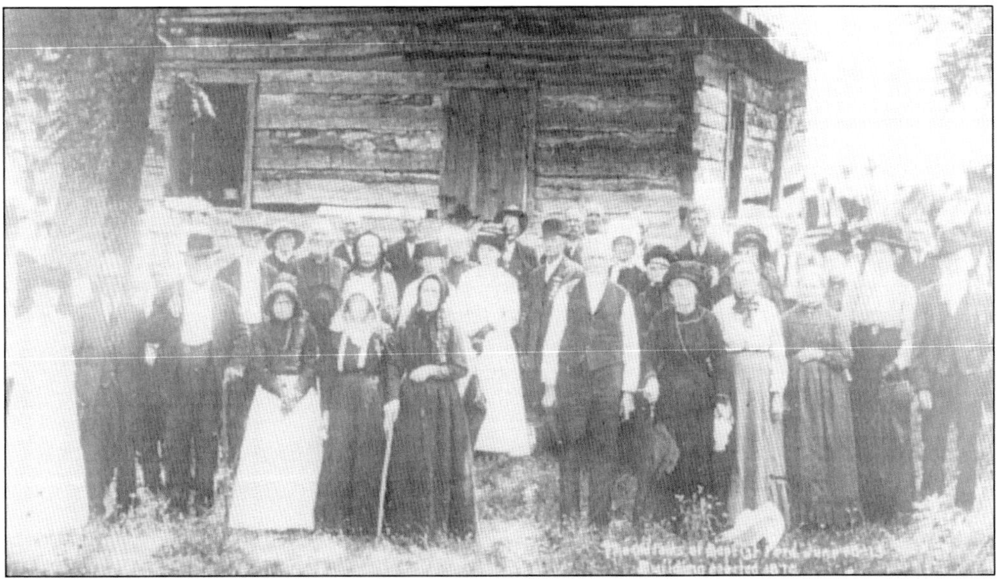

Baptist Ford Church was erected where the main north/south road out of Fayetteville forded the West Fork of the White River. It was not a Baptist church, but it served all denominations when it was built in 1870. Pictured is a gathering after Sunday services in 1913. School may have been held in this building, but no records are available.

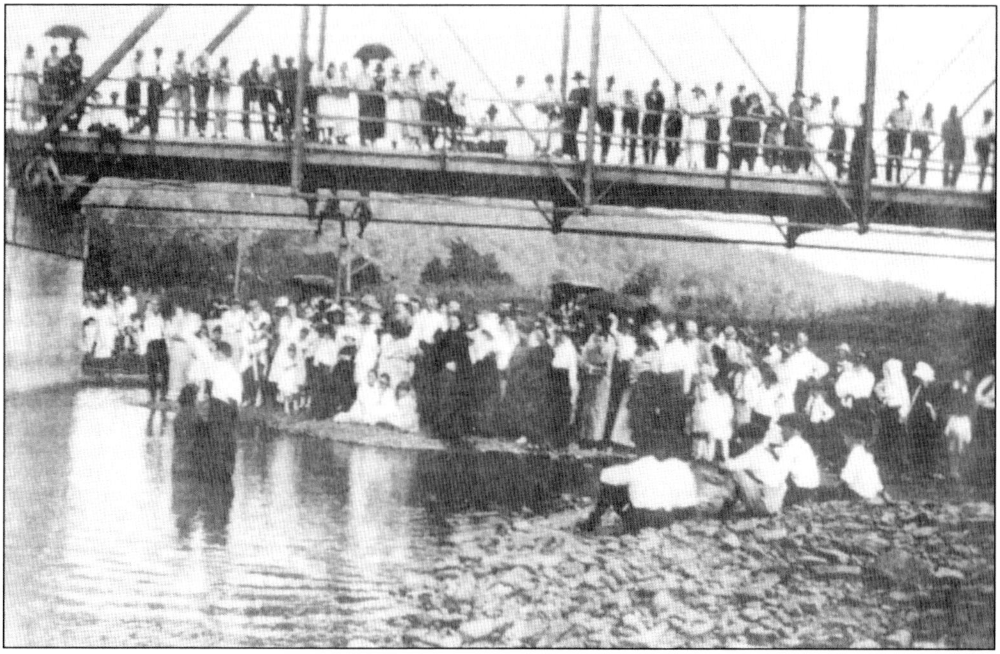

This old bridge that crossed a fork of the White River near West Fork was once a favorite gathering place for swimming, picture taking, and baptizings. On this day in August 1920, an evangelist for the Christian Church came over from Oklahoma and brought in a total of 42 area residents to the church rolls—37 by complete immersion and six by statement.

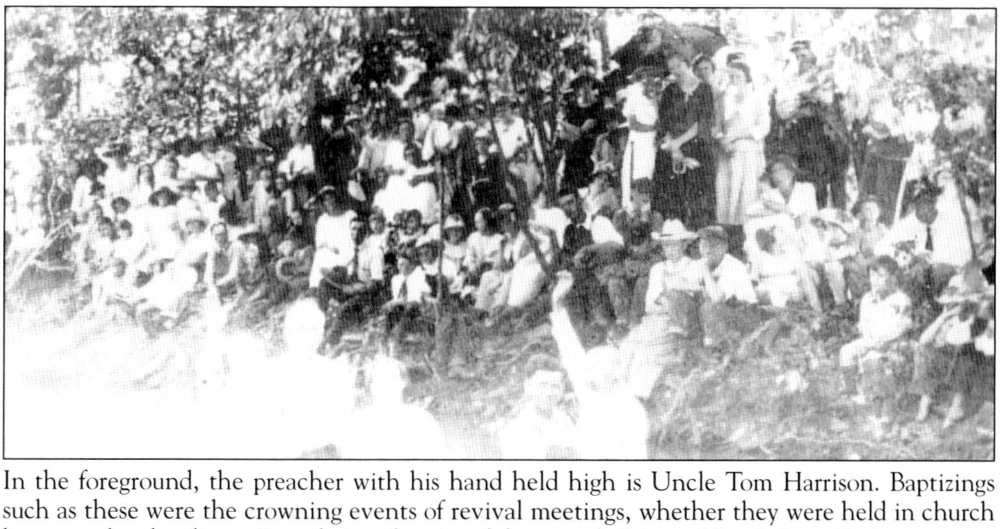

In the foreground, the preacher with his hand held high is Uncle Tom Harrison. Baptizings such as these were the crowning events of revival meetings, whether they were held in church houses or brush arbors. Considering the size of the crowd, this could truly be called a spectator event. This baptizing took place in Winn's Creek in July 1924, following a revival conducted at Blackburn by evangelist Irene Holcomb.

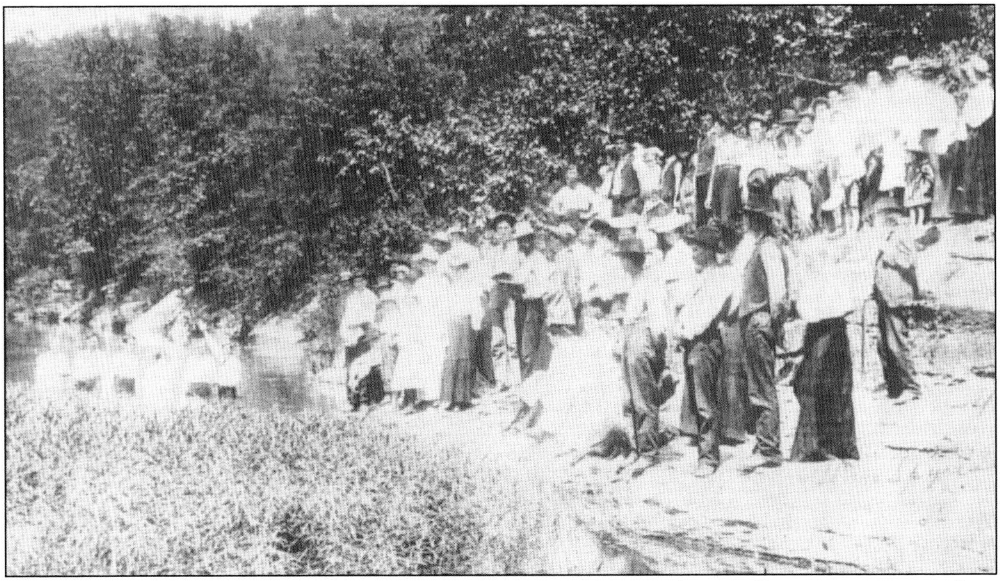

Though some of this old picture is blurred, it illustrates the popularity of baptizings, even when the creek bank was steep and treacherous. This one took place in Lee's Creek, below Old Bethlehem Church *c.* 1905. The two ministers are L.L. Johnson and Malen Spyres; the elderly man with a cane, Alex Carson, walked two miles from Blackburn to attend.

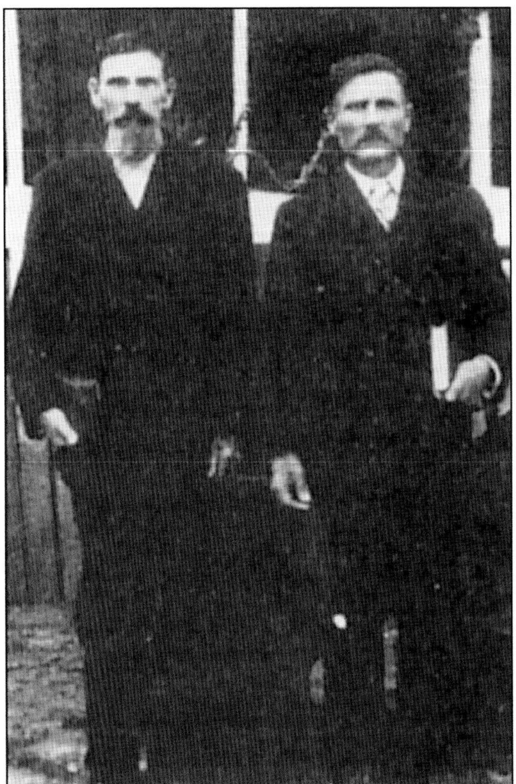

Ministers Malen Spyres (man with beard) and L.L. Johnson pose somberly before wading into the cold creek water to baptize the faithful. People stood in long lines, patiently waiting their turn. Spyres was a circuit-rider preacher. Tennie Spyres Tanner remembered that she was baptized on this day at the age of 11.

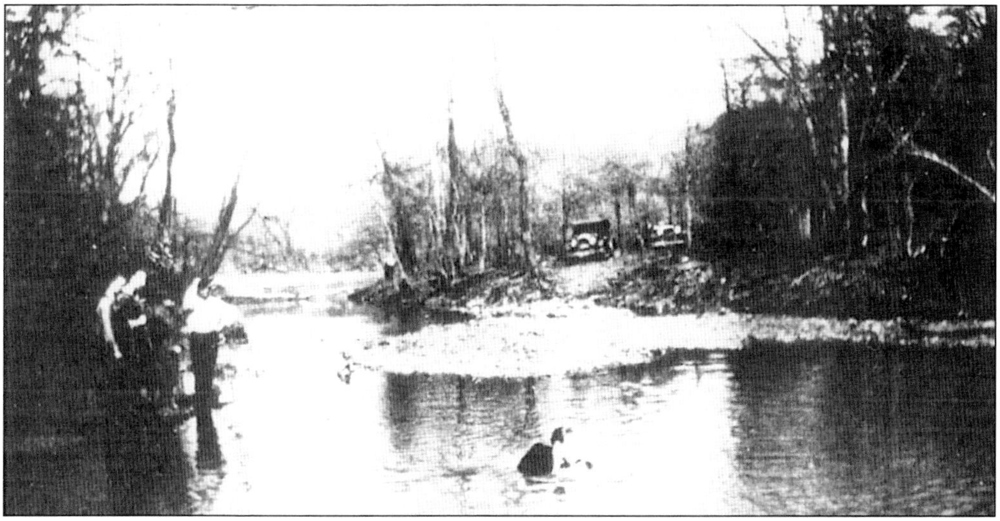

Though the photo is dark around the edges, the preacher is clearly seen in the center, immersing someone at Slicker. Folks truly demonstrated the power of their convictions by wading into ice-cold streams. Notice the pole held by one of the men on the bank. The minister would wade out, gauging the depth by probing with the stick.

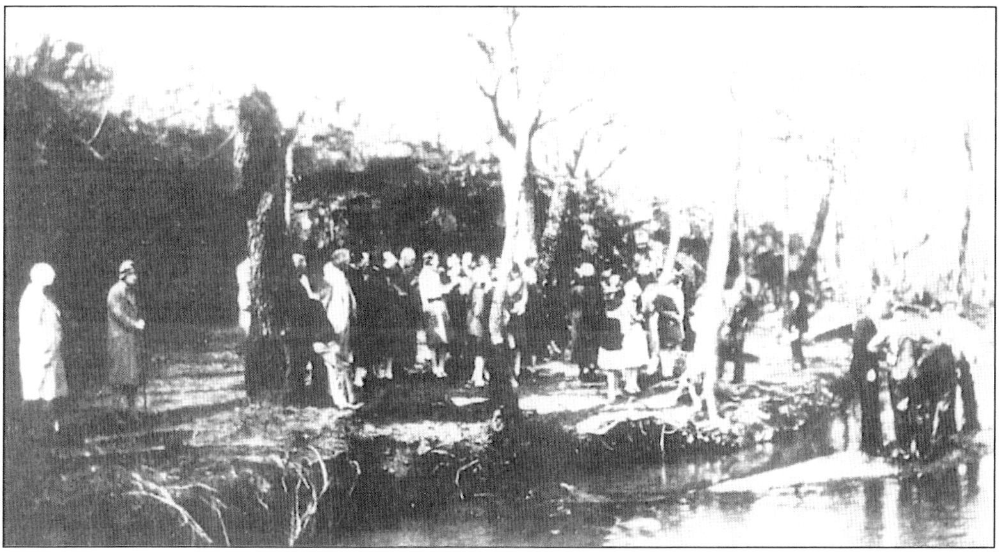

Here, at the same baptizing at Slicker, the cold weather is evidenced by the way people are bundled up in heavy, winter coats. The trees are completely void of foliage. This baptizing took place on a cold Sunday in April 1930. Though difficult to make out, curious onlookers line the top of the bluff to watch the ceremony.

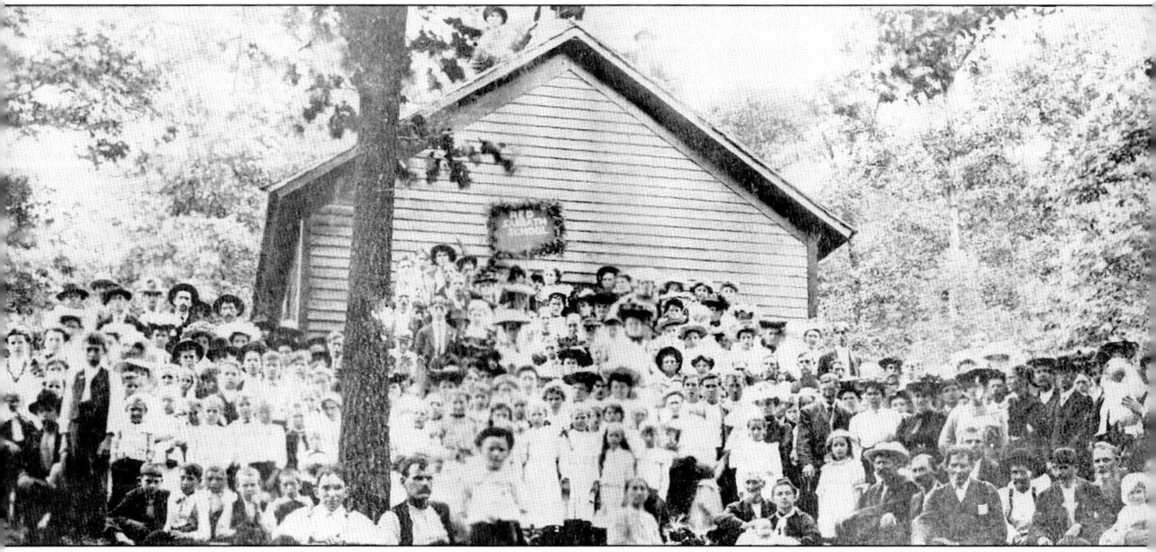

For generations, Sunday school rallies are events that have been an annual highlight for small, country churches. The year this photo was taken, around the turn of the century, a rally was held at Old Red. Groups in attendance included Bethlehem, Mt. Olive, Sycamore, and Blackburn, as well as many other area church communities. Old Red was located south of what is now Highway 74, the Winslow entrance road to Devil's Den, and east of Blackburn at a turn-off near the junction with Winn's Creek road from the north. Rallies included singing, preaching, a picnic dinner, and plenty of flies, ticks, and chiggers. A good time was had by all. Circuit-rider preachers in this photo include Grab Spyres and Tom Harrison; they probably had a go at "sermonizing" during the day-long meeting.

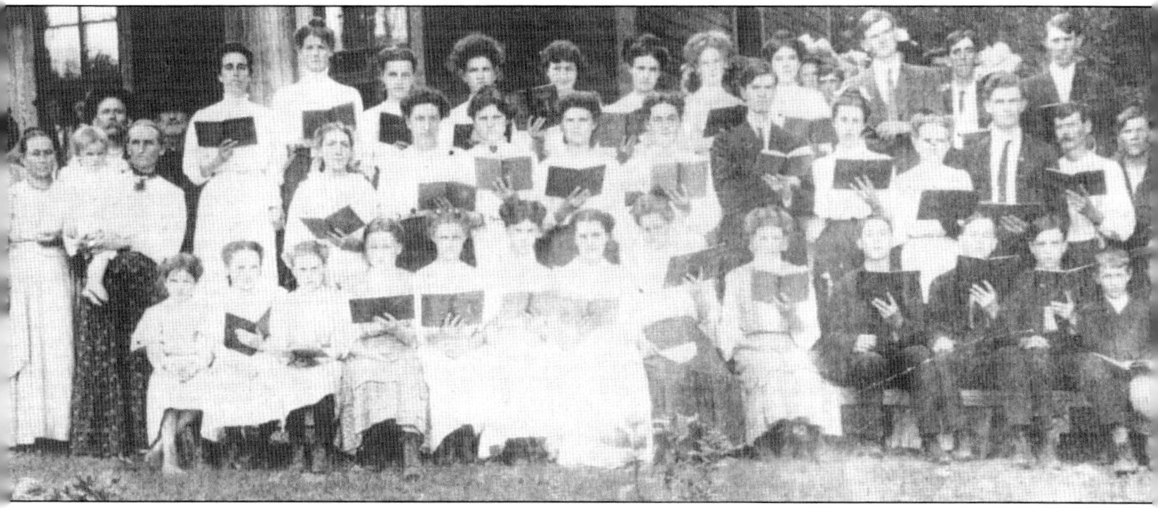

Singing Schools were also held at Old Red. This one shows the graduating class of 1907 at Grover Johnson's singing school. After the turn of the century, it was deemed important that young folks learned to sing by note. Entire families attended these singing schools, or as many members as could be spared from work at home. When the pump organ was played at church services or the family gathered around the parlor organ at home, the rafters would ring with traditional hymns as old and young showed off what they had learned at singing school. Many of the old hymnals used "shaped notes," and it was important that everyone learn how to read them and adapt their singing voice to follow the tune if it happened to be unfamiliar. Some of the youngsters holding song books appear to be no older than six or seven years of age.

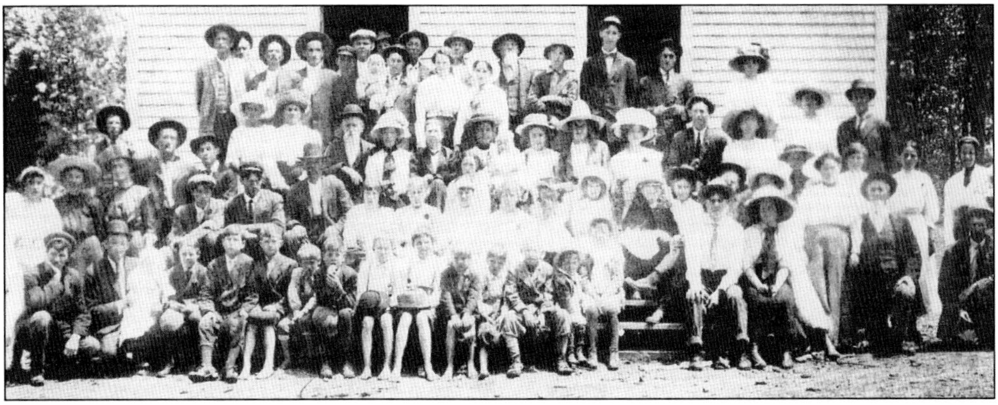

This interdenominational Sunday School Convention was held at Oak Grove sometime before 1910. Oak Grove, one of the community buildings that still remains standing, is located northwest of Winslow. It is occasionally used for singing events, reunions, and services. For two summers, about a decade ago, it was used as a school for area youngsters in which they could learn what classes were like in the past century.

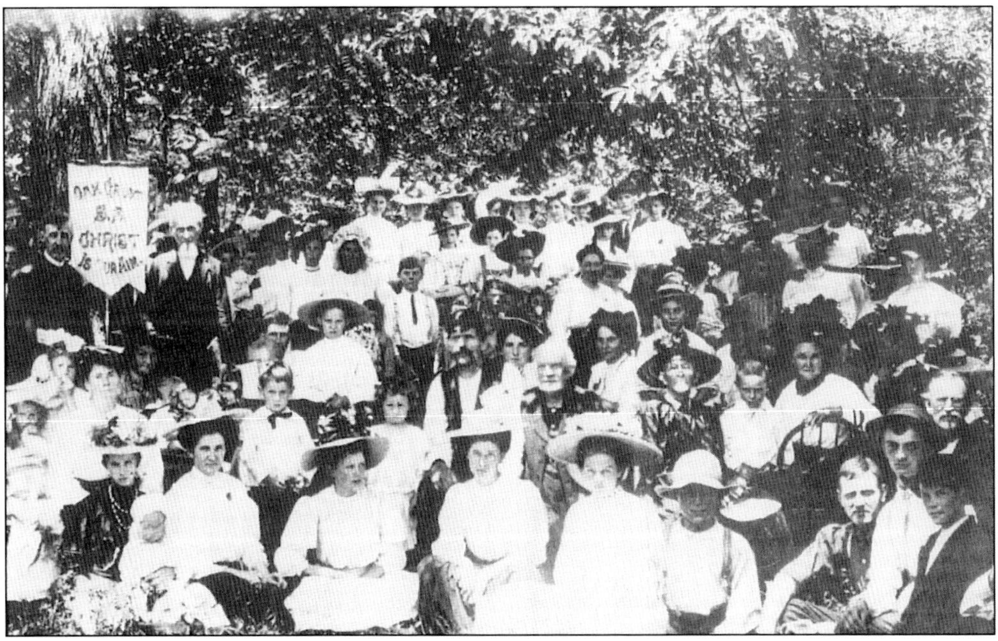

Another postcard produced by photographers early in the century includes this view of the Sunday School Convention held at Valley Grove on July 25, 1908. As evidenced by the banner from Oak Grove, several community churches were represented in what was apparently a one-day meeting.

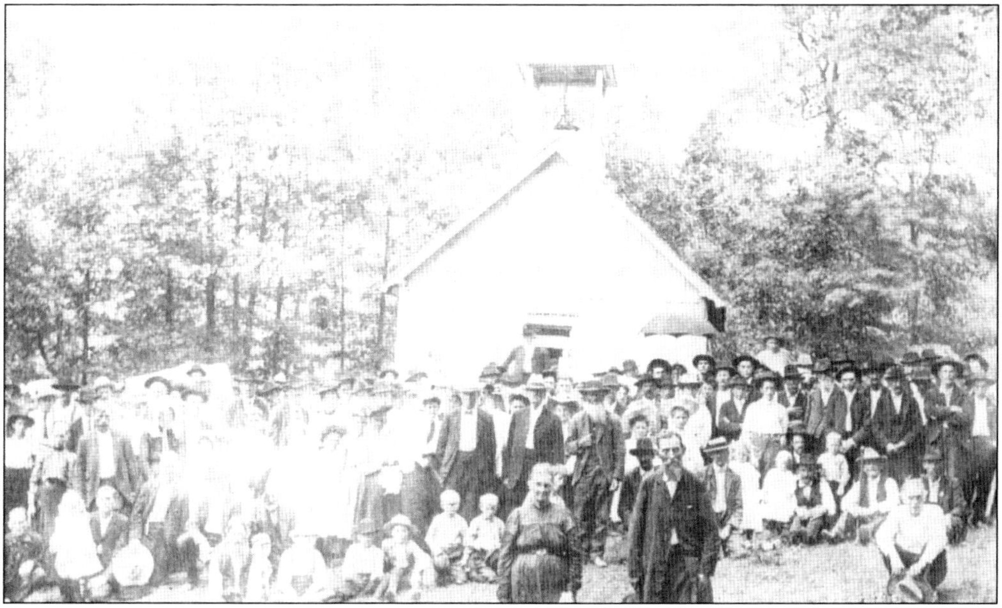

A hollow across Lee's Creek from Old Bethlehem is known as U.S. Hollow because a troop of Union soldiers spent a winter there under a bluff. The earlier log building dates back prior to that time, but this "little white church in the Wildwood," as it was often referred to, hosted this Sunday School Convention. Officially called the Missionary Baptist Church, it was one of the few around at the time. The date of the photo is 1906.

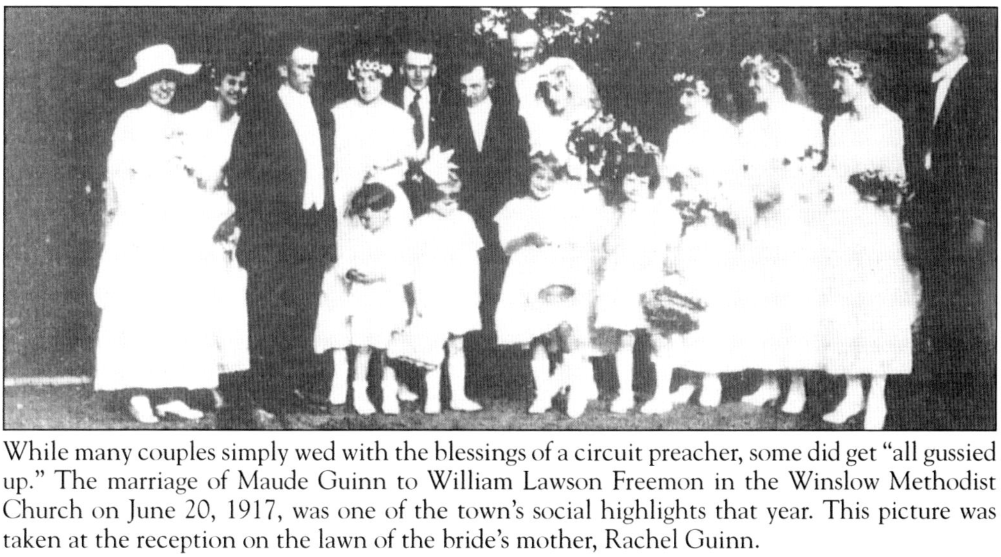

While many couples simply wed with the blessings of a circuit preacher, some did get "all gussied up." The marriage of Maude Guinn to William Lawson Freemon in the Winslow Methodist Church on June 20, 1917, was one of the town's social highlights that year. This picture was taken at the reception on the lawn of the bride's mother, Rachel Guinn.

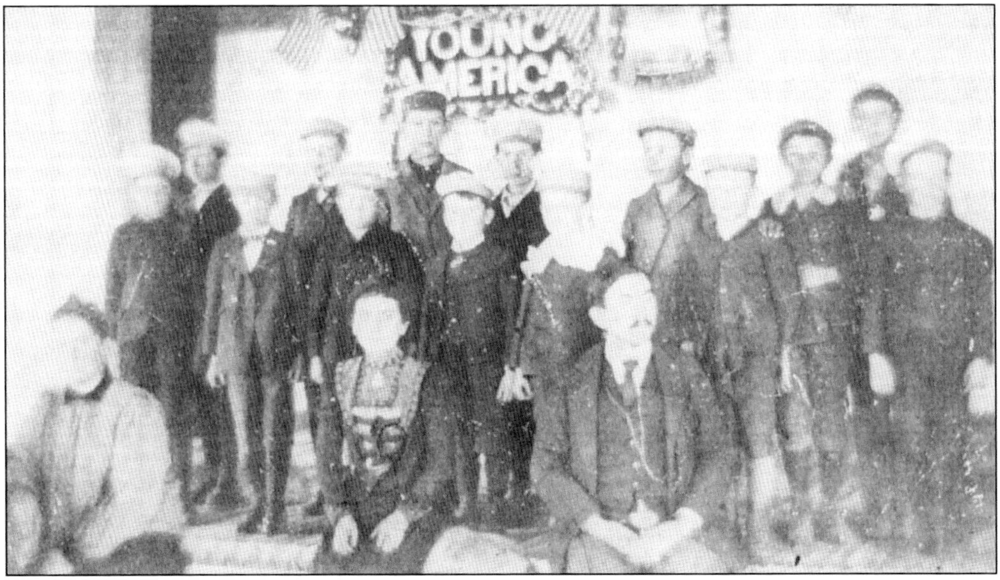

This 1898 photo is a view of Winslow lads who belonged to the patriotic organization known as Young America. The pair seated in front are Alma McClinton and her brother, Hurd. The latter taught school in Winslow. The lady at the far left is Elizabeth (Lizzie) Sharp Harris.

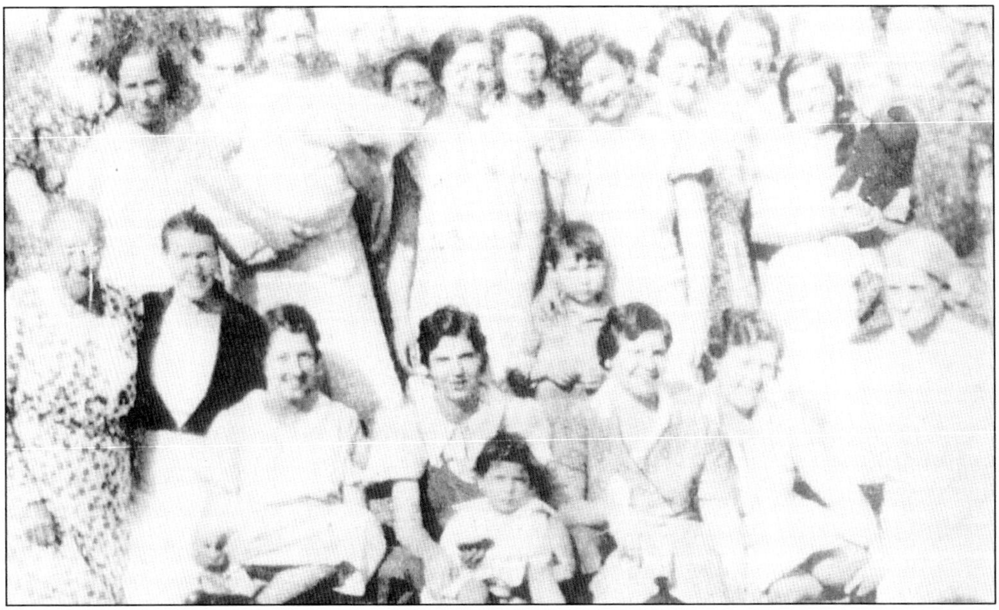

In the early 1930s, the town of Brentwood had an active Home Demonstration Club. From left to right are as follows: (front row) Mrs. Sid Brown, Mary Smith, Retta Talley, Gladys Cox, Nadine Cox, Mary Cox, Clara Bulger, and Mrs. Gus Morgan; (back row) Edna Smith, Iva Cox, Jessie May, Juanita Hilliard Duncan, Gertie Smith, Ethel Ramey, Mrs. Floy Coleman, Pauline Mills, Tommy Middleton, Mrs. Floy Parrish, Mrs. Middleton, Vera Smith, and Kary Smith. Retta Talley Neville celebrated her 96th birthday this October.

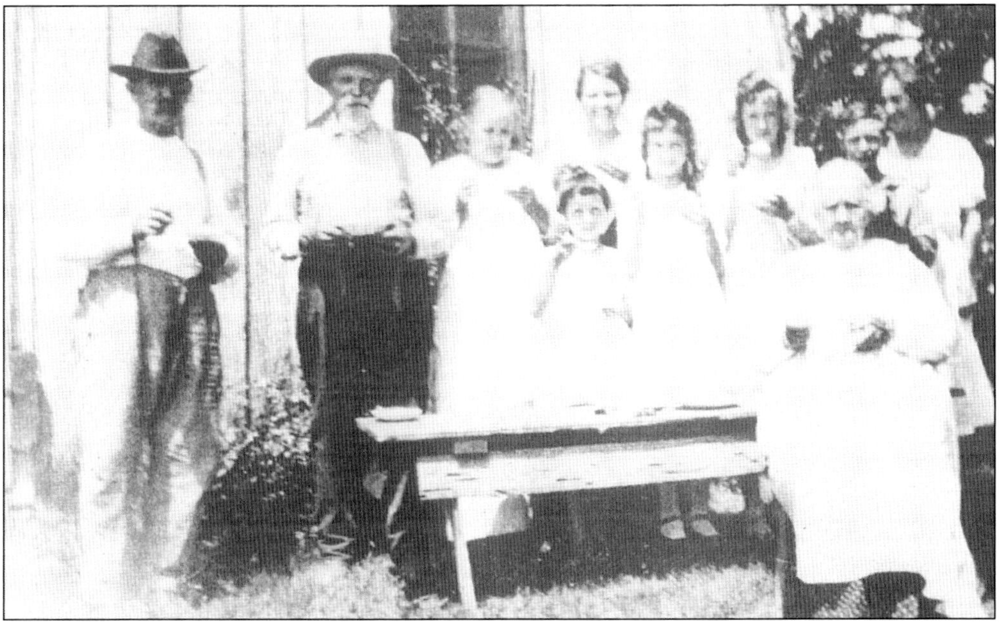

Before the days of mass entertainment, folks took advantage of every event to get together socially. Shortly after the turn of the century, the group above gathered one Sunday afternoon to celebrate the birthday of two of their friends. Those photographed at the old Larsen home near Brentwood, are, from left to right, as follows: Mr. Boone, Mr. and Mrs. Ole Larsen, Nelle Jett Duncan, Lottie Jett, Mildred Jett Waggoner, Ruby Olive, Hugh Jett, Gertie Larsen, and Grandma Tolbert (seated in front).

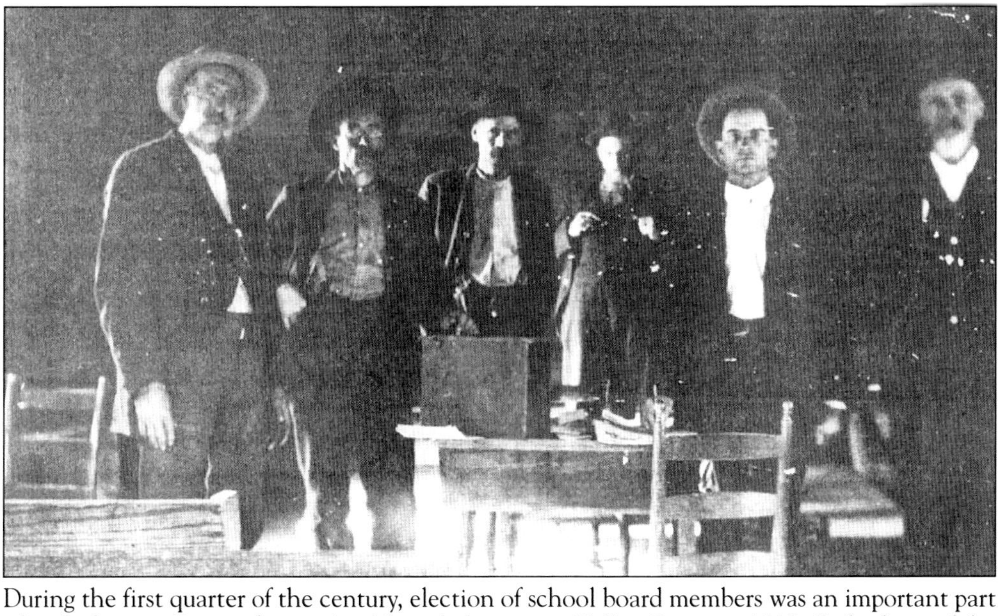

During the first quarter of the century, election of school board members was an important part of each district. Pictured is a school board election at Valley Grove c. 1910. Only three of the men are identified as election officials. Note the hand-made benches and cane bottom chairs; these are typical of the era.

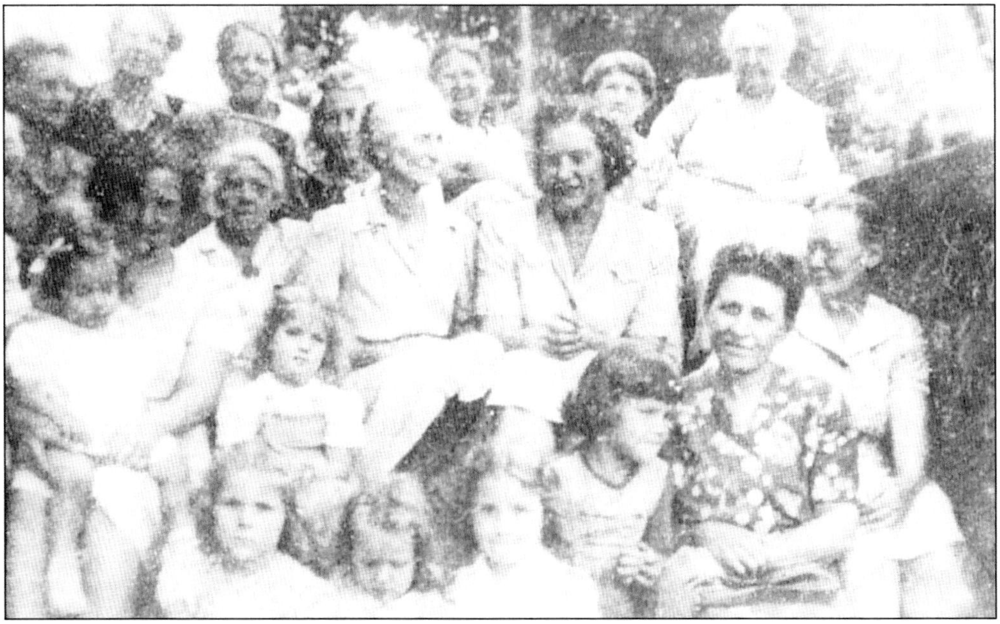

The basement of the Winslow Methodist Church was a beehive of activity for many years. In addition to its use for Sunday school classes, it was used during the week for community meetings such as those held weekly by this quilting group. They gathered on the steps in 1946 to have this picture taken.

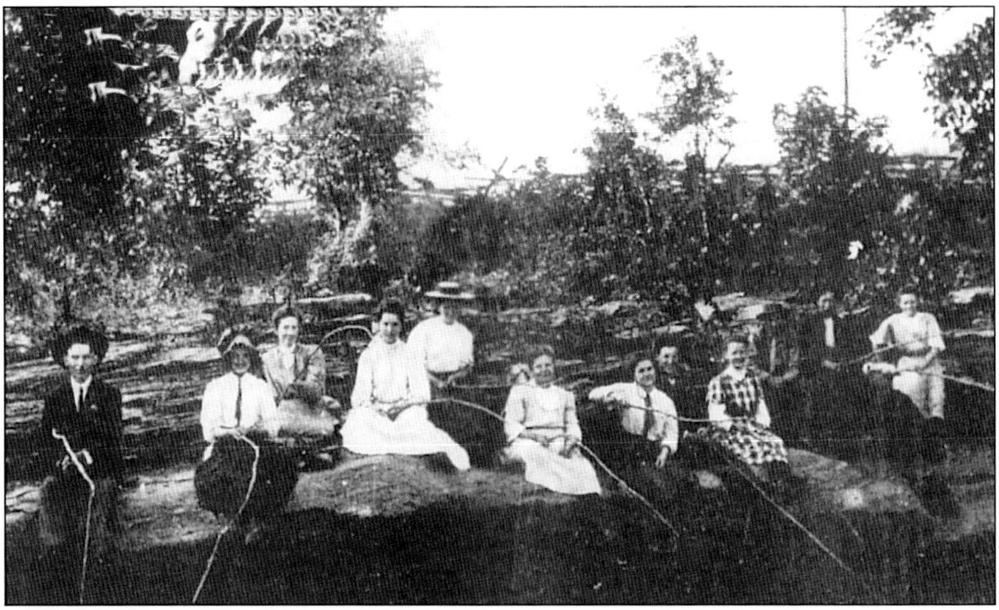

Slicker Swimming Hole was so named because of the slick rocks over which the stream flows into a pool. It was popular for swimming, baptizing, and as seen here, fishing. These young people probably didn't expect to catch much, but it was a wonderful way to spend a Sunday afternoon in the summer of 1907. From left to right are as follows: Emmet Lee, Maude Guinn, Martha McClendon, Grace Lehn, Mary Smith, Rose McClendon, Dolly Smith, Bess Guinn, Elmer Lehn, and Estelle Smith. The other men are not identified.

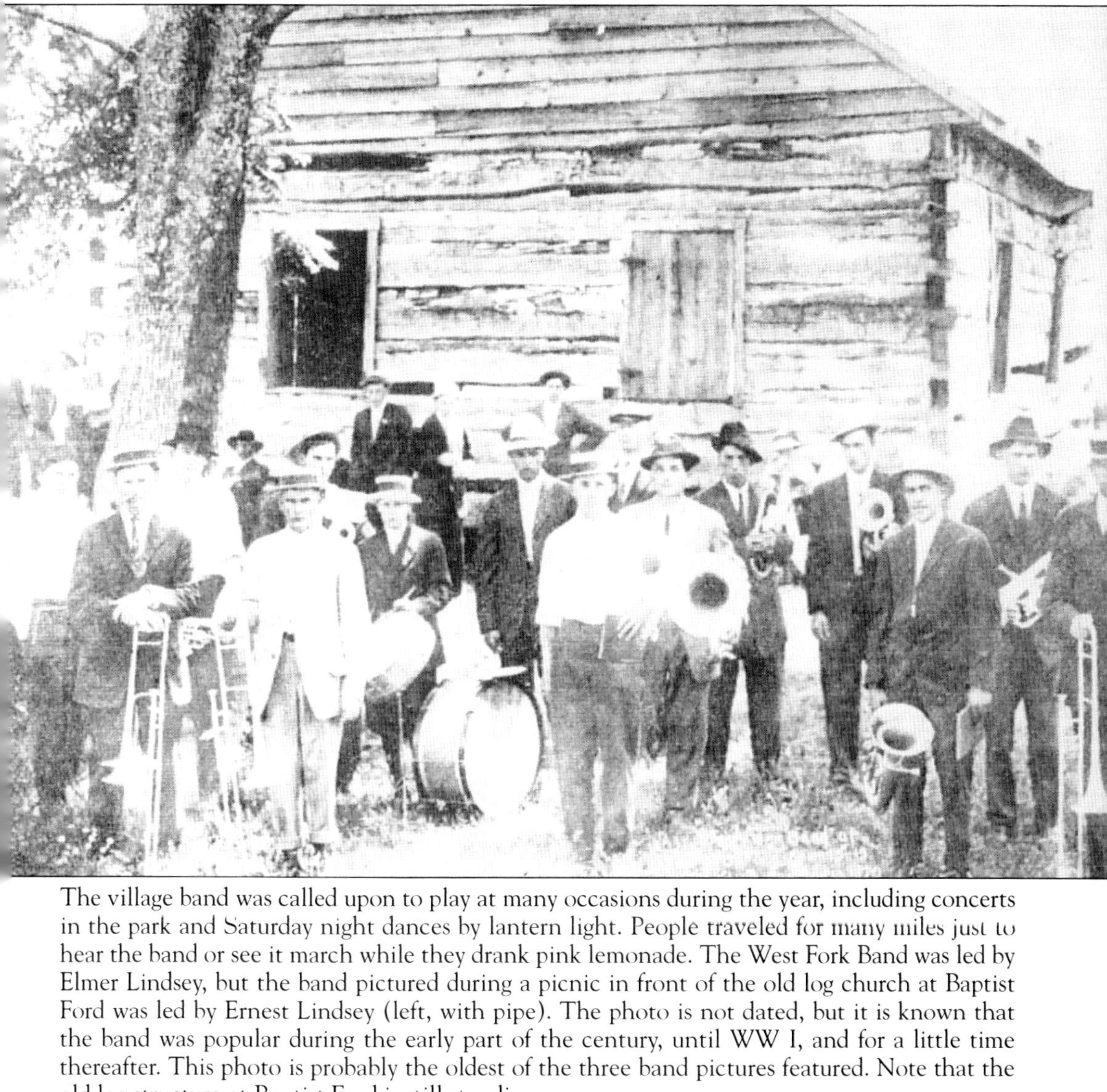

The village band was called upon to play at many occasions during the year, including concerts in the park and Saturday night dances by lantern light. People traveled for many miles just to hear the band or see it march while they drank pink lemonade. The West Fork Band was led by Elmer Lindsey, but the band pictured during a picnic in front of the old log church at Baptist Ford was led by Ernest Lindsey (left, with pipe). The photo is not dated, but it is known that the band was popular during the early part of the century, until WW I, and for a little time thereafter. This photo is probably the oldest of the three band pictures featured. Note that the old log structure at Baptist Ford is still standing.

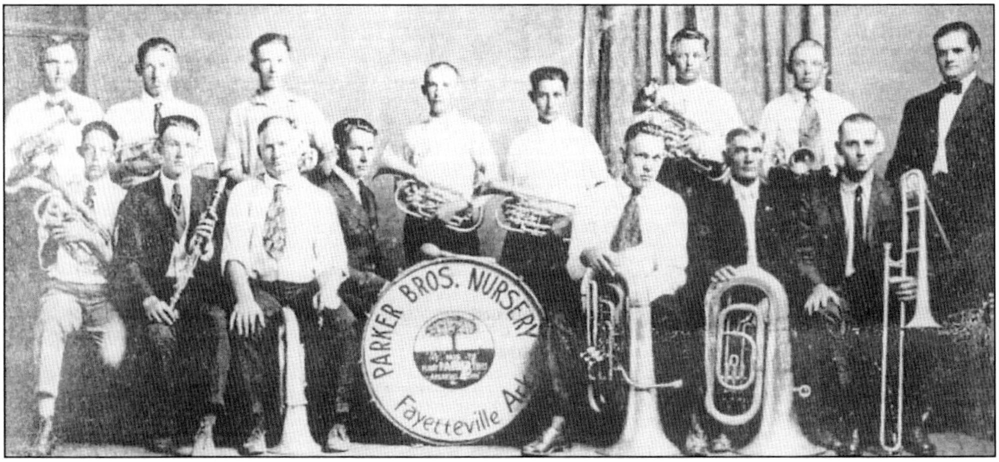

This band, known as Parker Brothers Nursery Band, included some West Fork and Greenland musicians. Elmer Lindsey was the band director. This group played for many picnics and other events and was one of the last adult bands to play as an organized group in the county. The photo was taken in the 1920s.

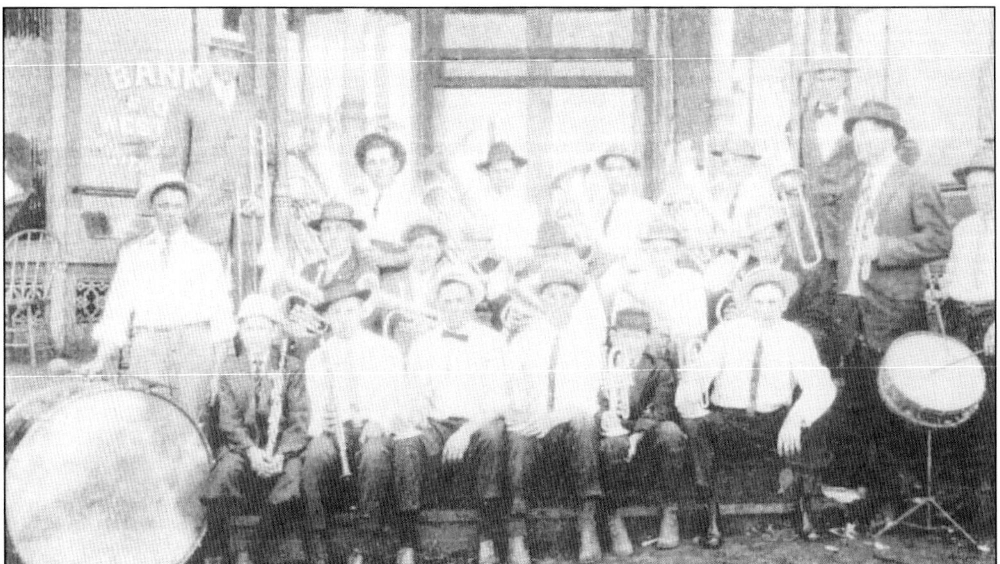

The West Fork Band is thought to have posed for this photo in front of the Bank of West Fork, a short time before the onset of WW I. Elmer Lindsey was also this band's leader. It is difficult to compare the photos and pick out the same musicians. None are identified in the photo taken at Baptist Ford.

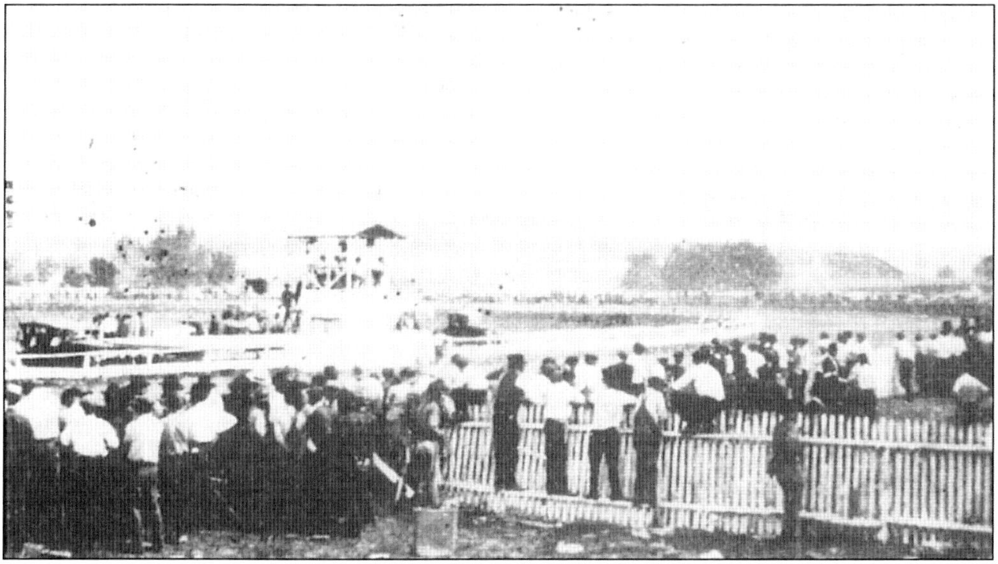

This photo shows the side of the racetrack at the 1920 county fair. Racing horses were owned by county farmers who competed for prizes. Although betting on the races was illegal, some old-timers recall that bets were placed. The crowd shown here stands in front of the grandstand, where visitors could watch the races without paying admission.

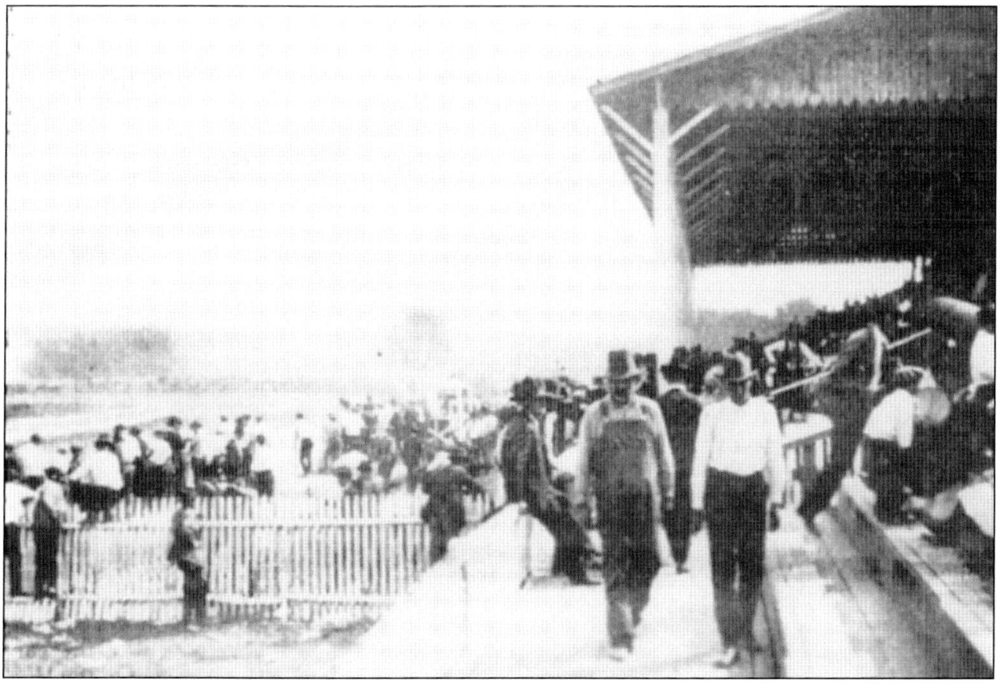

This view of the grandstand at the 1920 county fair also shows part of the racetrack (left). There were horse races every afternoon. Local bands provided music between races. Farmers brought their livestock, and entire families camped out for the five days of the fair, sleeping in covered wagons and cooking their meals over open fires.

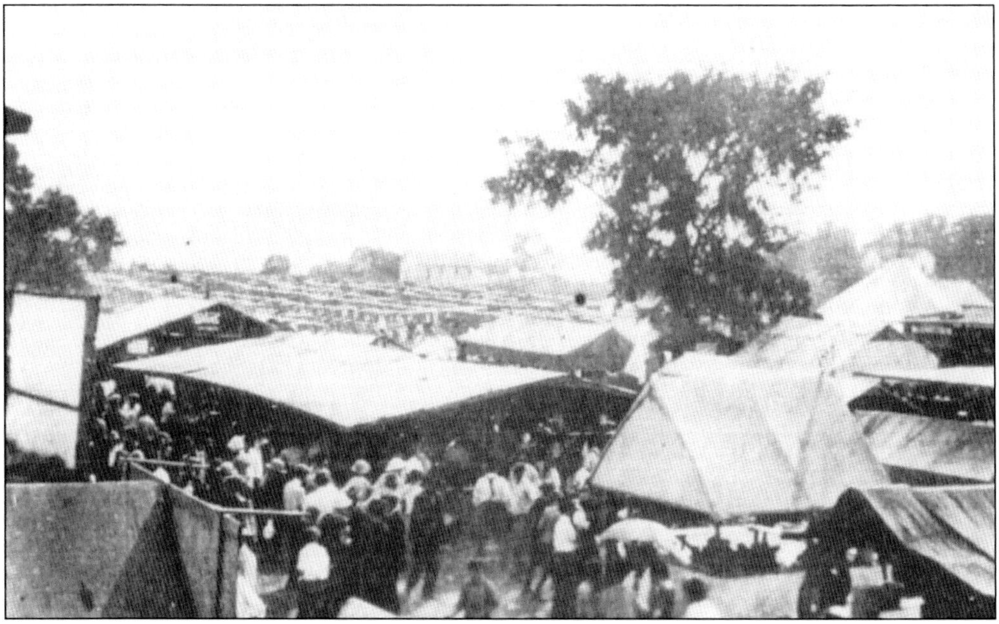

Shelters at the county fair were temporary covers for various stands and booths that were erected to keep out sun and rain. Because there was no lighting on the grounds, the gates were closed before sundown. The main carnival rides were a merry-go-round and a Ferris wheel, usually owned by some enterprising local farmer. In earlier days, they were powered by a mule or horse walking around a track.

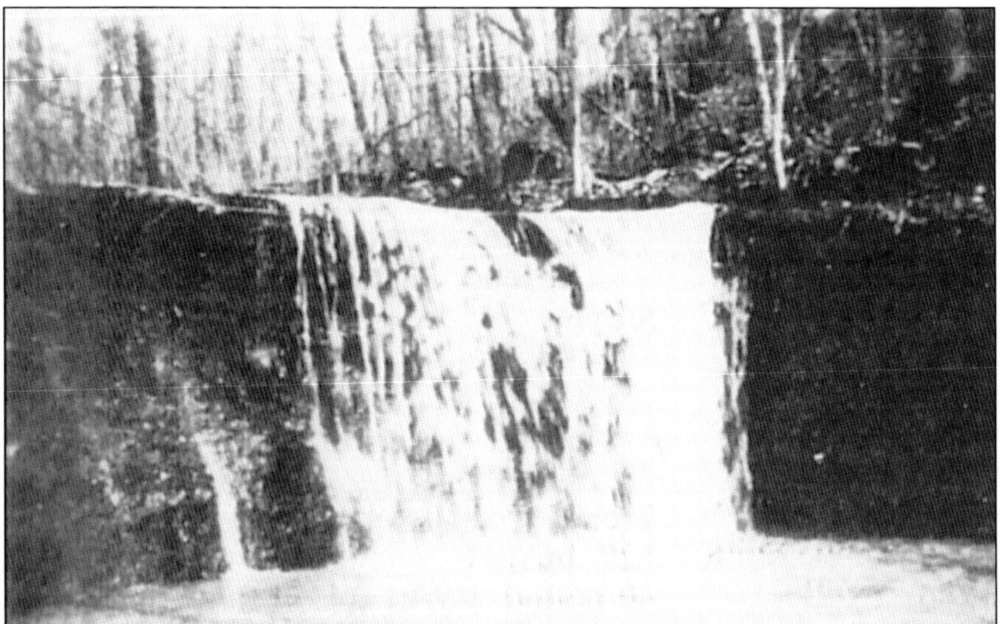

When youngsters in the Winslow area wanted to "walk out" together or spend the day on a picnic, they usually went to one of the several falls. This one, called Pennywinkle Falls, was located southwest of Winslow. It was not quite as spectacular as some.

Wheeler, or Winslow, Falls was by far the most popular because it could be reached by walking across a meadow. Long walks were just what young men enjoyed when in the company of a beautiful young lady, and she wasn't averse to the idea herself. Usually if he said, "Let's go to the falls," it was this one he meant. In this view, ice has frozen the water into lacy white crystals. Both photos were taken by Omer Winn in the 1920s.

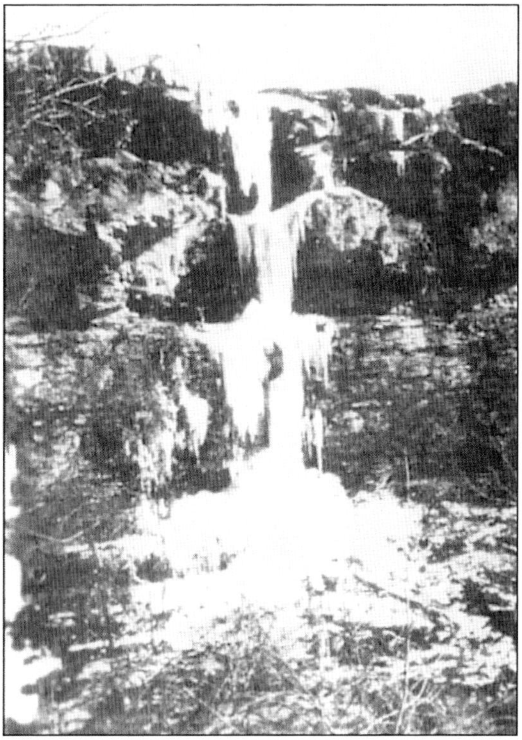

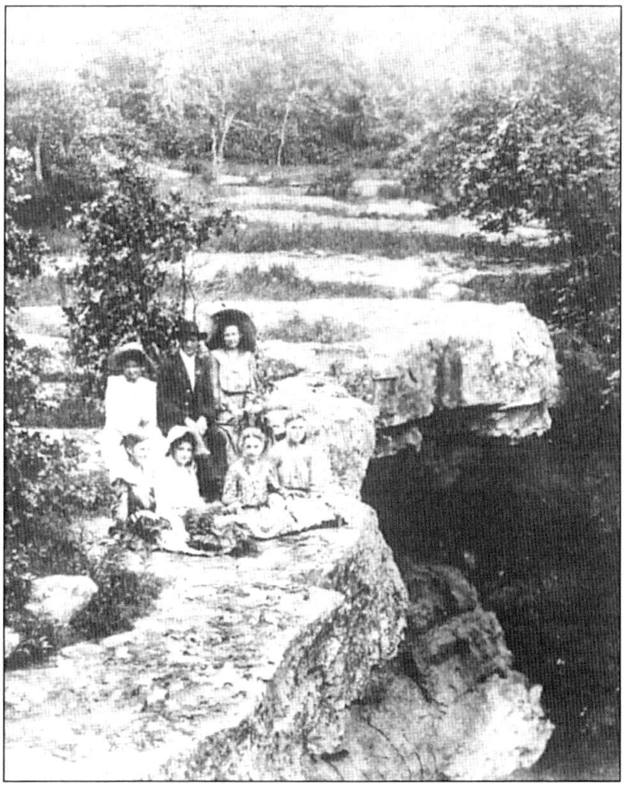

In 1905, five young ladies accompanied Oda Miller and his fiancé, Pearl Guinn, (right) on an outing to the falls. On the left is his future sister-in-law, Bess Guinn. Others pictured are seated from left to right as follows: Grace Karnes, Elizabeth Page, Maude Guinn, and Gertrude Gregg. The photographer must have been sure footed and brave to capture this pose.

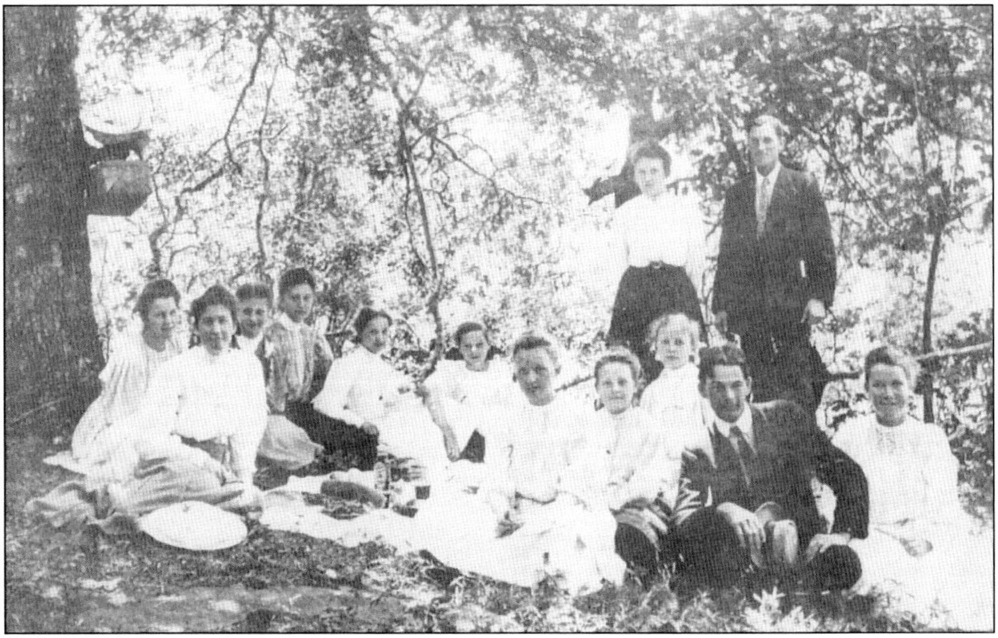

One of the most popular pastimes with young folks in the "good ole' days" was a picnic. This picnic at the falls near Winslow in 1903 was organized by the Guinn girls to honor their visiting cousin, William Wilson. Lunch is spread on the white cloth on the ground and a picnic basket is hanging from a tree limb in the background.

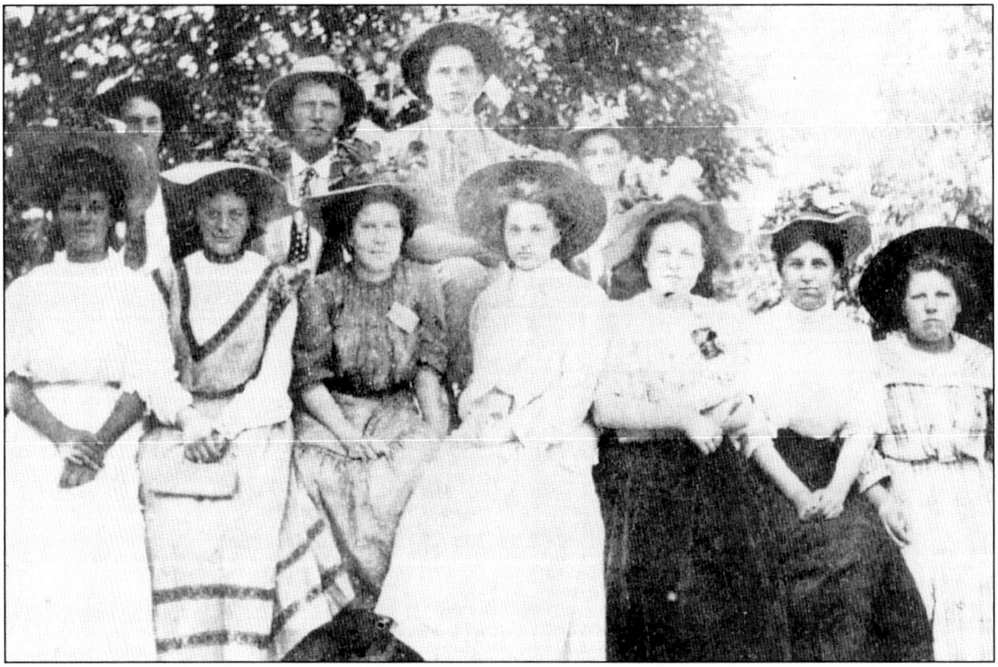

A Fourth of July picnic in 1910 was held near Coil Cemetery. Everyone is attired in the latest fashions and, while the wide-brimmed hats probably kept the sun off their faces, imagine the long skirts after walking in ankle deep dust on the unpaved road, along the two-or-three-mile walk to and from the picnic. The identifications on this photograph are uncertain.

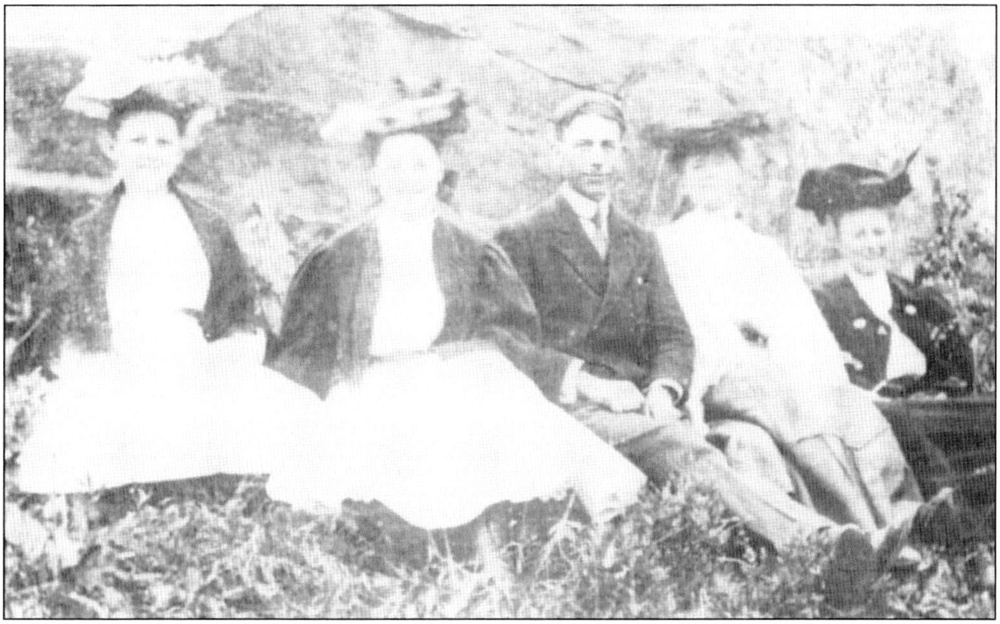

The young man is in good company on this Sunday afternoon outing in 1905. Note his wide lapels and the high, stiff, celluloid collar he is wearing. The girls piled their long hair high on their heads in order to secure the fashionable hats with large hat pins. From left to right are as follows: Bess Guinn Hansbury, Maude Guinn Freeman, Emmett Lee, Nellie Lee, and Pearl Guinn Miller.

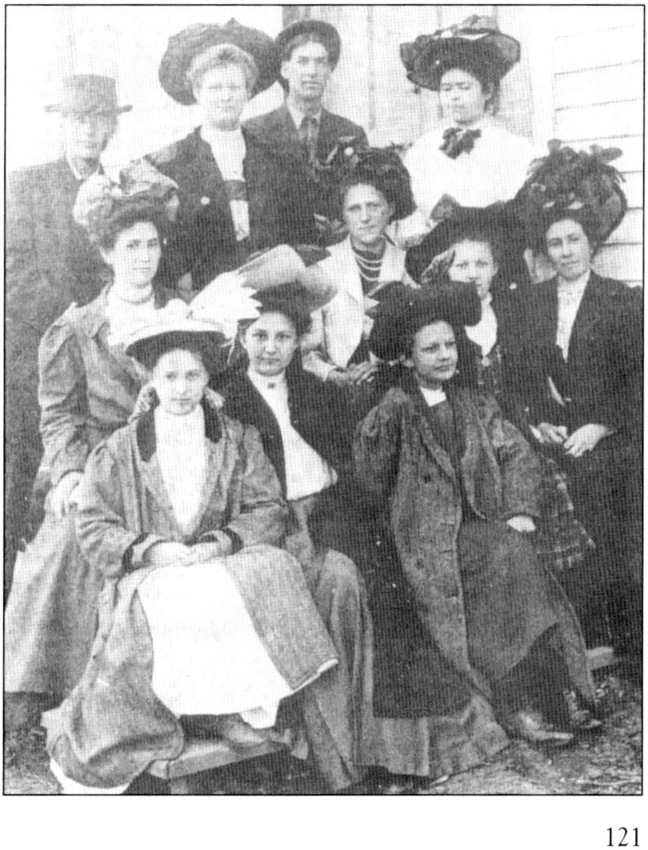

This early 1900s photo was taken on the front steps of the Winslow School house, obviously in mid-winter. Church and Sunday school had probably been conducted in the building that morning. From left to right are as follows: (front row) Maude Guinn, Jewell McClendon, and Rose McClendon; (middle row) Alice McClendon, Belle Coil, Bess Guinn, and Martha McClendon; (back row) Carl Mackey, Ollie Nickell, Vern Henby, and Nellie Lee.

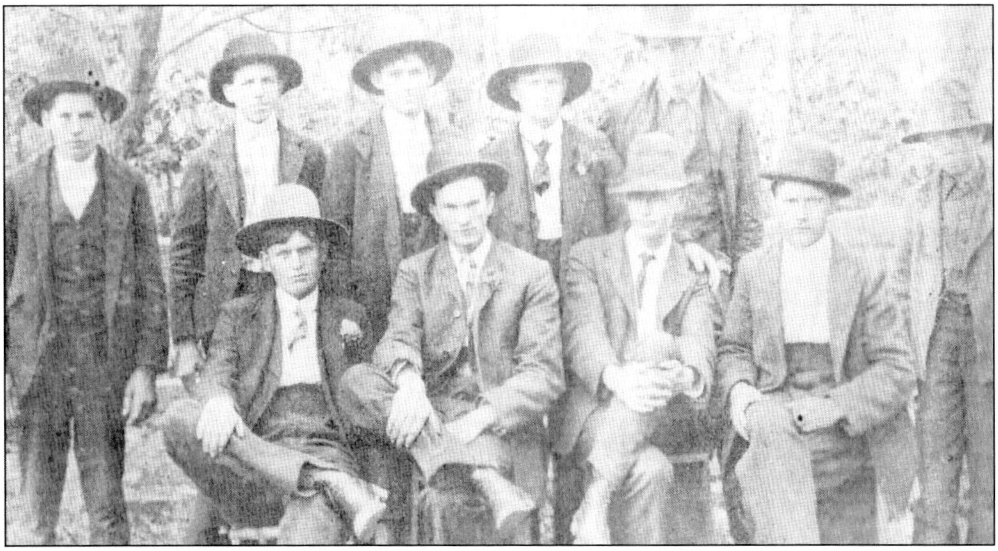

Attending Sunday school and church in 1910 was not only a spiritual experience but a social one as well. Entire families took part. The young ladies these lads had their "caps set for" would also be in attendance. These young men from Sassafras Pond were on their way to White School one cool fall Sunday when they stopped to have their picture taken. From left to right are as follows: (seated) Earnest Hobbs, Jim Bunyard, Carl Mackey, and Steve Poor; (standing) Ira Breeden, Manfred Kissinger, Noble Breeden, Albert Hobbs, Ed Rood, and John Rush.

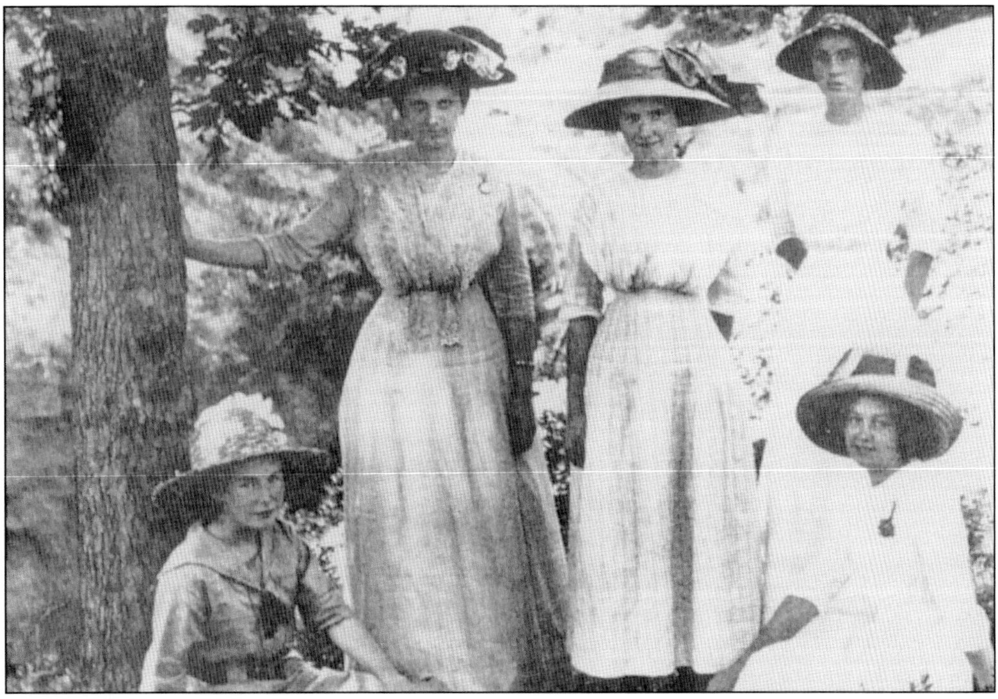

The fashions of well-dressed young ladies in Winslow in 1913 are depicted here by five Winn cousins who are out and about on a summer Sunday afternoon. From left to right are Lyda, Ethel, Martha, Stella, and Dora. Not all youngsters of that time could afford to dress in such a way or to have their pictures taken.

Young men about town in Winslow would inevitably pose beside the railroad tunnel. These fellows are standing at the north end in this 1911 photo. From left to right, they are as follows: Jim Nail, Lyndell Deatherage, Doyle Adkins, Edgar Jones, and Earl Parks (hanging from supports on the side of the tunnel).

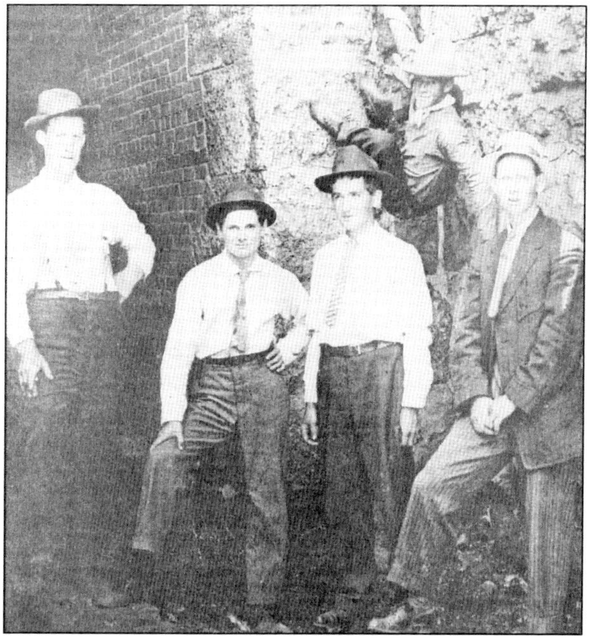

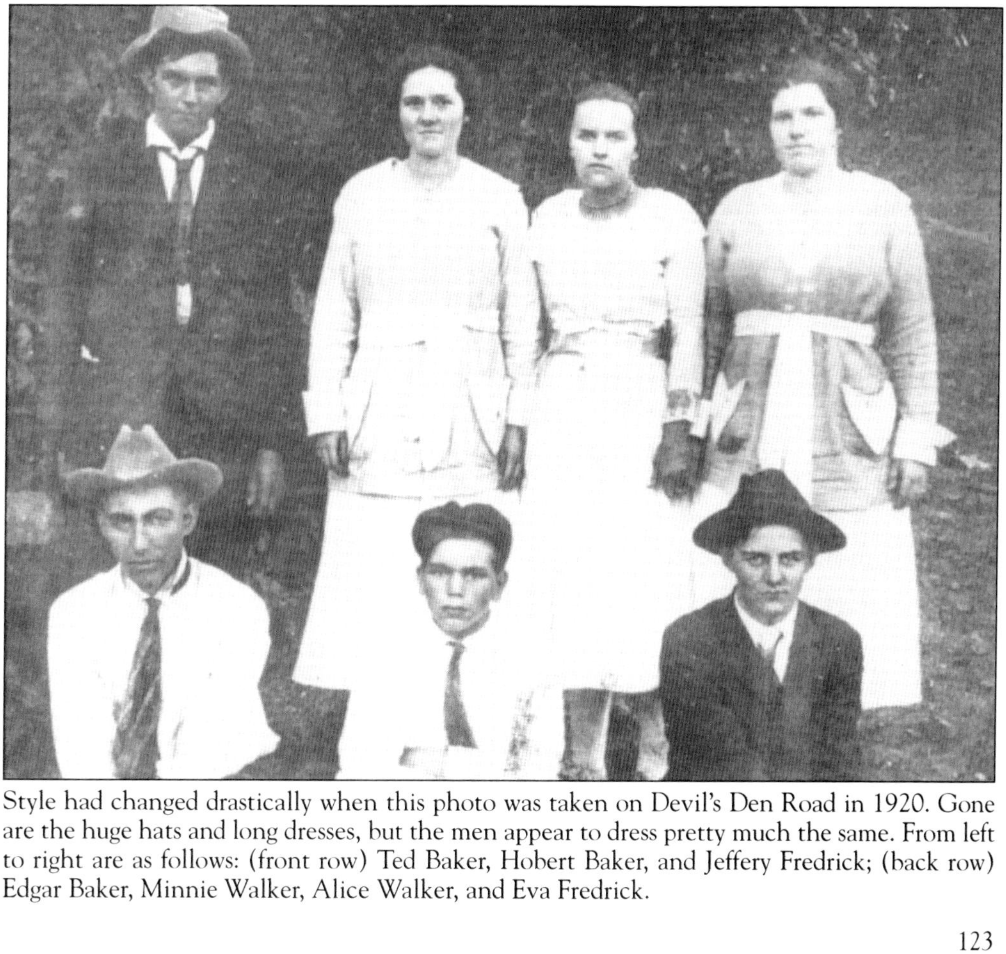

Style had changed drastically when this photo was taken on Devil's Den Road in 1920. Gone are the huge hats and long dresses, but the men appear to dress pretty much the same. From left to right are as follows: (front row) Ted Baker, Hobert Baker, and Jeffery Fredrick; (back row) Edgar Baker, Minnie Walker, Alice Walker, and Eva Fredrick.

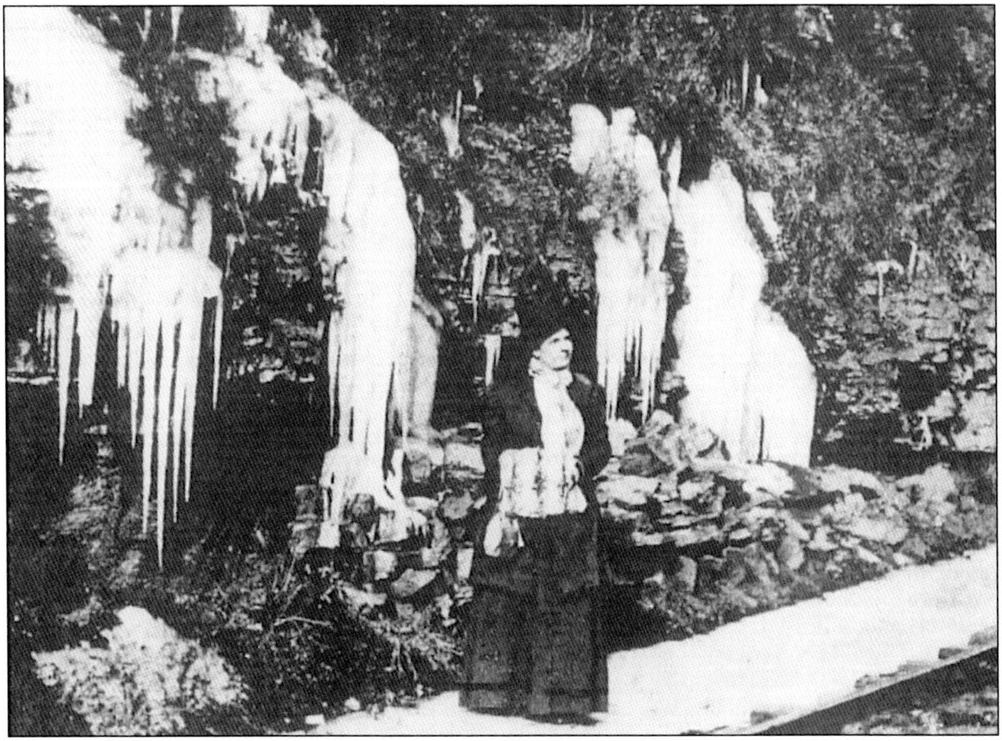

This view takes us back to 1900 and the winter fashion of a big muff carried by ladies to keep their hands warm. Rose Sample of Winslow is standing on the boardwalk that extended from the depot to a large spring, just north of the railroad tunnel. The springs were the source of water for the depot agent and his family who resided above the depot.

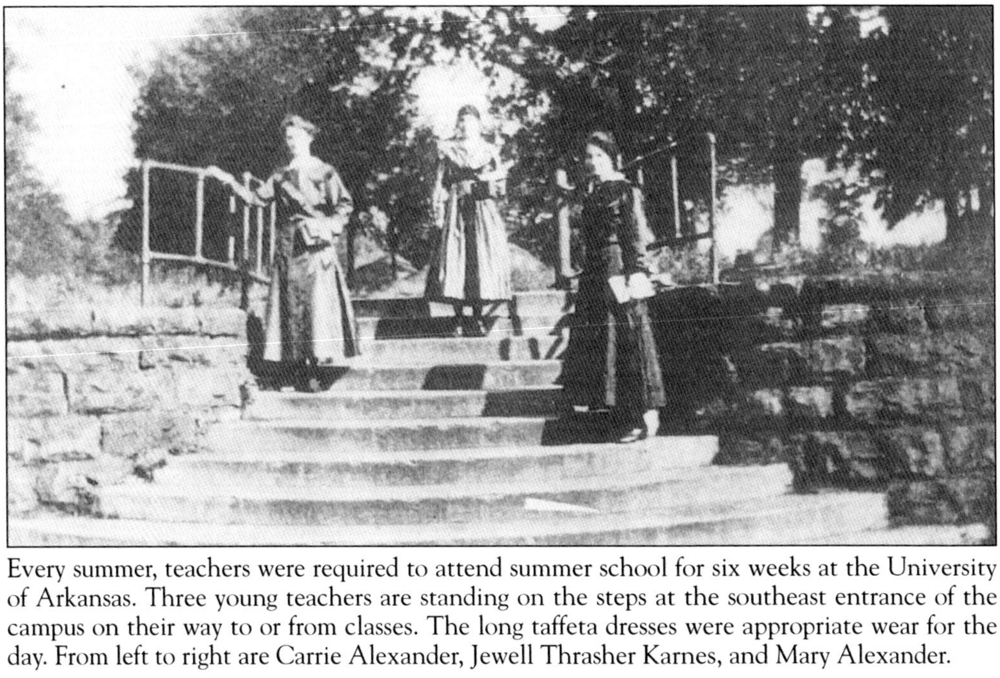

Every summer, teachers were required to attend summer school for six weeks at the University of Arkansas. Three young teachers are standing on the steps at the southeast entrance of the campus on their way to or from classes. The long taffeta dresses were appropriate wear for the day. From left to right are Carrie Alexander, Jewell Thrasher Karnes, and Mary Alexander.

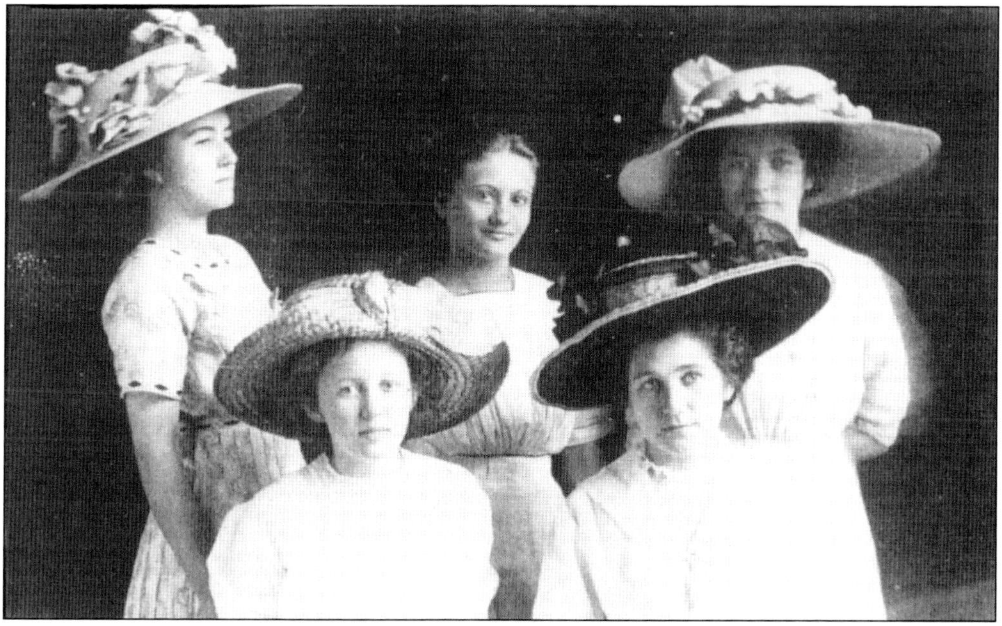

These young ladies are decked out in the latest 1910 fashion. Perhaps the young lady in the center (background) balked at such a get-up, or maybe one more large hat wouldn't fit in the picture. These delegates to the Methodist Church Epworth League Convention in Prairie Grove are, from left to right, as follows: Lena Carl, Kathy Shoffner (no hat), Bess Guinn (seated), and R. Lola Wilson. The other girl is not identified.

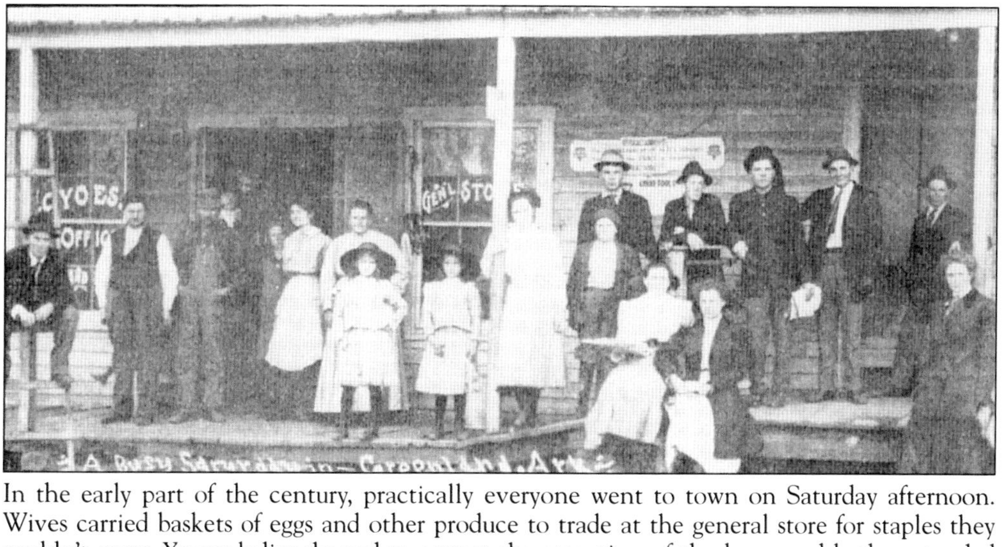

In the early part of the century, practically everyone went to town on Saturday afternoon. Wives carried baskets of eggs and other produce to trade at the general store for staples they couldn't grow. Young ladies dressed to attract the attention of the boys, and both pretended not to notice each other. This photo was taken on the porch in front of the general store of Jacob Yoes, a prominent Greenland merchant.

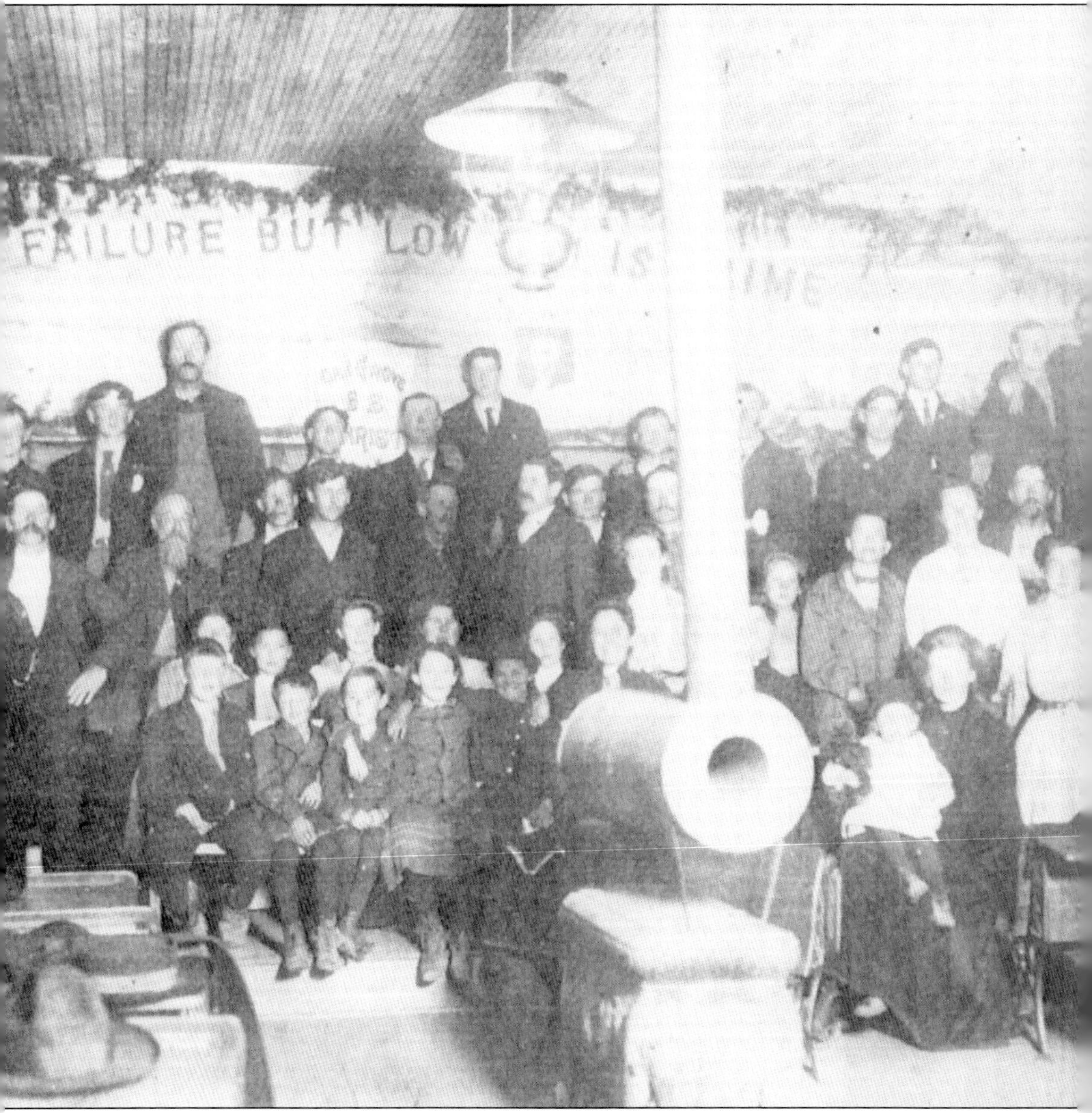

This is an excellent example of an early flash picture taken indoors. Powder poured in a trough was ignited to create the flash simultaneously with the taking of the picture. This is a c. 1907 Christmas celebration at Oak Grove School. The school motto on the wall, written there by teacher Grace Reese is "Not failure but low aim is crime." A drum on top of the wood-burning stove would have deflected more heat into the room. A kerosene lamp hangs from the ceiling. One of the most anticipated celebrations every year was presented in numerous county one-room schools around Christmastime. Many schools let out prior to that time, but the classes would plan and practice the program for weeks before school let out, usually around Thanksgiving. Everyone attended the event and pie suppers were held to raise money so that each child received a Christmas treat under the tree.

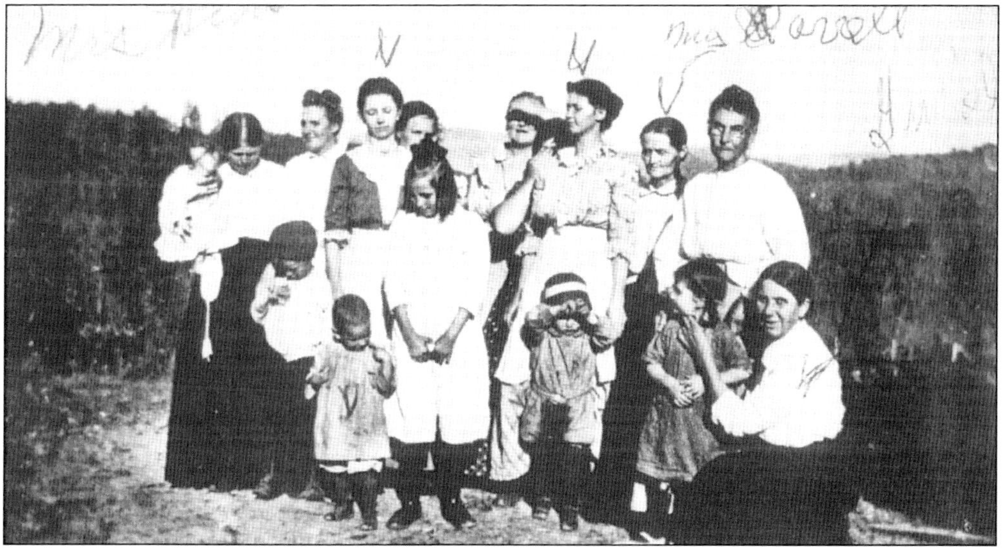

In pioneer days in the Ozarks, barn raisings were social community projects. When a family needed a new barn, help was readily available from neighbors. While the men built the barn, women visited and prepared a noon meal. This photo probably depicts one of the last such activities to take place in the county. It was taken just before WW I, on the Garrett family farm two miles north of Winslow.

This crew of barn raisers pauses here for a picture. The event gave men a chance to display their skills at raising and securing logs for the walls of the structure. Those pictured are identified as Mr. Garrett, Uncle Jimmie Langston, ElmerLehn,RufusGunnells, W.E. Langston, Mr. Gibson, Cleve Bogan (with son Paul in front). Others may be Ed and Bill Waterfield, and Pate and Jim Gunnells.

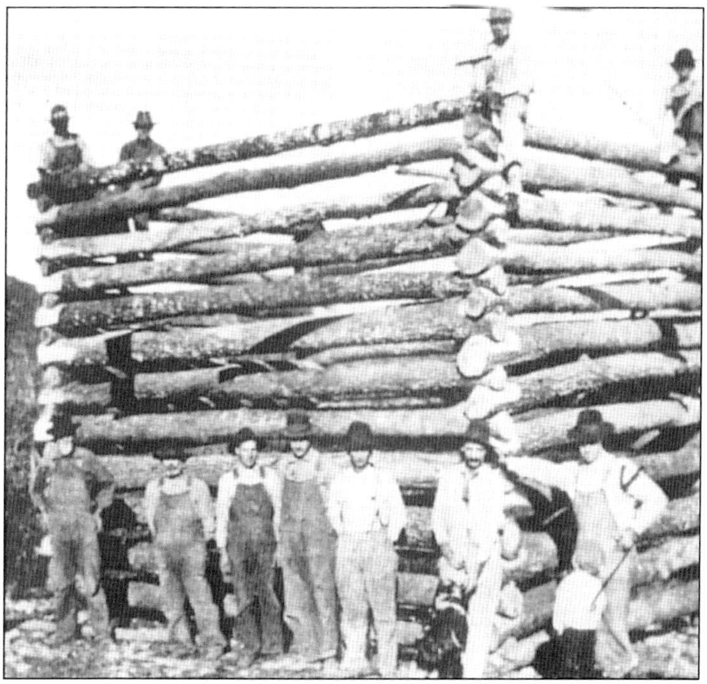

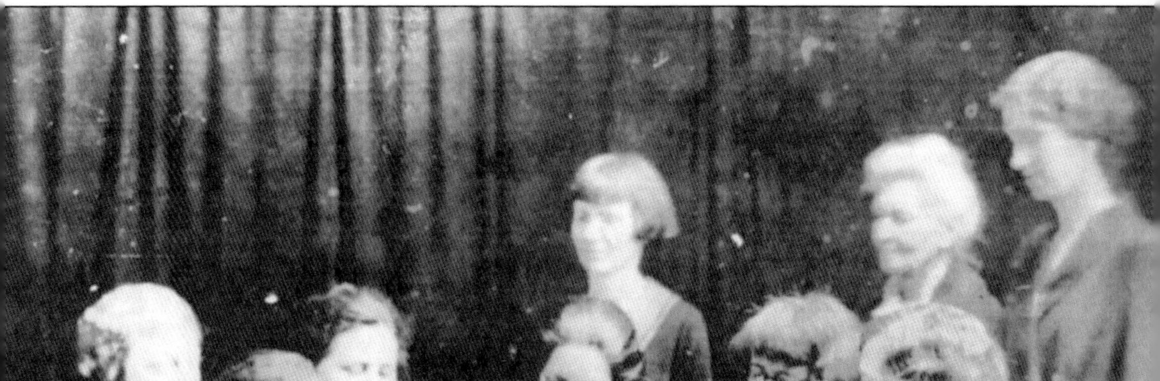

Winslow's Petticoat Government is claimed to have been the first in the United States. Members in this 1925 photo are, from left to right as follows: (seated) Her Honor, Mayor Maud Duncan (black hat), Lyda Cole, Florence Marley, Audie Crider, Bee Cherveny, Daisy Miller, and Etta Black; (standing) Treasurer Martha Winn, Virginia C. Dunlap (the "mother" of Winslow), and Postmistress Stella Winn. The women gained national acclaim for forming the first all-female city government. When they were re-elected in 1926, the *St. Louis Post Dispatch* ran the following headline: "Winslow Spruces Up, Gives Away Town Jail and Re-elects Its Petticoat Government." Hiring someone to haul off the jail building, 85-pound Mayor Duncan remarked, "If anyone breaks the law around here, they can answer to me." The women also had the steep mountain road west of town rerouted to enable them to drive forward rather than backing up the incline, which many could not manage with the cumbersome automobiles of the day. Following their second term, the ladies relinquished the reins of government to the men and graciously stepped down.